THE FIRST AND SECOND
BOOKS OF THE MACCABEES

THE IGNATIUS CATHOLIC STUDY BIBLE

REVISED STANDARD VERSION
SECOND CATHOLIC EDITION

THE FIRST AND SECOND
BOOKS OF THE MACCABEES

With Introduction, Commentary, and Notes

by

Matthew and Leeanne Thomas

with Scott Hahn and Curtis Mitch

and

with Study Questions by

Dennis Walters

IGNATIUS PRESS   SAN FRANCISCO

Original Revised Standard Version, Catholic Edition
Nihil Obstat: Thomas Hanlon, S.T.L., L.S.S., Ph.L.
Imprimatur: + Peter W. Bartholome, D.D.
Bishop of St. Cloud, Minnesota
May 11, 1966

Introduction, commentaries and notes:
Nihil Obstat: Ruth Ohm Sutherland, Ph.D., Censor Deputatus
Imprimatur: + The Most Reverend Salvatore Cordileone
Archbishop of San Francisco
March 2, 2022

The *nihil obstat* and *imprimatur* are official declarations that a book or pamphlet is free
of doctrinal or moral error. No implication is contained therein that those who have granted
the *nihil obstat* and *imprimatur* agree with the contents, opinions, or statements expressed.

Second Catholic Edition approved by the
National Council of the Churches of Christ in the USA

Cover art: *The Triumph of Judas Maccabeus*
By Peter Paul Reubens (1577–1640)
Photo: Gerard Blot
© RMN-Grand Palais, Art Resource, NY

Cover design by Riz Boncan Marsella

Published by Ignatius Press in 2023

Introductions, commentaries, notes, headings, and study questions
© 2023 by Ignatius Press, San Francisco
All rights reserved
ISBN 978-1-62164-325-8 (PB)
ISBN 978-1-64229-199-5 (eBook)
Printed in the United States of America ∞

CONTENTS

INTRODUCTION TO
THE IGNATIUS STUDY BIBLE
by Scott Hahn, Ph.D.

You are approaching the "word of God". This is the title Christians most commonly give to the Bible, and the expression is rich in meaning. It is also the title given to the Second Person of the Blessed Trinity, God the Son. For Jesus Christ became flesh for our salvation, and "the name by which he is called is The Word of God" (Rev 19:13; cf. Jn 1:14).

The word of God is Scripture. The Word of God is Jesus. This close association between God's *written* word and his *eternal* Word is intentional and has been the custom of the Church since the first generation. "All Sacred Scripture is but one book, and this one book is Christ, 'because all divine Scripture speaks of Christ, and all divine Scripture is fulfilled in Christ'"[1] (CCC 134). This does not mean that the Scriptures are divine in the same way that Jesus is divine. They are, rather, divinely inspired and, as such, are unique in world literature, just as the Incarnation of the eternal Word is unique in human history.

Yet we can say that the inspired word resembles the incarnate Word in several important ways. Jesus Christ is the Word of God incarnate. In his humanity, he is like us in all things, except for sin. As a work of man, the Bible is like any other book, except without error. Both Christ and Scripture, says the Second Vatican Council, are given "for the sake of our salvation" (*Dei Verbum* 11), and both give us God's definitive revelation of himself. We cannot, therefore, conceive of one without the other: the Bible without Jesus, or Jesus without the Bible. Each is the interpretive key to the other. And because Christ is the subject of all the Scriptures, St. Jerome insists, "Ignorance of the Scriptures is ignorance of Christ"[2] (CCC 133).

When we approach the Bible, then, we approach Jesus, the Word of God; and in order to encounter Jesus, we must approach him in a prayerful study of the inspired word of God, the Sacred Scriptures.

Inspiration and Inerrancy The Catholic Church makes mighty claims for the Bible, and our acceptance of those claims is essential if we are to read the Scriptures and apply them to our lives as the Church intends. So it is not enough merely to nod at words like "inspired", "unique", or "inerrant". We

have to understand what the Church means by these terms, and we have to make that understanding our own. After all, what we believe about the Bible will inevitably influence the way we read the Bible. The way we read the Bible, in turn, will determine what we "get out" of its sacred pages.

These principles hold true no matter what we read: a news report, a search warrant, an advertisement, a paycheck, a doctor's prescription, an eviction notice. How (or whether) we read these things depends largely upon our preconceived notions about the reliability and authority of their sources—and the potential they have for affecting our lives. In some cases, to misunderstand a document's authority can lead to dire consequences. In others, it can keep us from enjoying rewards that are rightfully ours. In the case of the Bible, both the rewards and the consequences involved take on an ultimate value.

What does the Church mean, then, when she affirms the words of St. Paul: "All Scripture is inspired by God" (2 Tim 3:16)? Since the term "inspired" in this passage could be translated "God-breathed", it follows that God breathed forth his word in the Scriptures as you and I breathe forth air when we speak. This means that God is the primary author of the Bible. He certainly employed human authors in this task as well, but he did not merely assist them while they wrote or subsequently approve what they had written. God the Holy Spirit is the *principal* author of Scripture, while the human writers are *instrumental* authors. These human authors freely wrote everything, and only those things, that God wanted: the word of God in the very words of God. This miracle of dual authorship extends to the whole of Scripture, and to every one of its parts, so that whatever the human authors affirm, God likewise affirms through their words.

The principle of biblical inerrancy follows logically from this principle of divine authorship. After all, God cannot lie, and he cannot make mistakes. Since the Bible is divinely inspired, it must be without error in everything that its divine and human authors affirm to be true. This means that biblical inerrancy is a mystery even broader in scope than infallibility, which guarantees for us that the Church will always teach the truth concerning faith and morals. Of course the mantle of inerrancy likewise covers faith and morals, but it extends even farther to ensure that all the facts and events of salvation history are accurately presented for us in

---

[1] Hugh of St. Victor, *De arca Noe* 2, 8: PL 176, 642: cf. ibid. 2, 9: PL 176, 642–43.
[2] *DV* 25; cf. Phil 3:8 and St. Jerome, *Commentariorum in Isaiam libri xviii*, prol.: PL 24, 17b.

the Scriptures. Inerrancy is our guarantee that the words and deeds of God found in the Bible are unified and true, declaring with one voice the wonders of his saving love.

The guarantee of inerrancy does not mean, however, that the Bible is an all-purpose encyclopedia of information covering every field of study. The Bible is not, for example, a textbook in the empirical sciences, and it should not be treated as one. When biblical authors relate facts of the natural order, we can be sure they are speaking in a purely descriptive and "phenomenological" way, according to the way things appeared to their senses.

Biblical Authority Implicit in these doctrines is God's desire to make himself known to the world and to enter a loving relationship with every man, woman, and child he has created. God gave us the Scriptures not just to inform or motivate us; more than anything he wants to save us. This higher purpose underlies every page of the Bible, indeed every word of it.

In order to reveal himself, God used what theologians call "accommodation". Sometimes the Lord stoops down to communicate by "condescension"—that is, he speaks as humans speak, as if he had the same passions and weakness that we do (for example, God says he was "sorry" that he made man in Genesis 6:6). Other times he communicates by "elevation"—that is, by endowing human words with divine power (for example, through the Prophets). The numerous examples of divine accommodation in the Bible are an expression of God's wise and fatherly ways. For a sensitive father can speak with his children either by condescension, as in baby talk, or by elevation, by bringing a child's understanding up to a more mature level.

God's word is thus saving, fatherly, and personal. Because it speaks directly to us, we must never be indifferent to its content; after all, the word of God is at once the object, cause, and support of our faith. It is, in fact, a test of our faith, since we see in the Scriptures only what faith disposes us to see. If we believe what the Church believes, we will see in Scripture the saving, inerrant, and divinely authored revelation of the Father. If we believe otherwise, we see another book altogether.

This test applies not only to rank-and-file believers but also to the Church's theologians and hierarchy, and even the Magisterium. Vatican II has stressed in recent times that Scripture must be "the very soul of sacred theology" (*Dei Verbum* 24). As Joseph Cardinal Ratzinger, Pope Benedict XVI echoed this powerful teaching with his own, insisting that "the *normative theologians* are the authors of Holy Scripture" (emphasis added). He reminded us that Scripture and the Church's dogmatic teaching are tied tightly together, to the point of being inseparable: "Dogma is by definition nothing other than an interpretation of Scripture." The defined dogmas of our faith, then, encapsulate the Church's infallible interpretation of Scripture, and theology is a further reflection upon that work.

The Senses of Scripture Because the Bible has both divine and human authors, we are required to master a different sort of reading than we are used to. First, we must read Scripture according to its *literal* sense, as we read any other human literature. At this initial stage, we strive to discover the meaning of the words and expressions used by the biblical writers as they were understood in their original setting and by their original recipients. This means, among other things, that we do not interpret everything we read "literalistically", as though Scripture never speaks in a figurative or symbolic way (it often does!). Rather, we read it according to the rules that govern its different literary forms of writing, depending on whether we are reading a narrative, a poem, a letter, a parable, or an apocalyptic vision. The Church calls us to read the divine books in this way to ensure that we understand what the human authors were laboring to explain to God's people.

The literal sense, however, is not the only sense of Scripture, since we interpret its sacred pages according to the *spiritual* senses as well. In this way, we search out what the Holy Spirit is trying to tell us, beyond even what the human authors have consciously asserted. Whereas the literal sense of Scripture describes a historical reality—a fact, precept, or event—the spiritual senses disclose deeper mysteries revealed through the historical realities. What the soul is to the body, the spiritual senses are to the literal. You can distinguish them; but if you try to separate them, death immediately follows. St. Paul was the first to insist upon this and warn of its consequences: "God ... has qualified us to be ministers of a new covenant, not in a written code but in the Spirit; for the written code kills, but the Spirit gives life" (2 Cor 3:5–6).

Catholic tradition recognizes three spiritual senses that stand upon the foundation of the literal sense of Scripture (see CCC 115). **(1)** The first is the *allegorical* sense, which unveils the spiritual and prophetic meaning of biblical history. Allegorical interpretations thus reveal how persons, events, and institutions of Scripture can point beyond themselves toward greater mysteries yet to come (OT) or display the fruits of mysteries already revealed (NT). Christians have often read the Old Testament in this way to discover how the mystery of Christ in the New Covenant was once hidden in the Old and how the full significance of the Old Covenant was finally made manifest in the New. Allegorical significance is likewise latent in the New Testament, especially in the life and deeds of Jesus recorded in the Gospels. Because Christ is the Head of the Church and the source of her spiritual life, what was accomplished in Christ the Head during his earthly life prefigures what he continually produces in his members through grace. The allegorical sense builds up the virtue of faith. **(2)** The second is the *tropological* or *moral* sense, which reveals how the actions of God's people in the Old Testament and the life of Jesus in the New Testament prompt us to form virtuous habits in our own lives. It therefore draws from Scripture warnings against sin and vice as well as inspirations to pursue holiness and purity. The moral sense is intended to build up the virtue of charity. **(3)** The third is the *anagogical* sense, which points upward to heavenly glory. It shows us how countless events in the Bible prefigure our final union with God in eternity and how things that are "seen" on earth are figures of things "unseen" in heaven. Because the anagogical sense leads us to contemplate our destiny, it is meant to build up the virtue of hope. Together with the literal sense, then, these spiritual senses draw out the fullness of what God wants to give us through his Word and as such comprise what ancient tradition has called the "full sense" of Sacred Scripture.

All of this means that the deeds and events of the Bible are charged with meaning beyond what is immediately apparent to the reader. In essence, that meaning is Jesus Christ and the salvation he died to give us. This is especially true of the books of the New Testament, which proclaim Jesus explicitly; but it is also true of the Old Testament, which speaks of Jesus in more hidden and symbolic ways. The human authors of the Old Testament told us as much as they were able, but they could not clearly discern the shape of all future events standing at such a distance. It is the Bible's divine Author, the Holy Spirit, who could and did foretell the saving work of Christ, from the first page of the Book of Genesis onward.

The New Testament did not, therefore, abolish the Old. Rather, the New fulfilled the Old, and in doing so, it lifted the veil that kept hidden the face of the Lord's bride. Once the veil is removed, we suddenly see the world of the Old Covenant charged with grandeur. Water, fire, clouds, gardens, trees, hills, doves, lambs—all of these things are memorable details in the history and poetry of Israel. But now, seen in the light of Jesus Christ, they are much more. For the Christian with eyes to see, water symbolizes the saving power of Baptism; fire, the Holy Spirit; the spotless lamb, Christ crucified; Jerusalem, the city of heavenly glory.

The spiritual reading of Scripture is nothing new. Indeed, the very first Christians read the Bible this way. St. Paul describes Adam as a "type" that prefigured Jesus Christ (Rom 5:14). A "type" is a real person, place, thing, or event in the Old Testament that foreshadows something greater in the New. From this term we get the word "typology", referring to the study of how the Old Testament prefigures Christ (CCC 128–30). Elsewhere St. Paul

draws deeper meanings out of the story of Abraham's sons, declaring, "This is an allegory" (Gal 4:24). He is not suggesting that these events of the distant past never really happened; he is saying that the events both happened *and* signified something more glorious yet to come.

The New Testament later describes the Tabernacle of ancient Israel as "a copy and shadow of the heavenly sanctuary" (Heb 8:5) and the Mosaic Law as a "shadow of the good things to come" (Heb 10:1). St. Peter, in turn, notes that Noah and his family were "saved through water" in a way that "corresponds" to sacramental Baptism, which "now saves you" (1 Pet 3:20–21). It is interesting to note that the expression translated as "corresponds" in this verse is a Greek term that denotes the fulfillment or counterpart of an ancient "type".

We need not look to the apostles, however, to justify a spiritual reading of the Bible. After all, Jesus himself read the Old Testament this way. He referred to Jonah (Mt 12:39), Solomon (Mt 12:42), the Temple (Jn 2:19), and the brazen serpent (Jn 3:14) as "signs" that pointed forward to him. We see in Luke's Gospel, as Christ comforted the disciples on the road to Emmaus, that "beginning with Moses and all the prophets, he interpreted to them in all the Scriptures the things concerning himself" (Lk 24:27). It was precisely this extensive spiritual interpretation of the Old Testament that made such an impact on these once-discouraged travelers, causing their hearts to "burn" within them (Lk 24:32).

Criteria for Biblical Interpretation We, too, must learn to discern the "full sense" of Scripture as it includes both the literal and spiritual senses together. Still, this does not mean we should "read into" the Bible meanings that are not really there. Spiritual exegesis is not an unrestrained flight of the imagination. Rather, it is a sacred science that proceeds according to certain principles and stands accountable to sacred tradition, the Magisterium, and the wider community of biblical interpreters (both living and deceased).

In searching out the full sense of a text, we should always avoid the extreme tendency to "overspiritualize" in a way that minimizes or denies the Bible's literal truth. St. Thomas Aquinas was well aware of this danger and asserted that "all other senses of Sacred Scripture are based on the literal" (*STh* I, 1, 10, *ad* 1, quoted in CCC 116). On the other hand, we should never confine the meaning of a text to the literal, intended sense of its human author, as if the divine Author did not intend the passage to be read in the light of Christ's coming.

Fortunately the Church has given us guidelines in our study of Scripture. The unique character and divine authorship of the Bible call us to read it "in the Spirit" (*Dei Verbum* 12). Vatican II outlines this teaching in a practical way by directing us to read the Scriptures according to three specific criteria:

1. We must "[b]e especially attentive 'to the content and unity of the whole Scripture'" (CCC 112).

2. We must "[r]ead the Scripture within 'the living Tradition of the whole Church'" (CCC 113).

3. We must "[b]e attentive to the analogy of faith" (CCC 114; cf. Rom 12:6).

These criteria protect us from many of the dangers that ensnare readers of the Bible, from the newest inquirer to the most prestigious scholar. Reading Scripture out of context is one such pitfall, and probably the one most difficult to avoid. A memorable cartoon from the 1950s shows a young man poring over the pages of the Bible. He says to his sister: "Don't bother me now; I'm trying to find a Scripture verse to back up one of my preconceived notions." No doubt a biblical text pried from its context can be twisted to say something very different from what its author actually intended.

The Church's criteria guide us here by defining what constitutes the authentic "context" of a given biblical passage. The first criterion directs us to the literary context of every verse, including not only the words and paragraphs that surround it, but also the entire corpus of the biblical author's writings and, indeed, the span of the entire Bible. The *complete* literary context of any Scripture verse includes every text from Genesis to Revelation—because the Bible is a unified book, not just a library of different books. When the Church canonized the Book of Revelation, for example, she recognized it to be incomprehensible apart from the wider context of the entire Bible.

The second criterion places the Bible firmly within the context of a community that treasures a "living tradition". That community is the People of God down through the ages. Christians lived out their faith for well over a millennium before the printing press was invented. For centuries, few believers owned copies of the Gospels, and few people could read anyway. Yet they absorbed the gospel—through the sermons of their bishops and clergy, through prayer and meditation, through Christian art, through liturgical celebrations, and through oral tradition. These were expressions of the one "living tradition", a culture of living faith that stretches from ancient Israel to the contemporary Church. For the early Christians, the gospel could not be understood apart from that tradition. So it is with us. Reverence for the Church's tradition is what protects us from any sort of chronological or cultural provincialism, such as scholarly fads that arise and carry away a generation of interpreters before being dismissed by the next generation.

The third criterion places scriptural texts within the framework of faith. If we believe that the Scriptures are divinely inspired, we must also believe them to be internally coherent and consistent with all the doctrines that Christians believe. Remember, the Church's dogmas (such as the Real Presence, the papacy, the Immaculate Conception) are not something *added* to Scripture; rather, they are the Church's infallible interpretation *of* Scripture.

Using This Study Guide This volume is designed to lead the reader through Scripture according to the Church's guidelines—faithful to the canon, to the tradition, and to the creeds. The Church's interpretive principles have thus shaped the component parts of this book, and they are designed to make the reader's study as effective and rewarding as possible.

Introductions: We have introduced the biblical book with an essay covering issues such as authorship, date of composition, purpose, and leading themes. This background information will assist readers to approach and understand the text on its own terms.

Annotations: The basic notes at the bottom of every page help the user to read the Scriptures with understanding. They by no means exhaust the meaning of the sacred text but provide background material to help the reader make sense of what he reads. Often these notes make explicit what the sacred writers assumed or held to be implicit. They also provide a great deal of historical, cultural, geographical, and theological information pertinent to the inspired narratives—information that can help the reader bridge the distance between the biblical world and his own.

Cross-References: Between the biblical text at the top of each page and the annotations at the bottom, numerous references are listed to point readers to other scriptural passages related to the one being studied. This follow-up is an essential part of any serious study. It is also an excellent way to discover how the content of Scripture "hangs together" in a providential unity. Along with biblical cross-references, the annotations refer to select paragraphs from the *Catechism of the Catholic Church*. These are not doctrinal "proof texts" but are designed to help the reader interpret the Bible in accordance with the mind of the Church. The *Catechism* references listed either handle the biblical text directly or treat a broader doctrinal theme that sheds significant light on that text.

Topical Essays, Word Studies, Charts: These features bring readers to a deeper understanding of select details. The *topical essays* take up major themes and explain them more thoroughly and theologically than the annotations, often relating them to the doctrines of the Church. Occasionally the annotations are supplemented by *word studies* that put readers in touch with the ancient languages of Scripture. These should help readers to understand better and appreciate the inspired terminology that runs throughout the sacred books. Also included are various *charts* that summarize biblical information "at a glance".

Icon Annotations: Three distinctive icons are interspersed throughout the annotations, each one corresponding to one of the Church's three criteria for biblical interpretation. Bullets indicate the passage or passages to which these icons apply.

Notes marked by the book icon relate to the "content and unity" of Scripture, showing how particular passages of the Old Testament illuminate the mysteries of the New. Much of the information in these notes explains the original context of the citations and indicates how and why this has a direct bearing on Christ or the Church. Through these notes, the reader can develop a sensitivity to the beauty and unity of God's saving plan as it stretches across both Testaments.

Notes marked by the dove icon examine particular passages in light of the Church's "living tradition". Because the Holy Spirit both guides the Magisterium and inspires the spiritual senses of Scripture, these annotations supply information along both of these lines. On the one hand, they refer to the Church's doctrinal teaching as presented by various popes, creeds, and ecumenical councils; on the other, they draw from (and paraphrase) the spiritual interpretations of various Fathers, Doctors, and saints.

Notes marked by the keys icon pertain to the "analogy of faith". Here we spell out how the mysteries of our faith "unlock" and explain one another. This type of comparison between Christian beliefs displays the coherence and unity of defined dogmas, which are the Church's infallible interpretations of Scripture.

Putting It All in Perspective Perhaps the most important context of all we have saved for last: the interior life of the individual reader. What we get out of the Bible will largely depend on how we approach the Bible. Unless we are living a sustained and disciplined life of prayer, we will never have the reverence, the profound humility, or the grace we need to see the Scriptures for what they really are.

You are approaching the "word of God". But for thousands of years, since before he knit you in your mother's womb, the Word of God has been approaching you.

One Final Note. The volume you hold in your hands is only a small part of a much larger work still in production. Study helps similar to those printed in this booklet are being prepared for *all* the books of the Bible and will appear gradually as they are finished. Our ultimate goal is to publish a single, one-volume Study Bible that will include the entire text of Scripture, along with all the annotations, charts, cross-references, maps, and other features found in the following pages. Individual booklets will be published in the meantime, with the hope that God's people can begin to benefit from this labor before its full completion.

We have included a long list of Study Questions in the back to make this format as useful as possible, not only for individual study, but for group settings and discussions as well. The questions are designed to help readers both "understand" the Bible and "apply" it to their lives. We pray that God will make use of our efforts and yours to help renew the face of the earth! «

INTRODUCTION TO THE FIRST BOOK OF THE MACCABEES

Author and Date The books of 1 and 2 Maccabees originate from the period following Alexander the Great's rapid conquest of the Eastern Mediterranean and Persia before his death in 323 B.C. They describe the suppression of Palestinian Judaism begun in 168 B.C. by one of Alexander's successors, the Seleucid king Antiochus IV Epiphanes, and the subsequent Jewish rebellion led by Mattathias and his sons. First Maccabees is an account of these events written by an anonymous author, who emulates the terse style of earlier biblical historiography—such as one finds in the books of Judges, Kings, and Chronicles—in recounting the story of the Jews' suffering and deliverance in this period. The author appears to have been a well-educated Jew in Palestine with access to official Jewish records as well as close familiarity with the region's geography and the Hebrew Scriptures. Scholars consider it most likely that 1 Maccabees was written sometime between the last decades of the second century B.C. and 63 B.C. These endpoints are set by the latter part of John Hyrcanus' high priesthood (134–104 B.C.), under whose leadership the book closes, and Pompey's conquest of Judea in 63 B.C., after which the positive portrayal of the Romans in 1 Mac 8 would seem unlikely to have been written.

Title The title of Maccabees, derived from the nickname of Judas Maccabeus (usually thought to mean "the hammer"), does not appear in the plural form within either of the two books themselves. Septuagint manuscripts carry the title *Makkabaiōn* ("Of the Maccabees"), which corresponds with early Christian attestation: Tertullian refers to the events taking place "in the times of the Maccabees", and St. Clement of Alexandria, St. Hippolytus, and Origen of Alexandria similarly use the plural of "Maccabees" when referring to the books. Origen's description of the Hebrew names of the books in the Jewish canon—which surprisingly has Maccabees appended at the end—attests that the Hebrew title is *Sarbeth Sabanaiel*, a seemingly garbled name that commentators speculate may have meant "Book of the House of the Hasmoneans" (the Maccabean family name), "Book of the House of God's Resisters", or "Prince of the House of God". Unlike books such as 1 and 2 Kings, 1 Maccabees is not the first part of a continuous narrative with 2 Maccabees but, rather, the first of two distinct works with unique perspectives on the events of the Hasmonean revolt and subsequent dynasty.

Place in the Canon The canonicity of 1 and 2 Maccabees was a matter of some dispute in the centuries after they were written, with most early Christians accepting them as Scripture and rabbinic Judaism eventually leaving them out of its canon. From a Christian standpoint, the Maccabean books were naturally accepted due to their inclusion among the writings of the Septuagint, the Old Testament translation made by Greek-speaking Jews that was regarded as inspired Scripture by nearly all the early Church. The books are thus cited just like other books of the Old Testament by early Church Fathers such as Tertullian, Origen, St. Cyprian, St. Hippolytus, and St. Ambrose. A minority of Church Fathers, such as St. Melito of Sardis and St. Jerome, held to the authority of the smaller Jewish canon instead of the broader Septuagint one. This left the status of the Maccabean books in a grey area for these writers, though those holding to the Jewish canon, like St. Jerome, are still often found to cite the Maccabean books in their writings. The majority position of using the broader Septuagint canon was affirmed at the early synods at Hippo (393) and Carthage (397, 419) and later at the Council of Florence in 1442, which was reaffirmed by the Council of Trent in 1546. Eastern Orthodox churches similarly follow the traditional canon of the Septuagint and thus include 1 and 2 Maccabees (along with 3 Maccabees, a story recounting the persecution of Jews in Egypt in the late third century B.C.).

From a Jewish standpoint, while little evidence remains of the argumentation that lay behind the inclusion and exclusion of various books in the canon, it is thought that 1 Maccabees' laudatory description of the Romans' strength in 1 Mac 8 would have rendered the books unfavorable once this strength turned against the Jews, as it did with the Roman conquest of Judea (63 B.C.) and the eventual destruction of the Temple (A.D. 70). While not preserved in the Jewish canon, the books of 1 and 2 Maccabees are the earliest historical witnesses to the Feast of Dedication (Hanukkah), creating the ironic modern situation whereby an important Jewish festival finds its scriptural attestation only in the Catholic (and Orthodox) Bible!

The canonicity of the Maccabean books again came into question among Christians during the period of the Reformation, at which time various Protestant groups followed Luther's example in accepting the Jewish canon as authoritative rather than the larger Catholic canon. While this meant downgrading the Maccabean books from an authoritative status as Scripture for Protestants, Luther himself held to a surprisingly high view of 1 Maccabees. In his preface to 1 Maccabees, he describes the book as not unworthy of a place among the Old

Testament writings, particularly for its value for interpreting Daniel 11, and he concludes his 2 Maccabees introduction by stating it is proper that the first book (but not the second) be included in the Scriptures. Despite Luther's appreciation for 1 Maccabees, few contemporary Protestants are familiar with the text.

The Maccabean books are found in two locations in contemporary Catholic Bibles, which reflects varying traditions for ordering the biblical books. One tradition, following the Vulgate (which this text follows), uses a chronological ordering that places these books at the end of the Old Testament. The other tradition, used by a number of modern Bibles (such as the NAB and Jerusalem Bible), follows the thematic ordering sometimes reflected in the Septuagint and thus places 1 and 2 Maccabees after Esther at the end of the historical books.

Structure First Maccabees is most commonly divided into four parts, corresponding with the leadership of Mattathias, Judas, Jonathan, and Simon: **(1)** Antiochus' suppression and Mattathias' revolt (1:1—2:70); **(2)** the leadership of Judas Maccabeus (3:1—9:22); **(3)** the leadership of Jonathan Maccabeus (9:23—12); and **(4)** the leadership of Simon Maccabeus (13:1—16:24). Alternative proposals include the suggestion that the book is framed around the climactic events of the purification of the Temple (4:36–59) and the recapture of the citadel (13:49–52), while others question whether any particular structure is actually intrinsic to the text. While both alternatives have merit—these two events, indeed, represent high points in the narrative, and the structure of 1 Maccabees is more subtle than explicit—the book's most natural framing is the inciting aggression of Antiochus and the rebellion of Mattathias, followed by the three successive campaigns of Judas, Jonathan, and Simon.

Literary Background Our earliest witnesses to the text of 1 Maccabees are in Greek (with Latin and Syriac versions following). Nevertheless, most scholars agree that the original of 1 Maccabees was written in Hebrew, a judgment based on a grammar and style that is more characteristic of Hebrew than Greek composition. This judgment is corroborated by the testimony of Origen and St. Jerome, who attest to familiarity with a Hebrew version of the text.

First Maccabees is the most important historical resource for our knowledge of this period and is the primary source of information utilized by later historians such as Josephus. Exact chronology in 1 Maccabees is difficult to establish, as the book records dates using two different Seleucid calendar systems, which are likely inherited from the author's own sources. Other historical questions include the reconciliation of 1 Maccabees' chronology with that of 2 Maccabees (such as the sequence of events around Antiochus' campaign in

Egypt and his eventual death) and the nature of the correspondence between the Jews and foreign powers that is recorded at various points in the book (Rome in chaps. 8 and 15; Sparta in chaps. 12 and 14; Seleucids in chaps. 10—11, 13, and 15). On the first question, scholars tend to give historical priority to the chronology of 1 Maccabees, particularly as 2 Maccabees is confessedly written in a style to make the history easy to read and memorize and to delight its readers (2 Mac 2:24–25; 15:39). On the second, it is difficult to assess the degree to which these exchanges with foreign powers are paraphrases or more-or-less verbatim transcriptions. In either case, such correspondence likely took place originally in Greek or Aramaic, then was translated into Hebrew by the author, before finally being rendered from Hebrew into Greek by the translator of 1 Maccabees.

Themes and Characteristics The author of 1 Maccabees follows the example of earlier biblical historians by presenting a terse narrative in which God's Providence is assumed throughout, but his direct judgment or intervention is saved for a few key instances (such as Jonathan's prayer and deliverance in 11:68–74). Outside of these rare occasions, it is left to the reader to assess the fidelity of the Maccabees to God's Law, and as with other great leaders in Israel's history—such as the Judges, David, or Solomon—the resulting picture carries some ambiguities. On the one hand, the author clearly regards the Maccabees as God's chosen agents to save the Jews and preserve God's covenant, describing their leadership in terms that evoke God's prior work through faithful Israelites like Phineas, Joshua, and Elijah. Further, it is clear from the author's standpoint that the Maccabees are fighting for God's glory and not their own, which is illustrated by the counterexample of Joseph and Azariah, who depart from Maccabean leadership in seeking to gain a name for themselves in battle and tragically die as a result (5:56–62). Indeed, though the book makes no messianic claims for the Hasmoneans, their deeds (and especially Simon's) are described with language that evokes Israel's eschatological promises of blessing found in passages like Micah 4 and Zechariah 8.

On the other hand, while the text does not directly criticize the Maccabees, the author largely refrains from offering defenses of the Maccabees' decisions, some of which come across as quite brutal in the text (such as Jonathan and Simon's raid upon the Nabateans in 1 Mac 9, which Josephus later clarifies as being in accordance with retributive justice). In keeping with earlier biblical ambivalence toward royalty (cf. 1 Sam 8), the presentation of the Maccabees' relation to power is also fascinating: while the Roman leaders are praised by the narrator for not wearing purple as a mark of pride (8:14), the Maccabees find themselves clothed in the royal color by other nations (10:62) before eventually mandating that purple be worn by their leader and forbidden to all others (14:43–45). In addition, a careful reader will not fail to notice that the author's affirmation of David's everlasting throne in 1 Mac 2:57 sits in tension with the accession of the non-Davidic Hasmoneans to political leadership by the end of the book. Thus, while the Maccabees clearly function as God's chosen servants in liberating Israel, the author also presents their claim to ongoing political and spiritual leadership as resting upon the grounds of popular acclamation rather than divine mandate (14:46), with no equivalent of Aaron's budding rod as a sign of perpetual election (cf. Num 17). Further, the Maccabean leadership arrangement is itself presented as subject to God's prophetic judgment in the future (14:41).

Another common theme of 1 Maccabees is the author's tracing of how the Providence of God subtly interweaves with the good and evil deeds of history's characters. On the one side stand the Maccabees, who are lifted up from a humble line of priests at the beginning of the story to become rulers of an independent Jewish kingdom whose borders astonishingly rival those of King David by the end. The author makes clear that such blessings coincide with the Maccabees' fidelity to God's Law, which they strive to follow at key points throughout the book (e.g., 2:21; 3:48; 4:47). Rewards for integrity are similarly bestowed upon foreign nations like the Romans, whose success corresponds with their honesty and humility—virtues that set them apart from the other Gentile empires. Even where the Maccabees suffer losses, these tend to result from the deceit of the Seleucids and their supporters, whose mischief profits them nothing more than temporary gains, followed by their destruction.

On the other side stand the Hellenistic empires and the Jewish apostates who support them. The defining characteristic of these figures is their faithlessness toward God and men, expressed in their willingness to employ deceit and war against God's covenant with Israel. While these figures are frequently able to gain temporary victories by breaking their word (e.g., 1:30; 6:62; 7:18; 11:53), these always prove to be short-lived, with God's justice never far behind them. This subtle administration of God's Providence in rewarding the faithful and punishing the wicked can be witnessed by comparing the life-spans of the Hasmonean and Seleucid rulers: while 1 Maccabees spans a single generation of Hasmonean brothers, the same period covers four generations of Seleucid kings with the same name (Antiochus IV–VII), interspersed with an array of other royal claimants whose lives are similarly characterized by violence, insolence, and brevity.

Christian Perspective If one thinks of Scripture as a symphony with successive movements, the Books of the Maccabees can be understood as an interlude that fills in the story following one movement (the Prophets) and sets up the events of the next (the Gospels). Indeed, a number of details in the time of Jesus and the apostles are far more intelligible against the background of the Maccabees:

(1) Why are Jewish messianic hopes in Christ's time so focused on military and political leadership (e.g., Mk 10:35–45; Jn 6:15; Acts 1:6)?

(2) Why do ideas like not maintaining separation from the Gentiles (e.g., Acts 21:27–29; cf. 1 Mac 1:11, 41) and God's favor being shown to foreigners (e.g., Lk 4:24–29; Acts 22:17–22) provoke such violent negative reactions from Jews in the first century?

(3) How has the Jewish high priesthood morphed into a seat of political power (14:27–45)?

(4) Why have the Jews—whose observance of the Torah during the time of the Prophets was often tepid at best—become so zealous for it by the time of Christ's advent (e.g., Acts 6:14; 15:1; 21:21)?

While valuable for understanding the historical background of the New Testament period, 1 Maccabees is not explicitly cited by any New Testament author. The likeliest allusion to the book in the New Testament comes in Heb 11:38, where the reference to the faithful who "[wandered] over deserts and mountains, and in dens and caves of the earth" matches the description of those who fled Antiochus' forced apostasy from the Law in 1 Mac 1:53; 2:28–31 (cf. 2 Mac 5:27; 6:11; 10:6). The Feast of Dedication (Hanukkah), which provides the context for Christ's identification as the light of the world in Jn 8–10, is drawn from the events described in 1 Mac 4.

For early patristic writers such as Tertullian, St. John Chrysostom, and St. Ambrose, the protagonists of 1 Maccabees served as examples of fidelity to God under extremely trying circumstances. If the early Christian imagination was most captured by the martyrs of 2 Mac 7, whose resistance was motivated by hope in the resurrection, the early Church regarded Mattathias and his sons in 1 Maccabees to be as noble as their earlier Old Testament forebears, whom they emulated in bravely fighting and dying to preserve the covenants and promises to the Patriarchs.

OUTLINE OF THE FIRST BOOK OF THE MACCABEES

1. Antiochus' Suppression and Mattathias' Revolt (1:1—2:70)
       A. Alexander the Great (1:1–9)
       B. Antiochus and His Persecution (1:10–64)
       C. Mattathias and His Resistance (2:1–70)

2. The Leadership of Judas Maccabeus (3:1—9:22)
       A. Judas' Initial Victories (3:1—4:35)
       B. Purification of the Temple (4:36–61)
       C. Judas' Subsequent Victories (5:1—7:50)
       D. Treaty with the Romans (8:1–32)
       E. Judas Dies in Battle (9:1–22)

3. The Leadership of Jonathan Maccabeus (9:23—12:53)
       A. Jonathan, Warrior and High Priest (9:23—11:74)
       B. Treaty with the Romans and Spartans (12:1–23)
       C. Jonathan Captured by Trypho (12:24–53)

4. The Leadership of Simon Maccabeus (13:1—16:24)
       A. Simon's Early Successes (13:1–53)
       B. Tribute to Simon (14:1–15)
       C. Renewed Alliance with Rome and Sparta (14:16–24)
       D. Simon's Honors (14:25—15:24)
       E. Simon Threatened, Murdered, and Succeeded by John (15:25—16:24)

THE FIRST BOOK OF THE

MACCABEES

Alexander the Great

1 After Alexander son of Philip, the Macedonian, who came from the land of Kittim, had defeated[a] Dari'us, king of the Persians and the Medes, he succeeded him as king. (He had previously become king of Greece.) [2]He fought many battles, conquered strongholds, and put to death the kings of the earth. [3]He advanced to the ends of the earth, and plundered many nations. When the earth became quiet before him, he was exalted, and his heart was lifted up. [4]He gathered a very strong army and ruled over countries, nations, and princes, and they became tributary to him.

5 After this he fell sick and perceived that he was dying. [6]So he summoned his most honored officers, who had been brought up with him from youth, and divided his kingdom among them while he was still alive. [7]And after Alexander had reigned twelve years, he died.

8 Then his officers began to rule, each in his own place. [9]They all put on crowns after his death, and so did their sons after them for many years; and they caused many evils on the earth.

Antiochus Epiphanes and Renegade Jews

10 From them came forth a sinful root, Anti'ochus Epiph'anes, son of Anti'ochus the king; he had been a hostage in Rome. He began to reign in the one hundred and thirty-seventh year of the kingdom of the Greeks.[b]

11 In those days lawless men came forth from Israel, and misled many, saying, "Let us go and make a covenant with the Gentiles round about us, for since we separated from them many evils have come upon us." [12]This proposal pleased them, [13]and some of the people eagerly went to the king. He authorized them to observe the ordinances of the Gentiles. [14]So they built a gymnasium in Jerusalem,

---

1:1–3 The book begins with background information on the Greek conqueror known as Alexander the Great (356–323 B.C.). His title is given in typical Hebrew fashion, naming him as the son of Philip and as a Macedonian (north of Greece) who came from Kittim, the Hebrew name for the island of Cyprus, which is also used to refer to someone who comes from Greece or the west more generally. Alexander's defeat of Darius III in 331 B.C. brings Greek rule to Palestine. At his death, Alexander's kingdom is divided among his former generals, and Judea becomes an area of conflict between the rulers of the Euphrates and Nile valleys. Babylon was taken in 312 B.C. by Seleucus, who founded the Seleucid dynasty, while Ptolemy controlled Egypt and founded the dynasty of Ptolemies. Originally, Judea was within the borders of the Ptolemaic empire, but in 198 B.C., the Seleucid king Antiochus III gained control of the region after defeating Scopas, the general of Ptolemy V.

1:4 became tributary: I.e., became a vassal nation forced to make annual payments to the conquering nation.

1:9 caused many evils: The author presents a consistently negative portrait of the Greek rulers, beginning with the lifted-up heart of Alexander and continuing with his officers. This foreshadows the later pride and wickedness of Antiochus and his own officers.

1:10 one hundred and thirty-seventh year: Counting from the beginning of the Seleucid empire in 312 B.C. Determining the date according to our own system is not straightforward, as two systems of dating were in use at this time: one according to Syrian usage (beginning in the fall), and another following Babylonian usage (beginning in the spring), which was used by the Jews. When the author uses Jewish sources for his account, the Babylonian dating is used, but Syrian dates can be found in the narrative as well.

1:11 lawless men: Introduces a group of Jews who sought to adopt Greek culture, commonly referred to as Hellenizers, who propose to make a covenant with the nations around them. • In light of the divine instructions given to Israel, these words serve as a warning to the reader that apostasy and its consequences are close at hand. (Cf. Ex 23:32: "You shall make no covenant with them or with their gods.... For if you serve their gods, it will surely be a snare to you"; similarly Ex 34:12; Deut 7:2.) While the covenant prohibition is specific to Israel's conquest of the land, the rationale against them is also illustrated in 1 Maccabees, as seen by the Hellenizers' desire to remove the marks of circumcision and abandon the holy covenant (1:15). For the maintenance of such boundaries after the return from exile, see Neh 10:28–31; 13:1–3.

1:13 some ... went to the king: The author of 1 Maccabees leaves out the name of Jason, their leader and the brother of Onias the High Priest, who is known from 2 Maccabees.

1:14 gymnasium: Where sporting activities were performed naked, which was especially offensive to Jewish custom. To remove the marks of one's circumcision was seen as a rejection of Judaism, since it was the primary way men identified as Jews.

The First and Second Books of the Maccabees

1 Maccabees deals with the history of the Jews in Palestine during the forty years from the accession of the Syrian king Antiochus Epiphanes to the death of Simon in 134 B.C. It was a life-and-death struggle between the Jews and the Syrians who wanted to impose Greek religion and culture on them. The book recounts the heroic deeds of the three great leaders, Judas Maccabeus and his brothers Jonathan and Simon, who were in turn at the head of the Jewish people until death overtook them. It was written with a strong religious purpose, and the high point is reached with a description of the rededication of the temple. Originally written in Hebrew about the year 100 B.C., the book now exists only in a Greek translation.

2 Maccabees is quite different. It is not a continuation of 1 Maccabees but concentrates on the period of about fifteen years covered by 1 Maccabees, chapters 1–7. It aims at bringing out even more strongly the religious lessons of the time, and the story is written in a way that is more like a sermon than a history. The historical facts are arranged to suit the religious purpose of the book. Several passages in the work are well known in reference to particular doctrines, e.g., the resurrection of the body (7:9, 11; 14:46); rewards and punishments after death (6:26); prayers for the dead (12:42–45); the intercession of the saints (15:12–16).

[a] Greek adds *and he defeated.*
[b] 175 B.C.

according to Gentile custom, [15]and removed the marks of circumcision, and abandoned the holy covenant. They joined with the Gentiles and sold themselves to do evil.

Antiochus in Egypt

16 When Anti'ochus saw that his kingdom was established, he determined to become king of the land of Egypt, that he might reign over both kingdoms. [17]So he invaded Egypt with a strong force, with chariots and elephants and cavalry and with a large fleet. [18]He engaged Ptol'emy king of Egypt in battle, and Ptolemy turned and fled before him, and many were wounded and fell. [19]And they captured the fortified cities in the land of Egypt, and he plundered the land of Egypt.

Persecution of the Jews

20 After subduing Egypt, Anti'ochus returned in the one hundred and forty-third year.[c] He went up against Israel and came to Jerusalem with a strong force. [21]He arrogantly entered the sanctuary and took the golden altar, the lampstand for the light, and all its utensils. [22]He took also the table for the bread of the Presence, the cups for drink offerings, the bowls, the golden censers, the curtain, the crowns, and the gold decoration on the front of the temple; he stripped it all off. [23]He took the silver and the gold, and the costly vessels; he took also the hidden treasures which he found. [24]Taking them all, he departed to his own land.

He committed deeds of murder,
    and spoke with great arrogance.
[25]Israel mourned deeply in every community,
[26]   rulers and elders groaned,
    maidens and young men became faint,
      the beauty of women faded.

[27]Every bridegroom took up the lament;
    she who sat in the bridal chamber was mourning.
[28]Even the land shook for its inhabitants,
    and all the house of Jacob was clothed with shame.

Occupation of Jerusalem

29 Two years later the king sent to the cities of Judah a chief collector of tribute, and he came to Jerusalem with a large force. [30]Deceitfully he spoke peaceable words to them, and they believed him; but he suddenly fell upon the city, dealt it a severe blow, and destroyed many people of Israel. [31]He plundered the city, burned it with fire, and tore down its houses and its surrounding walls. [32]And they took captive the women and children, and seized the cattle. [33]Then they fortified the city of David with a great strong wall and strong towers, and it became their citadel. [34]And they stationed there a sinful people, lawless men. These strengthened their position; [35]they stored up arms and food, and collecting the spoils of Jerusalem they stored them there, and became a great snare.

[36]It became an ambush against the sanctuary,
    an evil adversary of Israel continually.
[37]On every side of the sanctuary they shed innocent blood;
    they even defiled the sanctuary.
[38]Because of them the residents of Jerusalem fled;
    she became a dwelling of strangers;
  she became strange to her offspring,
    and her children forsook her.
[39]Her sanctuary became desolate as a desert;
    her feasts were turned into mourning,
  her sabbaths into a reproach,
    her honor into contempt.
[40]Her dishonor now grew as great as her glory;
    her exaltation was turned into mourning.

1:18 Ptolemy: The name given to all the rulers of the Ptolemaic dynasty. Here it refers to Ptolemy VI Philometor (reigned 180–145 B.C.), who reappears in 1 Mac 10–11.

1:20 came to Jerusalem: At least the second visit of Antiochus, as 2 Mac 4:22 records an earlier visit where Jason and the people received him favorably. 2 Mac 5:11 attributes his plundering of the city to Jason's revolt against Menelaus, who had outbid Jason for the high priesthood even though he was a Benjaminite (2 Mac 4:24), which was seen by Antiochus as a revolt against Syrian rule.

1:21–23 Gentiles were not allowed into the sanctuary. The hidden treasures Antiochus took suggest that he may have had help from those inside the Temple to locate them. 2 Mac 5:15 records that Menelaus served as Antiochus' guide when he entered the Temple.

1:24–28 The first of many poetic sections in 1 Maccabees. It is a lament composed either at the time of the events or soon afterward and alludes to Joel 2:12–17 and Amos 8:13. The allusion to Joel's call to repentance, along with the nation being "clothed in shame" (1:28), shows the author views the pillage of the Temple as due to the sin of the people, rather than the inability of their God to protect it.

1:29 chief collector of tribute: Likely a reference to Apollonius, the commander of the Mysian army (mercenaries from northwest Asia Minor), who is named in a similar account in 2 Mac 5:24. The original Hebrew for the "commander of the Mysian Army" (*sar hammussim*) and a "chief collector of tribute" (*sar hammissim*) are so similar that scholars suspect the text may have been mistranslated into Greek. On the other hand, this may have been an intentional pun to refer to Apollonius as a tax gatherer, indicating that Apollonius reduced Jerusalem from a city with its own officials to a status of direct taxation.

1:33 citadel: A fortress in Jerusalem that the Seleucids built up and fortified for their occupation of the area (cf. 14:36), which would have been populated by a combination of Seleucid forces and Hellenizing Jews (cf. 6:21). Here the author reminds the reader that this is the city of David as a way to indicate the citadel's true ownership.

1:36–40 A poetic lament matching the one in 1:24–28: as Antiochus oppresses the nation of Israel, so does the citadel oppress the city of Jerusalem. As Exodus 23 warned against making a covenant with the Gentiles (1:11), the citadel has become a great "snare", bringing about a reversal of all the Temple is meant to signify and accomplish among the people. According to 2 Mac 5:27, this is when Judas Maccabeus and his nine companions fled to the wilderness.

---

[c] 169 B.C.

Installation of Gentile Cults

41 Then the king wrote to his whole kingdom that all should be one people, 42and that each should give up his customs. 43All the Gentiles accepted the command of the king. Many even from Israel gladly adopted his religion; they sacrificed to idols and profaned the sabbath. 44And the king sent letters by messengers to Jerusalem and the cities of Judah; he directed them to follow customs strange to the land, 45to forbid burnt offerings and sacrifices and drink offerings in the sanctuary, to profane sabbaths and feasts, 46to defile the sanctuary and the priests, 47to build altars and sacred precincts and shrines for idols, to sacrifice swine and unclean animals, 48and to leave their sons uncircumcised. They were to make themselves abominable by everything unclean and profane, 49so that they should forget the law and change all the ordinances. 50"And whoever does not obey the command of the king shall die."

51 In such words he wrote to his whole kingdom. And he appointed inspectors over all the people and commanded the cities of Judah to offer sacrifice, city by city. 52Many of the people, every one who forsook the law, joined them, and they did evil in the land; 53they drove Israel into hiding in every place of refuge they had.

54 Now on the fifteenth day of Chis'lev, in the one hundred and forty-fifth year,ᵈ they erected a desolating sacrilege upon the altar of burnt offering.

They also built altars in the surrounding cities of Judah, 55and burned incense at the doors of the houses and in the streets. 56The books of the law which they found they tore to pieces and burned with fire. 57Where the book of the covenant was found in the possession of any one, or if any one adhered to the law, the decree of the king condemned him to death. 58They kept using violence against Israel, against those found month after month in the cities. 59And on the twenty-fifth day of the month they offered sacrifice on the altar which was upon the altar of burnt offering. 60According to the decree, they put to death the women who had their children circumcised, 61and their families and those who circumcised them; and they hung the infants from their mothers' necks.

62 But many in Israel stood firm and were resolved in their hearts not to eat unclean food. 63They chose to die rather than to be defiled by food or to profane the holy covenant; and they did die. 64And very great wrath came upon Israel.

Mattathias and His Sons

2 In those days Mattathi'as the son of John, son of Simeon, a priest of the sons of Jo'arib, moved from Jerusalem and settled in Mo'dein. 2He had five sons, John surnamed Gaddi, 3Simon called Thassi, 4Judas called Mac"cabe'us, 5Elea'zar called Av'aran, and Jonathan called Ap'phus. 6He saw

---

1:41–50 A decree against the Palestinian Jews, whose obedience to their Law through keeping Jewish sacrifices, Sabbath, and circumcision is causing unrest with the "lawless" leaders, who wish to abandon them. Judea's proximity to Egypt, the rival empire to the Seleucids, makes this unrest a particular political threat to Antiochus.

1:54 desolating sacrilege: Also known as the abomination of desolation. It refers to an act of Antiochus IV that desecrated the Jerusalem Temple, possibly the erection of a statue of the Greek god Zeus or a pagan altar within the sanctuary precincts. 2 Mac 6:2 records that the Temple was dedicated to the Olympian Zeus, which Antiochus may have assumed to be the Greek name for the Jewish god, thus conforming Israelite worship to Greek worship. The author is careful to give the exact date—December 6, 167 B.C., by modern dating—with sacrifice given upon it ten days later. • The abomination of desolation is also referred to in Dan 9:27; 11:21; and 12:11. It refers to a detestable entity that leads to damnation: although those who follow along with it now may be kept temporarily alive, in the future it will be death to them. This act of Antiochus leaves an indelible mark in Jewish memory, being used by Jesus in Mt 24:15–25 (cf. Mk 13:14) to describe the destruction that will come with the fall of Jerusalem in A.D. 70 and the trials at the end of time.

1:62–64 The response of the faithful in Israel, who are willing to die rather than "profane the holy covenant". 2 Mac 6 offers another account of this episode, detailing the brutality of the acts that enforced the decree. The author's conclusion— "And very great wrath came upon Israel"—is an example of how 1 Maccabees describes God's activity in a manner that is more implicit than explicit. If this is God's wrath coming

upon Israel, it likely ties back to 1:11, where the deeds of the "lawless men coming forth from Israel" are recorded. The mourning and shame expressed in the chapter's poetic sections also show that Israel viewed the calamity that had fallen upon it as punishment for sin. This aligns with 2 Maccabees, which explicitly states that these events were an illustration of God's kindness in punishing Israel before its sins had reached their fullness (2 Mac 6:12–15).

1:62 not to eat unclean food: The pious resolve to avoid unclean food and uphold God's covenant is simply demonstrated by Peter, who initially refuses to heed the heavenly vision at Joppa in Acts 10:9–16 because he has never eaten anything unclean. Only with God's insistence does Peter recognize that both the previously unclean foods and unclean foreign nations—represented by the descending wild beasts and Cornelius the centurion—have been made pure by Christ's atoning work. For laws on unclean foods, see Lev 11:1–47 and Deut 14:1–21.

2:1 priest of ... Joarib: Mattathias descends from the priestly family of Joarib (cf. 1 Chron 24:7). **Modein:** A town about 20 miles northwest of Jerusalem. Modein was Mattathias' ancestral home (2:70), and his return may have been precipitated by the persecution in Jerusalem (1:38).

2:2–5 The nicknames of each of Mattathias' sons are the subject of much conjecture, with respect both to their meaning and to whether they correspond with qualities of their namesake. Judas' surname (Maccabeus) is usually interpreted as "hammer", which fits well with his role in the narrative, while Jonathan's (Apphus, perhaps from the Syriac for "dissembler" or "diplomat") would correspond with the wise diplomacy exercised during his leadership. Others are less clear: John's (Gaddi) may mean "lucky", Simon's (Thassi) is speculated to be related to "wise" or "fiery", and Eleazar's (Avaran) could mean "alert" or "piercer".

ᵈ 167 B.C.

the blasphemies being committed in Judah and Jerusalem, [7]and said,

"Alas! Why was I born to see this,
   the ruin of my people, the ruin of the holy city,
and to dwell there when it was given over to the enemy,
   the sanctuary given over to aliens?
[8]Her temple has become like a man without honor;[e]
[9]   her glorious vessels have been carried into captivity.
Her infants have been killed in her streets,
   her youths by the sword of the foe.
[10]What nation has not inherited her palaces[f]
   and has not seized her spoils?
[11]All her adornment has been taken away;
   no longer free, she has become a slave.
[12]And behold, our holy place, our beauty,
   and our glory have been laid waste;
   the Gentiles have profaned it.
[13]   Why should we live any longer?"

14 And Mattathi'as and his sons tore their clothes, put on sackcloth, and mourned greatly.

Pagan Worship Refused

15 Then the king's officers who were enforcing the apostasy came to the city of Mo'dein to make them offer sacrifice. [16]Many from Israel came to them; and Mattathi'as and his sons were assembled. [17]Then the king's officers spoke to Mattathi'as as follows: "You are a leader, honored and great in this city, and supported by sons and brothers. [18]Now be the first to come and do what the king commands, as all the Gentiles and the men of Judah and those that are left in Jerusalem have done. Then you and your sons will be numbered among the friends of the king, and you and your sons will be honored with silver and gold and many gifts."

19 But Mattathi'as answered and said in a loud voice: "Even if all the nations that live under the rule of the king obey him, and have chosen to do his commandments, departing each one from the religion of his fathers, [20]yet I and my sons and my brothers will live by the covenant of our fathers. [21]Far be it from us to desert the law and the ordinances. [22]We will not obey the king's words by turning aside from our religion to the right hand or to the left."

23 When he had finished speaking these words, a Jew came forward in the sight of all to offer sacrifice upon the altar in Mo'dein, according to the king's command. [24]When Mattathi'as saw it, he burned with zeal and his heart was stirred. He gave vent to righteous anger; he ran and killed him upon the altar. [25]At the same time he killed the king's officer who was forcing them to sacrifice, and he tore down the altar. [26]Thus he burned with zeal for the law, as Phin'ehas did against Zimri the son of Sa'lu.

27 Then Mattathi'as cried out in the city with a loud voice, saying: "Let every one who is zealous for the law and supports the covenant come out with me!" [28]And he and his sons fled to the hills and left all that they had in the city.

29 Then many who were seeking righteousness and justice went down to the wilderness to dwell there, [30]they, their sons, their wives, and their cattle, because evils pressed heavily upon them. [31]And it was reported to the king's officers, and to the troops in Jerusalem the city of David, that men who had rejected the king's command had gone down to the

---

2:7-13 The third poetic lament is full of allusions to other tragedies in Israel's history, such as the destruction of Jerusalem and its Temple (cf. Lam 1:10; 2:11, 21) and Israel's enslavement in Egypt (2:11).

2:20-22 Mattathias' response that he will serve the Lord and not turn to the right or left alludes to Moses' and Joshua's words in Deut 17:20; 28:13-14; and Josh 1:7; 24:15. Mattathias' resolve will live on in his sons, who turn neither to right or to left in battle (cf. 5:46; 6:45).

2:23-26 Mattathias' zeal is modeled on that of Phinehas in Num 25:6-15. As a leader in the community, Mattathias has the responsibility to resist Antiochus' decrees and enforce the Jewish Law, which calls for the execution of apostates (cf. Deut 13:10). Like Phinehas, who was given a perpetual priesthood (cf. 2:54), the line of Mattathias will eventually form a dynasty of high priests under his son Jonathan (cf. 10:20). The likening of Mattathias to Phinehas serves to show this family's eligibility for the priesthood, which contrasts in this period with the high priests Jason and Menelaus, whose corruption and bribery have ended the Oniad line of priests (cf. 2 Mac 4). • While Christ's new covenant differs from the Mosaic Law regarding punishment for apostasy, both affirm the responsibility of civic leaders to preserve justice and constrain evil (cf. Rom 13:4; 1 Pet 2:14). Mattathias is singled out as Modein's leader by the Seleucid forces, and, rather than abandoning the covenant and collaborating with their oppressors, Mattathias fights back against those who were slaughtering the innocent (1:57-63) and those who were joining with them. Though not formulated until centuries later, such a defensive war to protect the innocent and restore justice anticipates later Christian teaching on just war (CCC 2302-17).

2:27-28 Mattathias' summons echoes the call of Moses after the golden calf apostasy in Ex 32:26, and the subsequent upholding of the covenant by force in 2:42-48 parallels the violent zeal of the sons of Levi who respond to Moses in Ex 32:27-29. The analogy with the Levites, who received the priesthood for their willingness to prioritize God over tribal or familial ties (Ex 32:29), here foreshadows the eventual Maccabean ascension to the high priesthood.

2:29-38 Commentators suggest that the people fled to the wilderness seeking justice in accordance with the prophecies of Isaiah 32, where 32:6 is interpreted as referring to Antiochus, and 32:16 promises justice in the desert. Isaiah 56:1-2 also creates a strong link between Sabbath observance and the arrival of salvation and justice. During this period of history, Jews interpreted the Sabbath laws to encompass a prohibition on war, even defensive warfare, on the Sabbath. This fact was exploited by their enemies. It is possible this group, often labeled the Pietists, were hoping for miraculous deliverance. Patristic readers like St. Hippolytus connected this group with "the wise" who are afflicted in Dan 11:33.

---

[e] The text of this verse is uncertain.
[f] Other authorities read *has not had a part in her kingdom.*

hiding places in the wilderness. ³²Many pursued them, and overtook them; they encamped opposite them and prepared for battle against them on the sabbath day. ³³And they said to them, "Enough of this! Come out and do what the king commands, and you will live." ³⁴But they said, "We will not come out, nor will we do what the king commands and so profane the sabbath day." ³⁵Then the enemy ᵍ hastened to attack them. ³⁶But they did not answer them or hurl a stone at them or block up their hiding places, ³⁷for they said, "Let us all die in our innocence; heaven and earth testify for us that you are killing us unjustly." ³⁸So they attacked them on the sabbath, and they died, with their wives and children and cattle, to the number of a thousand persons.

39 When Mattathi′as and his friends learned of it, they mourned for them deeply. ⁴⁰And each said to his neighbor: "If we all do as our brethren have done and refuse to fight with the Gentiles for our lives and for our ordinances, they will quickly destroy us from the earth." ⁴¹So they made this decision that day: "Let us fight against every man who comes to attack us on the sabbath day; let us not all die as our brethren died in their hiding places."

Counterattack

42 Then there united with them a company of Hasid′eans, mighty warriors of Israel, every one who offered himself willingly for the law. ⁴³And all who became fugitives to escape their troubles joined them and reinforced them. ⁴⁴They organized an army, and struck down sinners in their anger and lawless men in their wrath; the survivors fled to the Gentiles for safety. ⁴⁵And Mattathi′as and his friends went about and tore down the altars; ⁴⁶they forcibly circumcised all the uncircumcised boys that they found within the borders of Israel. ⁴⁷They hunted down the arrogant men, and the work prospered in their hands. ⁴⁸They rescued the law out of the hands of the Gentiles and kings, and they never let the sinner gain the upper hand.

Last Words of Mattathias

49 Now the days drew near for Mattathi′as to die, and he said to his sons: "Arrogance and reproach have now become strong; it is a time of ruin and furious anger. ⁵⁰Now, my children, show zeal for the law, and give your lives for the covenant of our fathers.

51 "Remember the deeds of the fathers, which they did in their generations; and receive great

---

2:39–41 Since war on the Sabbath was seen as violating the biblical commandment of rest, the author presents Mattathias' justification for defensive warfare: without fighting for their lives and ordinances, they will be destroyed from the earth. Warfare on the Sabbath was not entirely without precedent, as even Joshua, by divine command, appears to have marched against Jericho on the Sabbath (Josh 6:3–4). However, the Maccabees still observe the Sabbath in other instances when engaged in war (see 2 Mac 8:25–29). • Patristic readers such as Tertullian understood the Maccabees' example, like Joshua's, as an illustration of how the commandment

to observe the Sabbath was temporary and provisional, rather than eternal and absolute (*Against the Jews* 4).

2:42 Hasideans: Commentators disagree on who exactly the Hasideans were, and some speculate they were related to the group who died in the wilderness. Their name means "the pious" (from the Hebrew word *ḥesed*), and the Essenes and Pharisees are both usually traced back to this group. Later in 1 Maccabees (7:13), they desert the Maccabees when Alcimus is given the high priesthood.

2:49–69 Mattathias gives a farewell speech before his death, then is gathered to his ancestors in a manner similar to Jacob (Gen 49) and Moses (Deut 33).

2:51 great honor and an everlasting name: Unlike 2 Maccabees, 1 Maccabees gives no clear articulation of an expectation of the afterlife.

ᵍ Gk *they*.

WORD STUDY

Show Zeal (2:50)

zēloō (Gk.): A verb meaning "be zealous". By itself, zeal is morally neutral, representing a state of intense ardor or dedication that can be employed positively or negatively. We might use a phrase like "fired up" as an analogy: without appropriate cause, this can simply mean misplaced anger or jealousy, but it can also be the proper response to the violation of justice, and the absence of "fire" in such situations may actually represent an opposite error of indifference. Scripture thus presents both negative and positive examples of zealousness, with the misplaced anger of the Jewish leaders who did not recognize Christ described as being filled with "zeal" (translated "jealously" in Acts 5:17), and Jesus' forceful cleansing of the Temple in John 2 similarly described as "zeal" for God's house (Jn 2:17; cf. Ps 69:9). First Maccabees is filled with heroes who are zealous in the positive sense, who reject apathy and instead respond with resolve and conviction to injustice and oppression. Christians throughout the centuries have rightly regarded zealous figures like the Maccabees as heroes of the faith: not that each of their actions done under the Mosaic Law is to be emulated, but that they embody a complete fidelity to God and a complete rejection of the devil and all his works. It is such zeal to which Christ calls his disciples as well (cf. Mt 5:29–30; Eph 6:10–17) and, indeed, prefigures the zeal of the Son of God, who himself became incarnate "to destroy the works of the devil" (1 Jn 3:8).

honor and an everlasting name. ⁵²Was not Abraham found faithful when tested, and it was reckoned to him as righteousness? ⁵³Joseph in the time of his distress kept the commandment, and became lord of Egypt. ⁵⁴Phin'ehas our father, because he was deeply zealous, received the covenant of everlasting priesthood. ⁵⁵Joshua, because he fulfilled the command, became a judge in Israel. ⁵⁶Caleb, because he testified in the assembly, received an inheritance in the land. ⁵⁷David, because he was merciful, inherited the throne of the kingdom for ever. ⁵⁸Eli'jah because of great zeal for the law was taken up into heaven. ⁵⁹Hanani'ah, Azari'ah, and Mish'a-el believed and were saved from the flame. ⁶⁰Daniel because of his innocence was delivered from the mouth of the lions.

61 "And so observe, from generation to generation, that none who put their trust in him will lack strength. ⁶²Do not fear the words of a sinner, for his splendor will turn into dung and worms. ⁶³Today he will be exalted, but tomorrow he will not be found, because he has returned to the dust, and his plans will perish. ⁶⁴My children, be courageous and grow strong in the law, for by it you will gain honor.

65 "Now behold, I know that Simeon your brother is wise in counsel; always listen to him; he shall be your father. ⁶⁶Judas Mac"cabe'us has been a mighty warrior from his youth; he shall command the army for you and fight the battle against the peoples.ʰ ⁶⁷You shall rally about you all who observe the law, and avenge the wrong done to your people. ⁶⁸Pay back the Gentiles in full, and heed what the law commands."

69 Then he blessed them, and was gathered to his fathers. ⁷⁰He died in the one hundred and forty-sixth yearⁱ and was buried in the tomb of his fathers at Mo'dein. And all Israel mourned for him with great lamentation.

Early Victories of Judas Maccabeus

3 Then Judas his son, who was called Mac"cabe'us, took command in his place. ²All his brothers and all who had joined his father helped him; they gladly fought for Israel.

³He extended the glory of his people.
Like a giant he put on his breastplate;
he belted on his armor of war and waged battles,
protecting the host by his sword.
⁴He was like a lion in his deeds,
like a lion's cub roaring for prey.
⁵He searched out and pursued the lawless;
he burned those who troubled his people.
⁶Lawless men shrank back for fear of him;
all the evildoers were confounded;
and deliverance prospered by his hand.
⁷He embittered many kings,
but he made Jacob glad by his deeds,
and his memory is blessed for ever.
⁸He went through the cities of Judah;
he destroyed the ungodly out of the land;ʲ
thus he turned away wrath from Israel.
⁹He was renowned to the ends of the earth;
he gathered in those who were perishing.

10 But Apollo'nius gathered together Gentiles and a large force from Samar'ia to fight against Israel. ¹¹When Judas learned of it, he went out to meet him, and he defeated and killed him. Many were wounded and fell, and the rest fled. ¹²Then they seized their spoils; and Judas took the sword of Apollo'nius, and used it in battle the rest of his life.

13 Now when Se'ron, the commander of the Syrian army, heard that Judas had gathered a large company, including a body of faithful men who stayed with him and went out to battle, ¹⁴he said, "I will make a name for myself and win honor in the kingdom. I will make war on Judas and his companions, who scorn the king's command." ¹⁵And again a strong army of ungodly men went

---

2:52-60 Most of these examples from Israel's history are known for their faithfulness and zeal for the law. The description of David ("because he was merciful") appears as a bit of an outlier, which may be explained by *ḥesed* as the underlying Hebrew word, which also conveys covenant loyalty. Similar lists of the faithful occur in Heb 11 and Sir 44-50. See word study: *Merciful Love* at Ex 34:7.

2:64 be courageous and grow strong: Echoes Joshua's commissioning before the conquest of the Promised Land in Josh 1:6-9.

2:65 Simeon: The Hebrew form of Simon. **shall be your father:** This identification (along with his placement at the front) may correspond with Simon's later ascension to Israel's high priesthood and political leadership (14:41), which begins the Hasmonean dynasty.

3:3-9 The book's fourth poetic section is in honor of Judas. He is likened to a lion's cub in 3:4, echoing the description of Judah in Gen 49:9. According to 3:8, the wrath spoken of in 1:64 was turned away by Judas' destruction of the ungodly, which is another allusion to Phinehas, whose zeal similarly turned away God's anger from Israel (Num 25:11).

3:10-26 The battles against Apollonius and Seron are not mentioned in 2 Maccabees, possibly suggesting that they were guerrilla struggles and not yet full-fledged wars. Such battles would also necessitate the taking of spoils as a measure to arm Judas' nascent forces.

3:10 Apollonius: Identified by Josephus as the governor of Samaria. It is unknown whether or not he is the same Apollonius as the Mysian captain in 2 Mac 5:24 and alluded to in 1:29.

3:12 sword of Apollonius: Like David with Goliath, Judas takes the sword of his conquered enemy (1 Sam 17:51; 21:9).

3:13 Seron: A professional Syrian soldier. As the Syrian forces are near Antioch at this time as part of a review, Seron's army would likely consist of a number of Jews who are opposed to the Maccabean revolt.

ʰ Or *of the people.*
ⁱ 166 B.C.
ʲ Gk *it.*

up with him to help him, to take vengeance on the sons of Israel.

16 When he approached the ascent of Beth-ho'ron, Judas went out to meet him with a small company. [17]But when they saw the army coming to meet them, they said to Judas, "How can we, few as we are, fight against so great and strong a multitude? And we are faint, for we have eaten nothing today." [18]Judas replied, "It is easy for many to be hemmed in by few, for in the sight of Heaven there is no difference between saving by many or by few. [19]It is not on the size of the army that victory in battle depends, but strength comes from Heaven. [20]They come against us in great pride and lawlessness to destroy us and our wives and our children, and to despoil us; [21]but we fight for our lives and our laws. [22]He himself will crush them before us; as for you, do not be afraid of them."

23 When he finished speaking, he rushed suddenly against Se'ron and his army, and they were crushed before him. [24]They pursued them[k] down the descent of Beth-ho'ron to the plain; eight hundred of them fell, and the rest fled into the land of the Philis'tines. [25]Then Judas and his brothers began to be feared, and terror fell upon the Gentiles round about them. [26]His fame reached the king, and the Gentiles talked of the battles of Judas.

The Policy of Antiochus

27 When king Anti'ochus heard these reports, he was greatly angered; and he sent and gathered all the forces of his kingdom, a very strong army. [28]And he opened his coffers and gave a year's pay to his forces, and ordered them to be ready for any need. [29]Then he saw that the money in the treasury was exhausted, and that the revenues from the country were small because of the dissension and disaster which he had caused in the land by abolishing the laws that had existed from the earliest days. [30]He feared that he might not have such funds as he had before for his expenses and for the gifts which he used to give more lavishly than preceding kings. [31]He was greatly perplexed in mind, and determined to go to Persia and collect the revenues from those regions and raise a large fund.

32 He left Lys'ias, a distinguished man of royal lineage, in charge of the king's affairs from the river Euphrates to the borders of Egypt. [33]Lys'ias was also to take care of Anti'ochus his son until he returned. [34]And he turned over to Lys'ias[l] half of his troops and the elephants, and gave him orders about all that he wanted done. As for the residents of Judea and Jerusalem, [35]Lys'ias was to send a force against them to wipe out and destroy the strength of Israel and the remnant of Jerusalem; he was to banish the memory of them from the place, [36]settle aliens in all their territory, and distribute their land. [37]Then the king took the remaining half of his troops and departed from Antioch his capital in the one hundred and forty-seventh year.[m] He crossed the Euphrates river and went through the upper provinces.

Preparations for Battle

38 Lys'ias chose Ptol'emy the son of Dorym'enes, and Nica'nor and Gor'gias, mighty men among the friends of the king, [39]and sent with them forty

---

3:16 Beth-horon: A strategic battle location about 11 miles northwest of Jerusalem. The town controls the road to Jerusalem from the coastal plain, and the slope can also be used as a trap against armies and allow for a much smaller force to defeat a larger one. It is employed by Joshua in battle (Josh 10:10–11), and later the Romans suffer a defeat there in A.D. 66.

3:18 there is no difference … by few: An allusion to Jonathan's words in 1 Sam 14:6, before he and his armor-bearer rout the Philistines.

3:19 strength comes from Heaven: The use of "Heaven" with reference to God is a common example of 1 Maccabees' indirect way of speaking about divine aid and intervention in history. See also 4:10; 9:46; 12:15; 16:3.

3:22 He himself: Like the author's reference to God using "Heaven", here God is referred to with a simple pronoun ("he himself").

3:24 land of the Philistines: The descent moves westward toward what was in past times the land of the Philistines. The author's use of the phrase here presents the Maccabees as heirs to the centuries-long struggle of faithful Israel against its Gentile neighbors.

3:27–31 The author sets concerns over Judas' rebellion and Antiochus' lack of funds from his oppression of Jewish laws as the primary reasons for his expedition into Persia. Other reasons, derived from ancient sources, include Antiochus' concern to put the eastern provinces more firmly under his control and to exact taxes to prevent the funding of a possible usurper to his throne. The author's focus on Antiochus' actions as they relate to Israel shows that the snare Antiochus set for Israel has now become one for him as well and will lead to his eventual downfall.

3:32 Lysias: A distinguished Seleucid general, identified as Antiochus' guardian and kinsman in 2 Mac 11:1. **Euphrates to … Egypt:** Encompasses the land of Palestine.

3:33 his son: Antiochus' son, Antiochus V Eupator, who was at most nine years old.

3:37 Antioch: The western capital of the Seleucid empire, about 300 miles north of Jerusalem.

3:38 Ptolemy the son of Dorymenes: Another general of Antiochus. Elsewhere we learn that Ptolemy receives Menelaus' bribe (2 Mac 4:45) and is identified as the governor of Coele-syria, who sends out Nicanor and Gorgias (2 Mac 8:8–9). It is unclear whether this figure is the same as Ptolemy Macron in 2 Mac 10:12, whose kindness to the Jews contrasts with Ptolemy's aggression here. **Nicanor:** One of Antiochus' "chief friends" and "honored princes", who is said to have hated Israel (7:26; 2 Mac 8:9). He is identified as the governor of Cyprus and later Judea (2 Mac 12:2; 14:12) and is a recurring character in both Maccabean books. **Gorgias:** Another experienced Seleucid general who later becomes governor of Idumea (2 Mac 8:9; 10:14).

3:39 forty-thousand … seven thousand: Estimates from ancient historians regarding the size of military forces vary widely, and often figures are exaggerated. It is possible that the author is relating Judas to David, who similarly defeated a Syrian force of 40,000 infantry and 7,000 chariots (1 Chron 19:18). Jason of Cyrene numbers this army at 20,000 in 2 Mac 8:9.

---

[k] Other authorities read *him.*

[l] Gk *him.*

[m] 165 B.C.

thousand infantry and seven thousand cavalry to go into the land of Judah and destroy it, as the king had commanded. [40]So they departed with their entire force, and when they arrived they encamped near Emma'us in the plain. [41]When the traders of the region heard what was said of them, they took silver and gold in immense amounts, and shackles,[n] and went to the camp to get the sons of Israel for slaves. And forces from Syria and the land of the Philis'tines joined with them.

42 Now Judas and his brothers saw that misfortunes had increased and that the forces were encamped in their territory. They also learned what the king had commanded to do to the people to cause their final destruction. [43]But they said to one another, "Let us repair the destruction of our people, and fight for our people and the sanctuary." [44]And the congregation assembled to be ready for battle, and to pray and ask for mercy and compassion.
[45]Jerusalem was uninhabited like a wilderness;
    not one of her children went in or out.
The sanctuary was trampled down,
    and the sons of aliens held the citadel;
    it was a lodging place for the Gentiles.
Joy was taken from Jacob;
    the flute and the harp ceased to play.

46 So they assembled and went to Mizpah, opposite Jerusalem, because Israel formerly had a place of prayer in Mizpah. [47]They fasted that day, put on sackcloth and sprinkled ashes on their heads, and tore their clothes. [48]And they opened the book of the law to inquire into those matters about which the Gentiles were consulting the images of their idols. [49]They also brought the garments of the priesthood and the first fruits and the tithes, and they stirred up the Naz'irites who had completed their days; [50]and they cried aloud to Heaven, saying,
"What shall we do with these?
    Where shall we take them?
[51]Your sanctuary is trampled down and
        profaned,
    and your priests mourn in humiliation.
[52]And behold, the Gentiles are assembled
        against us to destroy us;
    you know what they plot against us.
[53]How will we be able to withstand them,
    if you do not help us?"

54 Then they sounded the trumpets and gave a loud shout. [55]After this Judas appointed leaders of the people, in charge of thousands and hundreds and fifties and tens. [56]And he said to those who were building houses, or were betrothed, or were planting vineyards, or were fainthearted, that each should return to his home, according to the law. [57]Then the army marched out and encamped to the south of Emma'us.

58 And Judas said, "Gird yourselves and be valiant. Be ready early in the morning to fight with these Gentiles who have assembled against us to destroy us and our sanctuary. [59]It is better for us to die in battle than to see the misfortunes of our nation and of the sanctuary. [60]But as his will in heaven may be, so he will do."

The Battle at Emmaus

4 Now Gor'gias took five thousand infantry and a thousand picked cavalry, and this division moved out by night [2]to fall upon the camp of the Jews and attack them suddenly. Men from the citadel were his guides. [3]But Judas heard of it, and he and his mighty men moved out to attack the king's force in Emma'us [4]while the division was still absent from the camp. [5]When Gor'gias entered the camp of Judas by night, he found no one there, so he looked for them in the hills, because he said, "These men are fleeing from us."

6 At daybreak Judas appeared in the plain with three thousand men, but they did not have armor and swords such as they desired. [7]And they saw the camp of the Gentiles, strong and fortified, with cavalry round about it; and these men were trained in war. [8]But Judas said to the men who were with him, "Do not fear their numbers or be afraid when they charge. [9]Remember how our fathers were saved at the Red Sea, when Pharaoh with his forces pursued them. [10]And now let us cry to Heaven, to see whether he will favor us and remember his covenant with our fathers and crush this army before us today. [11]Then all the Gentiles will know that there is one who redeems and saves Israel."

3:40 Emmaus: A town around 20 miles west of Jerusalem. It is uncertain whether this Emmaus corresponds with the site of Jesus' appearance in Lk 24. The Syrian forces may have occupied the coastal region in order to block Judas from seeking help from Ptolemy.

3:46–53 Since they could no longer go to the Temple, nor was there a prophet or a priest with Urim and Thummim to consult, Judas takes the people to Mizpah, where Samuel had prayed for victory over the Philistines (1 Sam 7:5). Here they consult the book of the Law for direction and ask for favor in battle so that they might be free to worship God in his Temple once again. • As St. John Chrysostom writes regarding

their fasting and petitions, the Maccabees reminded the people that God loves men and never takes away from them the salvation that comes from repentance (*Treatise on Psalm 44*).

3:49: Nazirites: Those who made a special vow dedicating themselves to God for a defined period of time. During this time, they were prohibited from drinking wine or juice from grapes, shaving their heads, and going near the dead. See Num 6:1–21.

3:55 in charge of thousands: Judas appoints leaders in the fashion of Moses (see Ex 18:25).

3:56 according to the law: This follows the injunctions in Deut 20:5–8, showing that Judas' concern for the law is greater than his need for numbers in the army.

3:60 as his will ... so he: See note on 3:22.

4:1 Gorgias: See note on 3:38.

---

[n]Syr: Gk *slaves*.

12 When the foreigners looked up and saw them coming against them, ¹³they went forth from their camp to battle. Then the men with Judas blew their trumpets ¹⁴and engaged in battle. The Gentiles were crushed and fled into the plain, ¹⁵and all those in the rear fell by the sword. They pursued them to Gaza′ra, and to the plains of Idume′a, and to Azo′tus and Jam′nia; and three thousand of them fell. ¹⁶Then Judas and his force turned back from pursuing them, ¹⁷and he said to the people, "Do not be greedy for plunder, for there is a battle before us; ¹⁸Gor′gias and his force are near us in the hills. But stand now against our enemies and fight them, and afterward seize the plunder boldly."

19 Just as Judas was finishing this speech, a detachment appeared, coming out of the hills. ²⁰They saw that their army° had been put to flight, and that the Jews° were burning the camp, for the smoke that was seen showed what had happened. ²¹When they perceived this they were greatly frightened, and when they also saw the army of Judas drawn up in the plain for battle, ²²they all fled into the land of the Philis′tines. ²³Then Judas returned to plunder the camp, and they seized much gold and silver, and cloth dyed blue and sea purple, and great riches. ²⁴On their return they sang hymns and praises to Heaven, for he is good, for his mercy endures for ever. ²⁵Thus Israel had a great deliverance that day.

First Campaign of Lysias

26 Those of the foreigners who escaped went and reported to Lys′ias all that had happened. ²⁷When he heard it, he was perplexed and discouraged, for things had not happened to Israel as he had intended, nor had they turned out as the king had commanded him. ²⁸But the next year he mustered sixty thousand picked infantrymen and five thousand cavalry to subdue them. ²⁹They came into

---

4:15 Gazara: Also known as Gezer (cf. Josh 16:10; 1 Kings 9:15), a city in the foothills of the Judean mountains, on the road from Jerusalem to the coastal city of Joppa. **Idumea:** Judea's neighbor to the south and home of the Edomites, traditionally the sons of Esau. The plains of Idumea extend northward toward the coastal cities of Azotus and Jamnia. **Azotus**

and Jamnia: Coastal cities west of Jerusalem that formerly belonged to the Philistines. Azotus, also known as Ashdod, was the site of Dagon's temple where the Philistines brought the captured Ark of the Covenant in 1 Sam 5.

4:24 his mercy endures for ever: Cf. Ps 118:1; 136:1. This song of thanksgiving credits their victory to divine assistance.

4:29 Beth-zur: A town 20 miles southwest of Jerusalem on the border between Idumea and Judea. It becomes a key location within the book and is the next place that Judas fortifies after Mount Zion (4:61).

°Gk *they.*

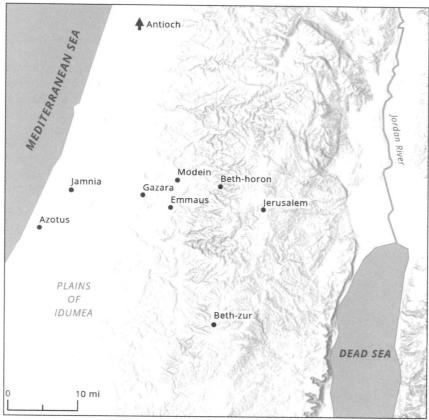

BATTLE SITES IN JUDEA

Idume'a and encamped at Beth-zur,* and Judas met
them with ten thousand men.
30 When he saw that the army was strong, he
prayed, saying, "Blessed are you, O Savior of Israel,
who did crush the attack of the mighty warrior by
the hand of your servant David, and did give the
camp of the Philis'tines into the hands of Jonathan,
the son of Saul, and of the man who carried his
armor. 31 So do you hem in this army by the hand of
your people Israel, and let them be ashamed of their
troops and their cavalry. 32 Fill them with cowardice;
melt the boldness of their strength; let them tremble
in their destruction. 33 Strike them down with the
sword of those who love you, and let all who know
your name praise you with hymns."
34 Then both sides attacked, and there fell of
the army of Lys'ias five thousand men; they fell
in action.[p] 35 And when Lys'ias saw the rout of his
troops and observed the boldness which inspired
those of Judas, and how ready they were either to
live or to die nobly, he departed to Antioch and
enlisted mercenaries, to invade Judea again with an
even larger army.

Cleansing and Dedication of the Temple

36 Then said Judas and his brothers, "Behold,
our enemies are crushed; let us go up to cleanse
the sanctuary and dedicate it." 37 So all the army
assembled and they went up to Mount Zion.
38 And they saw the sanctuary desolate, the altar
profaned, and the gates burned. In the courts they
saw bushes sprung up as in a thicket, or as on one
of the mountains. They saw also the chambers of
the priests in ruins. 39 Then they tore their clothes,
and mourned with great lamentation, and sprinkled
themselves with ashes. 40 They fell face down on the
ground, and sounded the signal on the trumpets,
and cried out to Heaven. 41 Then Judas detailed men
to fight against those in the citadel until he had
cleansed the sanctuary.
42 He chose blameless priests devoted to the law,
43 and they cleansed the sanctuary and removed the
defiled stones to an unclean place. 44 They deliberated
what to do about the altar of burnt offering, which
had been profaned. 45 And they thought it best to tear
it down, lest it bring reproach upon them, for the
Gentiles had defiled it. So they tore down the altar,
46 and stored the stones in a convenient place on the
temple hill until there should come a prophet to tell
what to do with them. 47 Then they took unhewn[q]
stones, as the law directs, and built a new altar like
the former one. 48 They also rebuilt the sanctuary
and the interior of the temple, and consecrated the
courts. 49 They made new holy vessels, and brought
the lampstand, the altar of incense, and the table
into the temple. 50 Then they burned incense on the
altar and lighted the lamps on the lampstand, and
these gave light in the temple. 51 They placed the
bread on the table and hung up the curtains. Thus
they finished all the work they had undertaken.
52 Early in the morning on the twenty-fifth day
of the ninth month, which is the month of Chis'lev, in
the one hundred and forty-eighth year,[r] 53 they rose
and offered sacrifice, as the law directs, on the new
altar of burnt offering which they had built. 54 At the
very season and on the very day that the Gentiles
had profaned it, it was dedicated with songs and
harps and lutes and cymbals. 55 All the people fell
on their faces and worshiped and blessed Heaven,
who had prospered them. 56 So they celebrated the
dedication of the altar for eight days, and offered
burnt offerings with gladness; they offered a
sacrifice of deliverance and praise. 57 They decorated
the front of the temple with golden crowns and small
shields; they restored the gates and the chambers for
the priests, and furnished them with doors. 58 There
was very great gladness among the people, and the
reproach of the Gentiles was removed.
59 Then Judas and his brothers and all the
assembly of Israel determined that every year at
that season the days of the dedication of the altar
should be observed with gladness and joy for eight
days, beginning with the twenty-fifth day of the
month of Chis'lev.
60 At that time they fortified Mount Zion with
high walls and strong towers round about, to keep
the Gentiles from coming and trampling them
down as they had done before. 61 And he stationed

4:30–33 Judas' prayer recalls the two examples of David (1 Sam 17) and Jonathan (1 Sam 14:1–14), who were granted victory by God despite their lack of size.

4:34–35 Second Maccabees 11 fills out this short summary, including negotiations with Lysias following the battle that grant greater freedom for Jewish worship and customs (2 Mac 11:13–38).

4:41 citadel: See note on 1:33.

4:46 until there should come a prophet: This brief comment, and the similar one in 14:41, allude to the Jewish expectation of a coming prophet, attested elsewhere in Deut 18:15 and Mal 4:5.

4:47 unhewn stones: Instructions for the altar are found in Ex 20:25 and Deut 27:6.

4:52–59 Three years after the abomination of desolation was erected in 167 B.C., Judas completes the restoration of the Temple and institutes Hanukkah (December 14 of 164 B.C.). The name is taken from the Hebrew *hanak,* meaning "to dedicate". Like the feasts of the Temple's dedication under Solomon (1 Kings 8:65–66) and Hezekiah (2 Chron 29:17), Hanukkah lasts for eight days. With the restoration of the sanctuary, the feasts that had turned into mourning (1 Mac 1:39) become feasts once more. For another account, see 2 Mac 10:1–8.

4:55 Heaven: See note on 3:19.

4:61 Beth-zur: See note on 4:29. While it is not actually part of the Jewish kingdom (cf. 6:7), Judas fortifies the city because of its strategic location between Judea and Idumea.

*4:29: Vulgate has "Judea" for *Idumea* and "Beth-horon" for *Beth-zur.*
[p] Or *and some fell on the opposite side.*
[q] Gk *whole.*
[r] 164 B.C.

a garrison there to hold it. He also[s] fortified Beth-zur, so that the people might have a stronghold that faced Idume'a.

Wars with Neighboring Peoples

5 When the Gentiles round about heard that the altar had been built and the sanctuary dedicated as it was before, they became very angry, [2]and they determined to destroy the descendants of Jacob who lived among them. So they began to kill and destroy among the people. [3]But Judas made war on the sons of Esau in Idume'a, at Ak"rabatte'ne, because they kept lying in wait for Israel. He dealt them a heavy blow and humbled them and despoiled them. [4]He also remembered the wickedness of the sons of Bae'an, who were a trap and a snare to the people and ambushed them on the highways. [5]They were shut up by him in their towers; and he encamped against them, vowed their complete destruction, and burned with fire their[t] towers and all who were in them. [6]Then he crossed over to attack the Am'monites, where he found a strong band and many people with Timothy as their leader. [7]He engaged in many battles with them and they were crushed before him; he struck them down. [8]He also took Ja'zer and its villages; then he returned to Judea.

Liberation of Galilean Jews

9 Now the Gentiles in Gilead gathered together against the Israelites who lived in their territory, and planned to destroy them. But they fled to the stronghold of Dath'ema, [10]and sent to Judas and his brothers a letter which said, "The Gentiles around us have gathered together against us to destroy us. [11]They are preparing to come and capture the stronghold to which we have fled, and Timothy is leading their forces. [12]Now then come and rescue us from their hands, for many of us have fallen, [13]and all our brethren who were in the land of Tob have been killed; the enemy[u] have captured their wives and children and goods, and have destroyed about a thousand men there."

14 While the letter was still being read, behold, other messengers, with their garments torn, came from Galilee and made a similar report; [15]they said that against them had gathered together men of Ptolema'is and Tyre and Si'don, and all Galilee of the Gentiles,[v] "to annihilate us." [16]When Judas and the people heard these messages, a great assembly was called to determine what they should do for their brethren who were in distress and were being attacked by enemies.[w] [17]Then Judas said to Simon his brother, "Choose your men and go and rescue your brethren in Galilee; I and Jonathan my brother will go to Gilead." [18]But he left Joseph, the son of Zechari'ah, and Azari'ah, a leader of the people, with the rest of the forces, in Judea to guard it; [19]and he gave them this command, "Take charge of this people, but do not engage in battle with the Gentiles until we return." [20]Then three thousand men were assigned to Simon to go to Galilee, and eight thousand to Judas for Gilead.

21 So Simon went to Galilee and fought many battles against the Gentiles, and the Gentiles were crushed before him. [22]He pursued them to the gate of Ptolema'is, and as many as three thousand of the Gentiles fell, and he despoiled them. [23]Then he took the Jews[x] of Galilee and Ar'batta, with their wives and children, and all they possessed, and led them to Judea with great rejoicing.

Judas and Jonathan in Gilead

24 Judas Mac"cabe'us and Jonathan his brother crossed the Jordan and went three days' journey into

---

5:1–8 Judas' campaigns in this chapter are spurred by the surrounding Gentiles' persecution of the Jews (such as the drowning at Joppa described in 2 Mac 12:3–4), which may have been occasioned by fears of Jewish expansion. While Judas assumes the role of a second Joshua, the motivation for his battles is presented as defense of his fellow Jews rather than conquest.

5:3 sons of Esau: Edomites. **Idumea:** See note on 4:15. **Akrabattene:** An uncertain location, possibly corresponding with the ascent of Akrabbim southwest of the Dead Sea (cf. Num 34:4; Josh 15:3).

5:4 sons of Baean: Otherwise unattested nomads in the Transjordan region (cf. Beon in Num 32:3).

5:6 Ammonites: A people to the east across the Jordan near present-day Amman. **Timothy:** The Seleucid commander over the Transjordan region, noted here and frequently in 2 Maccabees.

5:8 Jazer: A city in the Transjordan region, taken from the Amorites by Moses in Num 21:32. Its precise location is disputed.

5:9 Gilead: The region east of the Jordan between the Yarmuk and Arnon rivers. **Dathema:** A stronghold in Gilead. Its precise location is unknown, but it may be related to the land of Tob (5:13), where a military colony led by the Tobiad family was located.

5:13 land of Tob: The land to which Jephthah fled in Judg 11:3. Its precise location is uncertain: rabbinic tradition identifies it with Hippos, three miles east of the Sea of Galilee, while others identify it with a region in Gilead 12 miles southeast of the Sea.

5:14 Galilee: The region west of Lake Gennesaret (Sea of Galilee).

5:15 Ptolemais and Tyre and Sidon: Gentile cities northwest of Judea along the Mediterranean coast.

5:18 Joseph ... Azariah: On these two figures, see 5:55–60.

5:22 Ptolemais: A prominent city along the Mediterranean coast (also known as Acre), west of the Sea of Galilee.

5:23 Arbatta: An unattested location that some suspect refers to Narbata, a city in southwest Galilee.

5:24–55 For another version of this campaign of Judas, see 2 Mac 12:10–31.

---

[s] Greek adds *to hold it.*
[t] Gk *her.*
[u] Gk *they.*
[v] Gk *aliens.*
[w] Gk *them.*
[x] Gk *those.*

the wilderness. [25]They encountered the Nab"ate'ans, who met them peaceably and told them all that had happened to their brethren in Gilead: [26]"Many of them have been shut up in Bozrah and Bo'sor, in Al'ema and Chas'pho, Ma'ked and Carna'im"—all these cities were strong and large—[27]"and some have been shut up in the other cities of Gilead; the enemy[y] are getting ready to attack the strongholds tomorrow and take and destroy all these men in one day."

28 Then Judas and his army quickly turned back by the wilderness road to Bozrah; and he took the city, and killed every male by the edge of the sword; then he seized all its spoils and burned it with fire. [29]He departed from there at night, and they went all the way to the stronghold of Dath'ema.[z] [30]At dawn they looked up, and behold, a large company, that could not be counted, carrying ladders and engines of war to capture the stronghold, and attacking the Jews within.[a] [31]So Judas saw that the battle had begun and that the cry of the city went up to Heaven with trumpets and loud shouts, [32]and he said to the men of his forces, "Fight today for your brethren!" [33]Then he came up behind them in three companies, who sounded their trumpets and cried aloud in prayer. [34]And when the army of Timothy realized that it was Mac"cabe'us, they fled before him, and he dealt them a heavy blow. As many as eight thousand of them fell that day.

35 Next he turned aside to Al'ema,[b]* and fought against it and took it; and he killed every male in it, plundered it, and burned it with fire. [36]From there he marched on and took Chas'pho, Ma'ked, and Bo'sor, and the other cities of Gilead.

37 After these things Timothy gathered another army and encamped opposite Ra'phon on the other side of the stream. [38]Judas sent men to spy out the camp, and they reported to him, "All the Gentiles around us have gathered to him; it is a very large force. [39]They also have hired Arabs to help them, and they are encamped across the stream, ready to come and fight against you." And Judas went to meet them.

40 Now as Judas and his army drew near to the stream of water, Timothy said to the officers of his forces, "If he crosses over to us first, we will not be able to resist him, for he will surely defeat us. [41]But if he shows fear and camps on the other side of the river, we will cross over to him and defeat him." [42]When Judas approached the stream of water, he stationed the scribes of the people at the stream and gave them this command, "Permit no man to encamp, but make them all enter the battle." [43]Then he crossed over against them first, and the whole army followed him. All the Gentiles were defeated before him, and they threw away their arms and fled into the sacred precincts at Carna'im. [44]But he took the city and burned the sacred precincts with fire, together with all who were in them. Thus Carna'im was conquered; they could stand before Judas no longer.

The Return to Jerusalem

45 Then Judas gathered together all the Israel-ites in Gilead, the small and the great, with their wives and children and goods, a very large company, to go to the land of Judah. [46]So they came to E'phron. This was a large and very strong city on the road, and they could not go round it to the right or to the left; they had to go through it. [47]But the men of the city shut them out and blocked up the gates with stones. [48]And Judas sent them this friendly message, "Let us pass through your land to get to our land. No one will do you harm; we will simply pass by on foot." But they refused to open to him. [49]Then Judas ordered proclamation to be made to the army that each should encamp where he was. [50]So the men of the forces encamped, and he fought against the city all that day and all the night, and the city was delivered into his hands. [51]He destroyed every male by the edge of the sword, and razed and plundered the city. Then he passed through the city over the slain.

52 And they crossed the Jordan into the large plain before Beth-shan. [53]And Judas kept rallying the laggards and encouraging the people all the way till he came to the land of Judah. [54]So they went up to Mount Zion with gladness and joy, and offered burnt offerings, because not one of them had fallen before they returned in safety.

5:25 Nabateans: A nomadic Arab people, whose base was the city Petra in ancient Edom. See also 2 Mac 12:10–12, which may be another version of this meeting.

5:26 Bozrah ... Carnaim: All cities east of the Jordan River.

5:30 engines of war: Hellenistic-era warfare included the use of war machines, such as catapults, battering rams, cranes, and siege towers. The Maccabean forces become proficient with them as well (cf. 6:52; 11:20; 13:43).

5:37 Raphon: A town along a tributary of the Yarmuk River in Gilead.

5:39 Arabs: Hired here as mercenaries by Timothy. The Arabs are reported to make peace with Judas after their defeat in 2 Mac 12:10–12.

5:43 sacred precincts: Carnaim (known also as Ashteroth) was home to a temple of the Syrian fish goddess Atargatis, to which Timothy's soldiers flee in hope of asylum.

5:46 Ephron: Another city east of the Jordan River. The reasons for its hostility are unclear, though it may have been a Seleucid outpost, as evidenced by Lysias' dwelling there (2 Mac 12:27). Judas' actions here are modeled on the terms of peace and war in Deut 20:10–14.

5:52 Beth-shan: Also known as Scythopolis, a city south of the Sea of Galilee and 75 miles north of Jerusalem. The kindness of the people there to the Jews (in contrast with those of Ephron) is recounted in 2 Mac 12:29–31.

---

* 5:35: Vulgate reads "Maspha" (i.e., Mizpah) for *Alema;* cf. note b.
[y] Gk *they.*
[z] Greek lacks *of Dathema.* See verse 9.
[a] Gk *and they were attacking them.*
[b] The name is uncertain.

55 Now while Judas and Jonathan were in Gilead and Simon his brother was in Galilee before Ptolema'is, ⁵⁶Joseph, the son of Zechari'ah, and Azari'ah, the commanders of the forces, heard of their brave deeds and of the heroic war they had fought. ⁵⁷So they said, "Let us also make a name for ourselves; let us go and make war on the Gentiles around us." ⁵⁸And they issued orders to the men of the forces that were with them, and they marched against Jam'nia. ⁵⁹And Gor'gias and his men came out of the city to meet them in battle. ⁶⁰Then Joseph and Azari'ah were routed, and were pursued to the borders of Judea; as many as two thousand of the people of Israel fell that day. ⁶¹Thus the people suffered a great rout because, thinking to do a brave

deed, they did not listen to Judas and his brothers. ⁶²But they did not belong to the family of those men through whom deliverance was given to Israel.

63 The man Judas and his brothers were greatly honored in all Israel and among all the Gentiles, wherever their name was heard. ⁶⁴Men gathered to them and praised them.

Success at Hebron and Philistia
65 Then Judas and his brothers went forth and fought the sons of Esau in the land to the south. He struck He'bron and its villages and tore down its strongholds and burned its towers round about. ⁶⁶Then he marched off to go into the land of the Philis'tines, and passed through Mar'isa.ᶜ* ⁶⁷On

---

5:57 make a name for ourselves: The same proud motive of the tower builders at Babel (Gen 11:4) and Seron in 3:14, who meet similarly unfortunate results.
5:58 Jamnia: See note on 4:15.
5:59 Gorgias: See note on 3:38.
5:61–62 The first explicit mention of God's endorsement of the Maccabean family. Joseph and Azariah's errors are twofold: first, they have disobeyed the orders of the ones through

whom God has rescued the nation. Second, while the Maccabees fight in obedience to God, and so gain an everlasting name like Israel's past heroes (2:51; 5:63), Joseph and Azariah use Israel as a pretext to fight for their own glory and thus bring themselves and those who follow them to destruction.
5:63 Judas ... greatly honored: Mattathias' words in 2:64 have come to pass with his sons' courage and fidelity.
5:65 sons of Esau: The Idumaeans/Edomites of 5:3, though here they are fought in Hebron. **Hebron:** David's original capital, 20 miles south of Jerusalem.
5:66 Marisa: Also known as Mareshah, a Hellenized city west of Hebron along Judea's border with Idumea.

*5:66, 68: Vulgate has "aliens" and "strangers" for *Philistines*, and "Samaria" for *Marisa*; cf. note c.
ᶜ Other authorities read *Samaria*.

BATTLE SITES IN PALESTINE AND BEYOND

that day some priests, who wished to do a brave deed, fell in battle, for they went out to battle unwisely. ⁶⁸But Judas turned aside to Azo'tus in the land of the Philis'tines;* he tore down their altars, and the graven images of their gods he burned with fire; he plundered the cities and returned to the land of Judah.

The Last Days of Antiochus Epiphanes

6 King Anti'ochus was going through the upper provinces when he heard that Elyma'is in Persia was a city famed for its wealth in silver and gold. ²Its temple was very rich, containing golden shields, breastplates, and weapons left there by Alexander, the son of Philip, the Macedonian king who first reigned over the Greeks. ³So he came and tried to take the city and plunder it, but he could not, because his plan became known to the men of the city ⁴and they withstood him in battle. So he fled and in great grief departed from there to return to Babylon.

5 Then some one came to him in Persia and reported that the armies which had gone into the land of Judah had been routed; ⁶that Lys'ias had gone first with a strong force, but had turned and fled before the Jews;ᵈ that the Jewsᵉ had grown strong from the arms, supplies, and abundant spoils which they had taken from the armies they had cut down; ⁷that they had torn down the abomination which he had erected upon the altar in Jerusalem; and that they had surrounded the sanctuary with high walls as before, and also Beth-zur, his city.

8 When the king heard this news, he was astounded and badly shaken. He took to his bed and became sick from grief, because things had not turned out for him as he had planned. ⁹He lay there for many days, because deep grief continually gripped him, and he concluded that he was dying. ¹⁰So he called all his friends and said to them, "Sleep departs from my eyes and I am downhearted with worry. ¹¹I said to myself, 'To what distress I have

come! And into what a great flood I now am plunged! For I was kind and beloved in my power.' ¹²But now I remember the evils I did in Jerusalem. I seized all her vessels of silver and gold; and I sent to destroy the inhabitants of Judah without good reason. ¹³I know that it is because of this that these evils have come upon me; and behold, I am perishing of deep grief in a strange land."

14 Then he called for Philip, one of his friends, and made him ruler over all his kingdom. ¹⁵He gave him the crown and his robe and the signet, that he might guide Anti'ochus his son and bring him up to be king. ¹⁶Thus Anti'ochus the king died there in the one hundred and forty-ninth year.ᶠ ¹⁷And when Lys'ias learned that the king was dead, he set up Anti'ochus the king'sᵍ son to reign. Lysiasʰ had brought him up as a boy, and he named him Eu'pator.

Renewed Attacks from Syria

18 Now the men in the citadel kept hemming Israel in around the sanctuary. They were trying in every way to harm them and strengthen the Gentiles. ¹⁹So Judas decided to destroy them, and assembled all the people to besiege them. ²⁰They gathered together and besieged the citadelⁱ in the one hundred and fiftieth year;ʲ and he built siege towers and other engines of war. ²¹But some of the garrison escaped from the siege and some of the ungodly Israelites joined them. ²²They went to the king and said, "How long will you fail to do justice and to avenge our brethren? ²³We were happy to serve your father, to live by what he said and to follow his commands. ²⁴For this reason the sons of our people besieged the citadelᵏ and became hostile to us; moreover, they have put to death as many of us as they have caught, and they have seized our inheritances. ²⁵And not against us alone have they stretched out their hands, but also against all the lands on their borders. ²⁶And behold, today they have encamped against the citadel in Jerusalem to

---

5:68 Azotus: See note on 4:15. **tore down their altars:** These comments serve as a bookend with 5:1–2: while Jerusalem's rebuilt altar and sanctuary make the neighboring Gentiles determined to destroy the Jews, it is they who are defeated and have their altars destroyed.

6:1–17 Another account of this campaign and Antiochus' death appears in 2 Mac 9. First Maccabees records the death of Antiochus after the restoration of the Temple in 164 B.C.,

while 2 Mac places it in the chapter before the restoration, and a Babylonian king list records it as roughly contemporaneous (the month of Chislev 164 B.C., which covers November–December). For the author of 1 Mac, Antiochus serves as a counterexample to Judas: while Antiochus seeks riches and finds only defeat, Judas seeks honor and has riches added to him. Commentators also identify Dan 11:40–45 as corresponding with the events of Antiochus' demise.

6:7 Beth-zur: See note on 4:29.

6:14 Philip: A close friend of Antiochus IV who is given the authority previously belonging to Lysias (3:32–33), leading to their conflict in 6:55–56.

6:15 signet: The symbol of the king's authority. **Antiochus his son:** Known as Antiochus V Eupator ("of a good father"), who was between nine and twelve years old when he began to reign with Lysias in control of the government as his regent (cf. 2 Mac 13:2). His reign lasts until Demetrius I, the nephew of Antiochus IV, orders their deaths two years later (7:1–3).

6:18 citadel: See note on 1:33.

---

*5:66, 68: Vulgate has "aliens" and "strangers" for *Philistines*, and "Samaria" for *Marisa*; cf. note c.

ᵈ Gk *them*.

ᵉ Gk *they*.

ᶠ 163 B.C.

ᵍ Gk *his*.

ʰ *Gk He*.

ⁱ Gk *it*.

ʲ 162 B.C.

ᵏ The Greek text underlying *the sons...the citadel* is uncertain.

take it; they have fortified both the sanctuary and Beth-zur; [27]and unless you quickly prevent them, they will do still greater things, and you will not be able to stop them."

28 The king was enraged when he heard this. He assembled all his friends, the commanders of his forces and those in authority.[1] [29]And mercenary forces came to him from other kingdoms and from islands of the seas. [30]The number of his forces was a hundred thousand foot soldiers, twenty thousand horsemen, and thirty-two elephants accustomed to war. [31]They came through Idume'a and encamped against Beth-zur, and for many days they fought and built engines of war; but the Jews[m] sallied out and burned these with fire, and fought manfully.

The Battle at Beth-zechariah

32 Then Judas marched away from the citadel and encamped at Beth-zech"ari'ah, opposite the camp of the king. [33]Early in the morning the king rose and took his army by a forced march along the road to Beth-zech"ari'ah, and his troops made ready for battle and sounded their trumpets. [34]They showed the elephants the juice of grapes and mulberries, to arouse them for battle. [35]And they distributed the beasts among the phalanxes; with each elephant they stationed a thousand men armed with coats of mail, and with brass helmets on their heads; and five hundred picked horsemen were assigned to each beast. [36]These took their position beforehand wherever the beast was; wherever it went they went with it, and they never left it. [37]And upon the elephants[n] were wooden towers, strong and covered; they were fastened upon each beast by special harness, and upon each were four[o] armed men who fought from there, and also its Indian driver. [38]The rest of the horsemen were stationed on either side, on the two flanks of the army, to harass the enemy while being themselves protected by the phalanxes. [39]When the sun shone upon the shields of gold and brass, the hills were ablaze with them and gleamed like flaming torches.

40 Now a part of the king's army was spread out on the high hills, and some troops were on the plain, and they advanced steadily and in good order. [41]All who heard the noise made by their multitude, by the marching of the multitude and the clanking of their arms, trembled, for the army was very large and strong. [42]But Judas and his army advanced to the battle, and six hundred men of the king's army fell. [43]And Elea'zar, called Av'aran, saw that one of the beasts was equipped with royal armor. It was taller than all the others, and he supposed that the king was upon it. [44]So he gave his life to save his people and to win for himself an everlasting name. [45]He courageously ran into the midst of the phalanx to reach it; he killed men right and left, and they parted before him on both sides. [46]He got under the elephant, stabbed it from beneath, and killed it; but it fell to the ground upon him and there he died. [47]And when the Jews[p] saw the royal might and the fierce attack of the forces, they turned away in flight.

48 The soldiers of the king's army went up to Jerusalem against them, and the king encamped in Judea and at Mount Zion. [49]He made peace with the men of Beth-zur, and they evacuated the city, because they had no provisions there to withstand a siege, since it was a sabbatical year for the land. [50]So the king took Beth-zur and stationed a guard there to hold it. [51]Then he encamped before the sanctuary for many days. He set up siege towers, engines of war to throw fire and stones, machines to shoot arrows, and catapults. [52]The Jews[q] also made engines of war to match theirs, and fought for many days. [53]But they had no food in storage,[r] because it was the seventh year; those who found safety in Judea from the Gentiles had consumed the last of the stores. [54]Few men were left in the sanctuary,

---

6:28–31 The king (and Lysias; cf. 6:55) bring almost double the force that Lysias had in 4:28, along with elephants, and use the same strategy of attacking Judea from the south. For another account, see 2 Mac 13:9–26. The use of elephants by the Seleucid army was banned by Rome in the treaty of Apamea in 188 B.C., and their violation of this agreement leads the Romans to abandon support of Antiochus V and Lysias, opening the door for Demetrius I's takeover.

6:31 engines of war: See note on 5:30.

6:32 Beth-zechariah: Ten miles southwest of Jerusalem and six miles north of the fortification at Beth-zur.

6:34 juice of grapes: The use of wine to spur elephants for battle is also recorded in Jewish sources such as *3 Maccabees* and Josephus, where the intoxicated elephants attack their masters instead.

6:35 phalanxes: An interlocking formation of Greek infantry, with long spears pointing out from a front row covered with shields.

6:43–46 Eleazar, the fourth son of Mattathias, is the first of the Maccabees to die. The author records this event by alluding to Mattathias' words about the everlasting name given to their ancestors (2:51), and Eleazar's breaking through the phalanx to go directly to the enemy's heart evokes his father's resolve to turn neither to the right nor to the left (2:22). • St. Ambrose, writing on fortitude, infers that even though Eleazar's intuition proved incorrect, his valor was so great that it influenced Antiochus and Lysias' decision to withdraw from Judea and, thus, "left peace as the heir of his courage" (*On the Duties of the Clergy* 1, 40, 208).

6:49 A sabbatical year: Every seventh year the land is left uncultivated; see Ex 23:10–11; Lev 25:2–7.

6:50 Beth-zur: See note on 4:29.

---

[1] Gk *those over the reins.*
[m] Gk *they.*
[n] Gk *them.*
[o] Cn: Some authorities read *thirty*; others *thirty-two.*
[p] Gk *they.*
[q] Gk *They.*
[r] Other authorities read *in the sanctuary.*

because famine had prevailed over the rest and they had been scattered, each to his own place.

Syria Offers Terms

55 Then Lys'ias heard that Philip, whom King Anti'ochus while still living had appointed to bring up Antiochus his son to be king, [56]had returned from Persia and Med'ia with the forces that had gone with the king, and that he was trying to seize control of the government. [57]So he quickly gave orders to depart, and said to the king, to the commanders of the forces, and to the men, "We daily grow weaker, our food supply is scant, the place against which we are fighting is strong, and the affairs of the kingdom press urgently upon us. [58]Now then let us come to terms with these men, and make peace with them and with all their nation, [59]and agree to let them live by their laws as they did before; for it was on account of their laws which we abolished that they became angry and did all these things."

60 The speech pleased the king and the commanders, and he sent to the Jews[s] an offer of peace, and they accepted it. [61]So the king and the commanders gave them their oath. On these conditions the Jews[t] evacuated the stronghold. [62]But when the king entered Mount Zion and saw what a strong fortress the place was, he broke the oath he had sworn and gave orders to tear down the wall all around. [63]Then he departed with haste and returned to Antioch. He found Philip in control of the city, but he fought against him, and took the city by force.

Expedition of Bacchides and Alcimus

7 In the one hundred and fifty-first year[u] Deme'trius the son of Seleu'cus set forth from Rome, sailed with a few men to a city by the sea, and there began to reign. [2]As he was entering the royal palace of his fathers, the army seized Anti'ochus and Lys'ias to bring them to him. [3]But when this act became known to him, he said, "Do not let me see their faces!" [4]So the army killed them, and Deme'trius took his seat upon the throne of his kingdom.

5 Then there came to him all the lawless and ungodly men of Israel; they were led by Al'cimus, who wanted to be high priest. [6]And they brought to the king this accusation against the people: "Judas and his brothers have destroyed all your friends, and have driven us out of our land. [7]Now then send a man whom you trust; let him go and see all the ruin which Judas[v] has brought upon us and upon the land of the king, and let him punish them and all who help them."

8 So the king chose Bacchi'des, one of the king's friends, governor of the province Beyond the River; he was a great man in the kingdom and was faithful to the king. [9]And he sent him, and with him the ungodly Al'cimus, whom he made high priest; and he commanded him to take vengeance on the sons of Israel. [10]So they marched away and came with a large force into the land of Judah; and he sent messengers to Judas and his brothers with peaceable but treacherous words. [11]But they paid no attention to their words, for they saw that they had come with a large force.

12 Then a group of scribes appeared in a body before Al'cimus and Bacchi'des to ask for just terms. [13]The Hasid'eans were first among the sons of Israel to seek peace from them, [14]for they said, "A priest of the line of Aaron has come with the army, and he will not harm us." [15]And he spoke peaceable words to them and swore this oath to them, "We will not seek to injure you or your friends." [16]So they trusted him; but he seized sixty of them and killed them in one day, in accordance with the word which was written,

---

6:55–61 Despite its defeats and weakened condition, the nation's faithful observance of the Sabbath year eventually contributes to its deliverance, as Antiochus and Lysias' army is similarly affected by the lack of food (6:57), and Philip's timely return to Antioch to seize control of the kingdom forestalls any attack on Jerusalem. The Seleucids are thus forced to grant the Jews the freedoms Antiochus IV took away, corresponding with the promises in Lev 26:7–8 of victory over one's enemies, even when outnumbered, for faithful Sabbath observance.

6:62 he broke the oath: An example of Seleucid deceit, first witnessed under Antioch IV in 1:30 and frequently repeated both by Greeks and Hellenizing Jewish leaders in 1 Maccabees.

7:1 Demetrius: Demetrius I Soter was the son of King Seleucus IV, who reigned over the empire from 187 to 175 B.C. before being displaced by his younger brother Antiochus IV. As the son of Seleucus, Demetrius would have had a stronger claim to the throne than Antiochus V. He was a hostage in Rome from age nine (serving as a substitute for Antiochus IV), until his escape and return to Antioch at 25.

7:3 Do not let me see their faces: An indirect way of ordering their deaths.

7:5 Alcimus: A priest who is among the Hellenizers, but who has a strong enough claim as being from the "line of Aaron" to win the support of the Hasideans (7:14; see also 2 Mac 14:3–10). The last of the line of the Oniad family (which traditionally held the high priesthood) has fled to Egypt, and only later with Jonathan do the Hasmoneans take the high priestly office (10:20).

7:8 Bacchides: A Seleucid governor who becomes a great enemy of the Jews. **province Beyond the River:** Also known as Coele-syria (cf. 10:69), the term reflects a Mesopotamian viewpoint, describing all of the land west of the Euphrates River out to the Mediterranean Sea and stretching down to the border of Egypt. The term Coele-syria is also used more narrowly to describe the land north of Palestine, encompassing modern Lebanon and Syria.

7:13 Hasideans: Previously aligned with the Maccabees but here giving support to the pro-Seleucid high priest Alcimus, which is immediately shown to be misplaced. See note on 2:42.

---

[s] Gk *them.*
[t] Gk *they.*
[u] 161 B.C.
[v] Gk *he.*

[17]"The flesh of your saints and their blood
   they poured out round about Jerusalem,
   and there was none to bury them."
[18]Then the fear and dread of them fell upon all the people, for they said, "There is no truth or justice in them, for they have violated the agreement and the oath which they swore."

19 Then Bacchi'des departed from Jerusalem and encamped in Beth-za'ith. And he sent and seized many of the men who had deserted to him,[w] and some of the people, and killed them and threw them into the great pit. [20]He placed Al'cimus in charge of the country and left with him a force to help him; then Bacchi'des went back to the king.

21 Al'cimus strove for the high priesthood, [22]and all who were troubling their people joined him. They gained control of the land of Judah and did great damage in Israel. [23]And Judas saw all the evil that Al'cimus and those with him had done among the sons of Israel; it was more than the Gentiles had done. [24]So Judas[x] went out into all the surrounding parts of Judea, and took vengeance on the men who had deserted, and he prevented those in the city[y] from going out into the country. [25]When Al'cimus saw that Judas and those with him had grown strong, and realized that he could not withstand them, he returned to the king and brought wicked charges against them.

Nicanor in Judea

26 Then the king sent Nica'nor, one of his honored princes, who hated and detested Israel, and he commanded him to destroy the people. [27]So Nica'nor came to Jerusalem with a large force, and treacherously sent to Judas and his brothers this peaceable message, [28]"Let there be no fighting between me and you; I shall come with a few men to see you face to face in peace." [29]So he came to Judas, and they greeted one another peaceably. But the enemy were ready to seize Judas. [30]It became known to Judas that Nica'nor[x] had come to him with treacherous intent, and he was afraid of him and would not meet him again. [31]When Nica'nor learned that his plan had been disclosed, he went out to meet Judas in battle near Caph"arsal'ama. [32]About five hundred men of the army of Nica'nor fell, and the rest[z] fled into the city of David.

Nicanor Threatens the Temple

33 After these events Nica'nor went up to Mount Zion. Some of the priests came out of the sanctuary, and some of the elders of the people, to greet him peaceably and to show him the burnt offering that was being offered for the king. [34]But he mocked them and derided them and defiled them and spoke arrogantly, [35]and in anger he swore this oath, "Unless Judas and his army are delivered into my hands this time, then if I return safely I will burn up this house." And he went out in great anger. [36]Then the priests went in and stood before the altar and the temple, and they wept and said,
[37]"You chose this house to be called by your name,
   and to be for your people a house of prayer
      and supplication.
[38]Take vengeance on this man and on his army,
   and let them fall by the sword;
   remember their blasphemies,
      and let them live no longer."

The Death of Nicanor

39 Now Nica'nor went out from Jerusalem and encamped in Beth-ho'ron, and the Syrian army joined him. [40]And Judas encamped in Ad'asa with three thousand men. Then Judas prayed and said, [41]"When the messengers from the king spoke blasphemy, your angel went forth and struck down one hundred and eighty-five thousand of the Assyrians.[a] [42]So also crush this army before us today; let the rest learn that Nica'nor[b] has spoken wickedly against your sanctuary, and judge him

---

7:17 The flesh ... bury them: A quotation from Ps 79:2–3. Bacchides' actions here and following are intended to terrorize the population, as leaving bodies unburied in ancient culture was a dishonor without parallel.
   7:18 they have violated the agreement: Like Antiochus V in 6:62, the Seleucid leadership and those aligned with them employ deceit as standard procedure.
   7:19 Beth-zaith: Fifteen miles south of Jerusalem, near Beth-zur.
   7:23 more than the Gentiles: On the especially damaging sin of scandal within God's people, see CCC 2284–87.

7:26 Nicanor: Made a covenant with Judas, which he was forced to abandon on account of Alcimus' schemes. The account in 1 Mac passes over this and goes straight to Nicanor's attempt to trap Judas. A longer account of the relationship between Nicanor and Judas is given in 2 Mac 14. See also note on 3:38.
   7:31 Capharsalama: Location uncertain but most likely near Jerusalem, because of the soldiers' flight to the city of David, either seven miles northwest or five miles northeast.
   7:32 city of David: On the citadel, see note on 1:33.
   7:39 Beth-horon: See note on 3:16.
   7:40 Adasa: On the road from Beth-horon five miles northwest of Jerusalem. Here Judas is recorded as having only 3,000 men, compared to the 11,000 in 5:20 that were divided between Judas and Simon. After the near defeat by Lysias, Judas has managed with his small remaining army to check the arrogance of the Syrians once again.
   7:41 When the messengers ... Assyrians: Judas' prayer likens Nicanor to Sennacherib, who similarly blasphemed the God of Israel and whose army was struck down outside Jerusalem in 701 B.C. See 2 Kings 18–19; Is 36–37.

---

[w]Or *many of his men who had deserted.*
[x]Gk *he.*
[y]Gk *they were prevented.*
[x]Gk *he.*
[z]Gk *they.*
[a]Gk *of them.*
[b]Gk *he.*

according to this wickedness." [43]So the armies met in battle on the thirteenth day of the month of Adar'. The army of Nica'nor was crushed, and he himself was the first to fall in the battle. [44]When his army saw that Nica'nor had fallen, they threw down their arms and fled. [45]The Jews[c] pursued them a day's journey, from Ad'asa as far as Gaza'ra, and as they followed kept sounding the battle call on the trumpets. [46]And men came out of all the villages of Judea round about, and they outflanked the enemy[d] and drove them back to their pursuers,[e] so that they all fell by the sword; not even one of them was left. [47]Then the Jews[f] seized the spoils and the plunder, and they cut off Nica'nor's head and the right hand which he so arrogantly stretched out, and brought them and displayed them just outside Jerusalem. [48]The people rejoiced greatly and celebrated that day as a day of great gladness. [49]And they decreed that this day should be celebrated each year on the thirteenth day of Adar'. [50]So the land of Judah had rest for a few days.

An Eulogy of the Romans

8 Now Judas heard of the fame of the Romans, that they were very strong and were well-disposed toward all who made an alliance with them, that they pledged friendship to those who came to them, [2]and that they were very strong. Men told him of their wars and of the brave deeds which they were doing among the Gauls, how they had defeated them and forced them to pay tribute, [3]and what they had done in the land of Spain to get control of the silver and gold mines there, [4]and how they had gained control of the whole region by their planning and patience, even though the place was far distant from them. They also subdued the kings who came against them from the ends of the earth, until they crushed them and inflicted great disaster upon them; the rest paid them tribute every year. [5]Philip, and Per'seus king of the Macedonians,[g] and the others who rose up against them, they crushed in battle and conquered. [6]They also defeated Anti'ochus the Great, king of Asia, who went to fight against them with a hundred and twenty elephants and with cavalry and chariots and a very large army. He was crushed by them; [7]they took him alive and decreed that he and those who should reign after him should pay a heavy tribute and give hostages and surren-der some of their best provinces, [8]the country of India and Med'ia and Lyd'ia. These they took from him "and gave to Eu'menes the king. [9]The Greeks planned to come and destroy them, [10]but this became known to them, and they sent a general against the Greeks[h] and attacked them. Many of them were wounded and fell, and the Romans[i] took captive their wives and children; they plundered them, conquered the land, tore down their strongholds, and enslaved them to this day. [11]The remaining kingdoms and islands, as many as ever opposed them, they destroyed and enslaved; [12]but with their friends and those who rely on them they have kept friendship. They have subdued kings far and near, and as many as have heard of their fame have feared them. [13]Those whom they wish to help and to make kings, they make kings, and those whom they wish they depose; and they have been greatly exalted. [14]Yet for all this not one of them has put on a crown or worn purple as a mark of pride, [15]but they have built for themselves a senate chamber, and every day three hundred and twenty senators constantly deliberate concerning the people, to govern them well. [16]They trust one man each year to rule over them and to control all their land; they all heed the one man, and there is no envy or jealousy among them.

7:45 Gazara: See note on 4:15.

7:49 celebrated each year: This feast, known as Nicanor Day, was celebrated at least until the time of Josephus in the first century A.D., but is not kept by Jews today. See also 2 Mac 15:36.

7:50 rest ... few days: This phrase speaks of the amount of conflict that the land of Judah experiences within this period of history. The defeat of Nicanor in 160 or 161 B.C. means it could have literally been days before early in the year 152 (160 B.C.) when Bacchides was sent to them a second time.

8:1–16 A positive portrayal of the Romans, which suggests that 1 Mac was written before 63 B.C., when the Roman general Pompey marched on Jerusalem and the Romans became the oppressors of the Jews. By the time of the New Testament, Rome has become the Jews' most prominent enemy. The reader will note contrasts between the Romans and the Seleucids that were attractive to the Jews, such as the Roman leaders' refusal to exalt their own personal power (8:14–16) and their honesty in keeping oaths (8:1, 12). At the same time, the Romans' expansive tendencies noted here do share parallels with those of Alexander (cf. 1:1–4), which would prove ominous a century later when Judea was made subject to Roman power.

8:5 Philip, and Perseus: Philip V (reigned 221–179 B.C.) and his son Perseus (179–168 B.C.), kings of Macedon, who were defeated in a series of wars with the Romans.

8:6 Antiochus the Great: The Seleucid King Antiochus III (reigned 222–187 B.C.), the father of Antiochus IV Epiphanes, who was defeated by the Romans in Asia Minor in 189 B.C.

8:8 India and Media and Lydia: Territories originally conquered under Alexander the Great, corresponding with northwest India, northwest Iran, and western Turkey. **Eumenes:** Eumenes II of Pergamum (ruled 197–158 B.C.), a city near the western coast of Asia Minor that was allied with the Romans.

---

[c] Gk *They*.
[d] Gk *them*.
[e] Gk *these*.
[f] Gk *they*.
[g] Or *Kittim*.
[h] Gk *them*.
[i] Gk *they*.

An Alliance with Rome

17 So Judas chose Eupol'emus the son of John, son of Ac'cos, and Jason the son of Elea'zar, and sent them to Rome to establish friendship and alliance, 18and to free themselves from the yoke; for they saw that the kingdom of the Greeks was completely enslaving Israel. 19They went to Rome, a very long journey; and they entered the senate chamber and spoke as follows: 20"Judas, who is also called Mac"cabe'us, and his brothers and the people of the Jews have sent us to you to establish alliance and peace with you, that we may be enrolled as your allies and friends." 21The proposal pleased them, 22and this is a copy of the letter which they wrote in reply, on bronze tablets, and sent to Jerusalem to remain with them there as a memorial of peace and alliance:

23 "May all go well with the Romans and with the nation of the Jews at sea and on land for ever, and may sword and enemy be far from them. 24If war comes first to Rome or to any of their allies in all their dominion, 25the nation of the Jews shall act as their allies wholeheartedly, as the occasion may indicate to them. 26And to the enemy who makes war they shall not give or supply grain, arms, money, or ships, as Rome has decided; and they shall keep their obligations without receiving any return. 27In the same way, if war comes first to the nation of the Jews, the Romans shall willingly act as their allies, as the occasion may indicate to them. 28And to the enemy allies shall be given no grain, arms, money, or ships, as Rome has decided; and they shall keep these obligations and do so without

deceit. 29Thus on these terms the Romans make a treaty with the Jewish people. 30If after these terms are in effect both parties shall determine to add or delete anything, they shall do so at their discretion, and any addition or deletion that they may make shall be valid.

31 "And concerning the wrongs which King Deme'trius is doing to them we have written to him as follows, 'Why have you made your yoke heavy upon our friends and allies the Jews? 32If now they appeal again for help against you, we will defend their rights and fight you on sea and on land.'"

Bacchides Returns to Judea

9 When Deme'trius heard that Nica'nor and his army had fallen in battle, he sent Bacchi'des and Al'cimus into the land of Judah a second time, and with them the right wing of the army. 2They went by the road which leads to Gilgal and encamped against Mes'aloth in Arbe'la, and they took it and killed many people. 3In the first month of the one hundred and fifty-second year[j] they encamped against Jerusalem; 4then they marched off and went to Bere'a with twenty thousand foot soldiers and two thousand cavalry.

5 Now Judas was encamped in El'asa, and with him were three thousand picked men. 6When they saw the huge number of the enemy forces, they were greatly frightened, and many slipped away from the camp, until no more than eight hundred of them were left.

7 When Judas saw that his army had slipped away and the battle was imminent, he was crushed

---

8:17–21 Like Joshua, who regarded it as lawful to make a covenant with the Gibeonites when he believed they were a "very long journey" away from home (Josh 9:3–15), so Judas finds it lawful to make an alliance with the Romans who are also "a very long journey" away (8:19). For more on covenants, see note on 1:11.

8:17 Eupolemus: Descended from a priestly family mentioned in Ezra 2:61 (there called Hakkoz). He is noted again in 2 Mac 4:11. Eupolemus was also the name of a Jewish historian in the mid-second century B.C., whose writings, preserved in fragmentary form by early Christian writers, describe Moses as the original source for later Greek learning. Many identify that figure with the Eupolemus noted here. **Jason:** Perhaps the son of the martyr Eleazar in 2 Mac 6:18–20. Jason and Eupolemus bear Greek names, while their fathers' names are Hebrew, perhaps showing a more recent acceptance of Greek influence.

8:22 bronze tablets: A conventional way of memorializing treatises, attested elsewhere in the second century B.C. in Rome's treaty with the city of Kibyra in Asia Minor.

8:23–30 This treaty closely parallels others between Rome and much smaller powers in this period, such as the one found preserved in a stone engraving in Astypalaia, a small Greek island that allied with Rome in 105 B.C. Similar features include the wish for mutual well-being on land and sea forever, the promises to defend each other and not support one another's enemies, and brief terms for amending the treaty in the future.

8:31–32 This section may be a later addendum, which, in either case, the Romans did not appear to enforce with Demetrius' renewed aggression.

9:2 Gilgal: Either the Gilgal close to Jericho, a misreading of Galilee (similar in Hebrew and in close proximity to Arbela), or another Gilgal not yet known. **Mesaloth in Arbela:** Mesaloth is similar to the word for "steps" in Hebrew, perhaps meaning the incline up to Arbela, a mountain west of the Sea of Galilee. Josephus similarly recounts an attack by Bacchides on Jews hiding in the hillside caves at Arbela.

9:4 Berea: An uncertain location, with the likeliest candidate being el-Bireh ten miles north of Jerusalem.

9:5–6 Judas' men become afraid, even though previously they have won battles against greater odds (40,000 infantry and 7,000 cavalry against Judas' 3,000 men in 3:39; 4:6–15; 60,000 against Judas' 10,000 in 4:28). The text does not provide an explicit cause, and one proposal is that since the nation now holds religious freedoms previously denied them, the people have less resolve to fight for political freedom as well.

9:5 Elasa: An uncertain location, with the strongest candidate being Khirbet el-Assi, which lies across a valley near el-Bireh.

9:7–22 In a book written in A.D. 391, St. Ambrose illustrates the cardinal virtue of fortitude with the example of Judas, who, by his persistence in attacking the enemy's strength even in overwhelming adversity, secured more glory in his death than he did in any of his triumphs (*On the Duties of the Clergy* 1, 41, 209).

[j] 160 B.C.

in spirit, for he had no time to assemble them. ⁸He became faint, but he said to those who were left, "Let us rise and go up against our enemies. We may be able to fight them." ⁹But they tried to dissuade him, saying, "We are not able. Let us rather save our own lives now, and let us come back with our brethren and fight them; we are too few." ¹⁰But Judas said, "Far be it from us to do such a thing as to flee from them. If our time has come, let us die bravely for our brethren, and leave no cause to question our honor."

The Last Battle of Judas
11 Then the army of Bacchi′des* marched out from the camp and took its stand for the encounter. The cavalry was divided into two companies, and the slingers and the archers went ahead of the army, as did all the chief warriors. ¹²Bacchi′des was on the right wing. Flanked by the two companies, the phalanx advanced to the sound of the trumpets; and the men with Judas also blew their trumpets. ¹³The earth was shaken by the noise of the armies, and the battle raged from morning till evening.

14 Judas saw that Bacchi′des and the strength of his army were on the right; then all the stout-hearted men went with him, ¹⁵and they crushed the right wing, and he pursued them as far as Mount Azo′tus. ¹⁶When those on the left wing saw that the right wing was crushed, they turned and followed close behind Judas and his men. ¹⁷The battle became desperate, and many on both sides were wounded and fell. ¹⁸Judas also fell, and the rest fled.

19 Then Jonathan and Simon took Judas their brother and buried him in the tomb of their fathers at Mo′dein, ²⁰and wept for him. And all Israel made great lamentation for him; they mourned many days and said,

²¹"How is the mighty fallen,
　the savior of Israel!"
²²Now the rest of the acts of Judas, and his wars and the brave deeds that he did, and his greatness, have not been recorded, for they were very many.

Jonathan Succeeds Judas
23 After the death of Judas, the lawless emerged in all parts of Israel; all the doers of injustice appeared. ²⁴In those days a very great famine occurred, and the country deserted with them to the enemy. ²⁵And Bacchi′des chose the ungodly and put them in charge of the country. ²⁶They sought and searched for the friends of Judas, and brought them to Bacchi′des, and he took vengeance on them and made sport of them. ²⁷Thus there was great distress in Israel, such as had not been since the time that prophets ceased to appear among them.

28 Then all the friends of Judas assembled and said to Jonathan, ²⁹"Since the death of your brother Judas there has been no one like him to go against our enemies and Bacchi′des, and to deal with those of our nation who hate us. ³⁰So now we have chosen you today to take his place as our ruler and leader, to fight our battle." ³¹And Jonathan at that time accepted the leadership and took the place of Judas his brother.

The Campaigns of Jonathan
32 When Bacchi′des learned of this, he tried to kill him. ³³But Jonathan and Simon his brother and all who were with him heard of it, and they fled into the wilderness of Teko′a and camped by the water of the pool of As′phar. ³⁴Bacchi′des found this out on the sabbath day, and he with all his army crossed the Jordan.

35 And Jonathan¹ sent his brother as leader of the multitude and begged the Nab″ate′ans, who were his

---

9:15 Mount Azotus: Different from the Azotus in 4:15, which was on a plain. The location mentioned here is disputed, and one suggestion is that the Hebrew original was actually the word for "slopes" (i.e., the slopes of a mountain north of Jerusalem), which is distinguished from "Azotus" by a single letter and is confused in translation in other instances. Josephus calls this location Mount Aza, a name that is likewise unattested in ancient sources.

9:19 Modein: See note on 2:1. In order to get Judas' body, Jonathan and Simon would likely have made a truce with Bacchides.

9:21-22 The death of Judas recalls the deeds of Israel's past leaders. "How are the mighty fallen" is a refrain in David's mourning of Saul and Jonathan in 2 Sam 1:19-27, and references to a "savior" or "deliverer" are common in Judges (cf. 3:9, 15, 31). Unlike the records of the kings of Judah, which are written in the annals, the deeds of Judas were so numerous they could not be recorded (cf. Jn 21:25).

9:27 prophets ceased: Likely referring to the last of the postexilic prophets, Malachi, so the early fifth century B.C. The

text bears witness to both the Jews' recognition of an intermission in prophecy and their expectation for at least one prophet to come again (cf. 4:46; 14:41).

9:30 ruler and leader: Jonathan rises to power at the urging of the people rather than by his own self-assertion. The ascension of Jonathan to lead the resistance marks the beginning of the third major section of the book.

9:33 Tekoa: Fifteen miles southeast of Jerusalem. It was also a place of refuge for Saul and Jonathan and the home of the prophet Amos. **pool of Asphar:** Probably a cistern in the region.

9:35-42 Jonathan and Simon ambush a wedding procession in revenge for their brother's capture. Josephus' recounting of these bleak events provides further details: the seizing of John and all he has in 9:36 entails, not just the plundering of their goods, but also the murder of John and all his companions, numbering about four hundred in total. This, then, corresponds with the number of Jambri's tribe killed in Jonathan and Simon's counterattack, thus fulfilling the law of limited retribution (cf. Ex 21:23-25; Lev 24:19-20; Deut 19:21). The death of John leaves Jonathan and Simon as the only remaining sons of Mattathias.

9:35 Nabateans: See note on 5:25.

Gk the army.
¹*Gk he.*

friends, for permission to store with them the great amount of baggage which they had. ³⁶But the sons of Jam'bri from Med'eba came out and seized John and all that he had, and departed with it.

37 After these things it was reported to Jonathan and Simon his brother, "The sons of Jam'bri are celebrating a great wedding, and are conducting the bride, a daughter of one of the great nobles of Canaan, from Nad'abath* with a large escort." ³⁸And they remembered the blood of John their brother, and went up and hid under cover of the mountain. ³⁹They raised their eyes and looked, and saw a tumultuous procession with much baggage; and the bridegroom came out with his friends and his brothers to meet them with tambourines and musicians and many weapons. ⁴⁰Then they rushed upon them from the ambush and began killing them. Many were wounded and fell, and the rest fled to the mountain; and they took all their goods. ⁴¹Thus the wedding was turned into mourning and the voice of their musicians into a funeral dirge. ⁴²And when they had fully avenged the blood of their brother, they returned to the marshes of the Jordan.

43 When Bacchi'des heard of this, he came with a large force on the sabbath day to the banks of the Jordan. ⁴⁴And Jonathan said to those with him, "Let us rise up now and fight for our lives, for today things are not as they were before. ⁴⁵For look! the battle is in front of us and behind us; the water of the Jordan is on this side and on that, with marsh and thicket; there is no place to turn. ⁴⁶Cry out now to Heaven that you may be delivered from the hands of our enemies." ⁴⁷So the battle began, and Jonathan stretched out his hand to strike Bacchi'des, but he eluded him and went to the rear. ⁴⁸Then Jonathan and the men with him leaped into the Jordan and swam across to the other side, and the enemy[m] did not cross the Jordan to attack them. ⁴⁹And about one thousand of Bacchi'des' men fell that day.

Bacchides Builds Fortifications

50 Bacchi'des[n] then returned to Jerusalem and built strong cities in Judea: the fortress in Jericho, and Emma'us, and Beth-ho'ron, and Beth'el, and Tim'nath, and[o] Phar'athon, and Teph'on, with high walls and gates and bars. ⁵¹And he placed garrisons in them to harass Israel. ⁵²He also fortified the city of Beth-zur, and Gaza'ra, and the citadel, and in them he put troops and stores of food. ⁵³And he took the sons of the leading men of the land as hostages and put them under guard in the citadel at Jerusalem.

54 In the one hundred and fifty-third year,[p] in the second month, Al'cimus gave orders to tear down the wall of the inner court of the sanctuary. He tore down the work of the prophets! ⁵⁵But he only began to tear it down, for at that time Al'cimus was stricken and his work was hindered; his mouth was stopped and he was paralyzed, so that he could no longer say a word or give commands concerning his house. ⁵⁶And Al'cimus died at that time in great agony. ⁵⁷When Bacchi'des saw that Al'cimus was dead, he returned to the king, and the land of Judah had rest for two years.

The End of the War

58 Then all the lawless plotted and said, "See! Jonathan and his men are living in quiet and

---

9:36 Jambri from Medeba: Medeba lies 12 miles east of the north end of the Dead Sea and is situated on the road to the Nabatean center, Petra. It is unknown who the sons of Jambri are, and various translations of the text differ in the rendering of their name, reflecting uncertainty about their identity. They may have been a bedouin tribe of the Arabs or Amorites.

9:37 Nadabath: Location unknown, perhaps corresponding with the Aramaic name for nearby Mount Nebo.

9:43–49 Bacchides was evidently trying to see if Jonathan would fight on the Sabbath, and Jonathan's speech evokes his father Mattathias' words in 2:41. Judas won a similar victory over Timothy in 5:40–43. See notes on 2:29–38 and 2:39–41.

9:50 Jericho: Ten miles northeast of Jerusalem. **Emmaus:** See note on 3:40. **Beth-horon:** See note on 3:16. **Bethel:** Twelve miles north of Jerusalem. **Timnath, and Pharathon, and Tephon:** Cities of southern Samaria, north of Judea.

9:52 Beth-zur: See note on 4:29. **Gazara:** See note on 4:15. **citadel:** See note on 1:33.

9:54 inner court: Alcimus sets out to tear down the wall that separated the Temple's inner court—accessible only to Jews—from the outer court of the Gentiles, acting in line with the Hellenizers' aims to make Jerusalem like any other Greek city. The two courts are noted in 2 Kings 21:5 and Ezek 44:19, and the division was marked in Herod's Temple with the following inscription: "No foreigner is to enter inside the barrier and the fence around the sanctuary. Whosoever should be caught will be the cause of his own ensuing death." In Acts 21:27–36, Paul is nearly killed by those who mistakenly believed he had brought Trophimus the Ephesian into this inner court. **work of the prophets:** Likely a reference to Haggai and Zechariah, under whose leadership the Temple was rebuilt (cf. Ezra 5:1–2). • A surprising pattern in Scripture is seen in Satan often leading people to pursue ends that are similar to God's own, but with impure motives and means that are contrary to God's ways. The first example is found in Gen 3:5, where the serpent tells Eve she will become like God by eating the forbidden fruit; while God indeed desires for us to be like him (Mt 5:48; Eph 5:1) and even become "partakers of the divine nature" (2 Pet 1:4), this only comes about by trusting and obeying him, following, not Eve's example, but that of Mary. Similarly, the high priest Alcimus here pursues a goal of breaking down the division between Jew and Greek, following the wishes of a foreign king rather than those of God. Nevertheless, Alcimus' misguided attempt paradoxically foreshadows the work of the eternal high priest, Jesus Christ, whose atoning work brings about the blessing to all nations promised to Abraham (Gen 12:3) and breaks down this very dividing wall by making peace between Jew and Gentile, reconciling both to God by his own blood (Eph 2:11–22). See also essay: *Paul and the Maccabees*.

---

*9:37: Vulgate reads "Madaba" (i.e., Medeba, as in verse 36) for *Nadabath*.
[m] Gk *they*.
[n] Gk *He*.
[o] Some authorities omit *and*.
[p] 159 B.C.

confidence. So now let us bring Bacchi'des back, and he will capture them all in one night." [59]And they went and consulted with him. [60]He started to come with a large force, and secretly sent letters to all his allies in Judea, telling them to seize Jon-ath an and his men; but they were unable to do it, because their plan became known. [61]And Jonathan's men[q] seized about fifty of the men of the country who were leaders in this treachery, and killed them.

62 Then Jonathan with his men, and Simon, withdrew to Beth-ba'si in the wilderness; he rebuilt the parts of it that had been demolished, and they fortified it. [63]When Bacchi'des learned of this, he assembled all his forces, and sent orders to the men of Judea. [64]Then he came and encamped against Beth-ba'si; he fought against it for many days and made machines of war.

65 But Jonathan left Simon his brother in the city, while he went out into the country; and he went with only a few men. [66]He struck down Odomer'a and his brothers and the sons of Pha'siron in their tents. [67]Then he[r] began to attack and went into battle with his forces; and Simon and his men sallied out from the city and set fire to the machines of war. [68]They fought with Bacchi'des, and he was crushed by them. They distressed him greatly, for his plan and his expedition had been in vain. [69]So he was greatly enraged at the lawless men who had counseled him to come into the country, and he killed many of them. Then he decided to depart to his own land.

70 When Jonathan learned of this, he sent ambassadors to him to make peace with him and obtain release of the captives. [71]He agreed, and did as he said; and he swore to Jonathan[s] that he would not try to harm him as long as he lived. [72]He restored to him the captives whom he had formerly taken from the land of Judah; then he turned and departed to his own land, and came no more into their territory. [73]Thus the sword ceased from Israel. And Jonathan dwelt in Mich'mash. And Jonathan began to judge the people, and he destroyed the ungodly out of Israel.

Revolt of Alexander Epiphanes

10 In the one hundred and sixtieth year[t] Alexander Epiph'anes, the son of Anti'ochus, landed and occupied Ptolema'is. They welcomed him, and there he began to reign. [2]When Deme'trius the king heard of it, he assembled a very large army and marched out to meet him in battle. [3]And Deme'trius sent Jonathan a letter in peaceable words to honor him; [4]for he said, "Let us act first to make peace with him[u] before he makes peace with Alexander against us, [5]for he will remember all the wrongs which we did to him and to his brothers and his nation." [6]So Deme'trius[v] gave him authority to recruit troops, to equip them with arms, and to become his ally; and he commanded that the hostages in the citadel should be released to him.

7 Then Jonathan came to Jerusalem and read the letter in the hearing of all the people and of the men in the citadel. [8]They were greatly alarmed when they heard that the king had given him authority to recruit troops. [9]But the men in the citadel released the hostages to Jonathan, and he returned them to their parents.

10 And Jonathan dwelt in Jerusalem and began to rebuild and restore the city. [11]He directed those who were doing the work to build the walls and encircle Mount Zion with squared stones, for better fortification; and they did so.

12 Then the foreigners who were in the strongholds that Bacchi'des had built fled; [13]each left his

---

9:62 Beth-basi: A village identified with modern-day Khirbet Beit Bassa, six miles south of Jerusalem between Bethlehem and Tekoa.

9:64 machines of war: See note on 5:30.

9:66 Odomera ... sons of Phasiron: These would seem to be nomadic tribesmen in the region who were fighting alongside the Seleucids, as Josephus places them within Bacchides' camp. They are otherwise unknown.

9:68–69 The Hellenizers' dependence upon Seleucid aid and their lack of success at gaining leadership of Judea against the Maccabeans have finally exhausted the patience of the Seleucids.

9:73 Michmash: Nine miles northwest of Jerusalem. Jonathan's dwelling here signals that Jerusalem was still under Seleucid control. In 1 Sam 14, Michmash is also the site of Jonathan's surprise rout of the Philistines. **Jonathan began to judge:** An allusion to the time of Judges as an analogy for Jonathan's own rule.

10:1 Alexander Epiphanes: Commonly known outside 1 Maccabees as Alexander Balas, who claimed to be the son of Antiochus IV, though his legitimacy as such is unlikely. **Ptolemais:** See note on 5:22. **They welcomed him:** Josephus relates that Demetrius has become a recluse in his own palace and, thus, deeply unpopular among those in his kingdom.

10:3–5 Despite Jonathan's residence being in Michmash rather than Jerusalem, Demetrius recognizes Jonathan as the one who is able to aid him in Judea instead of the Hellenizers. This marks a twofold reversal: not only have the Seleucids abandoned support for the Hellenizing party, but they themselves are now seeking the help of the Maccabees.

10:9 released the hostages: Even though Bacchides released the captives that he had taken from them (9:53, 72), the hostages in the citadel must have been retained up to now.

10:10–11: Jonathan moves from Michmash to Jerusalem and begins rebuilding the wall that Lysias and Antiochus V tore down in 6:62.

---

[q] Gk *they.*
[r] Other authorities read *they.*
[s] Gk *him.*
[t] 152 B.C.
[u] Gk *them.*
[v] Gk *he.*

place and departed to his own land. [14]Only in Beth-zur did some remain who had forsaken the law and the commandments, for it served as a place of refuge.

15 Now Alexander the king heard of all the promises which Deme'trius had sent to Jonathan, and men told him of the battles that Jonathan[w] and his brothers had fought, of the brave deeds that they had done, and of the troubles that they had endured. [16]So he said, "Shall we find another such man? Come now, we will make him our friend and ally." [17]And he wrote a letter and sent it to him, in the following words:

Jonathan Becomes High Priest

18 "King Alexander to his brother Jonathan, greeting. [19]We have heard about you, that you are a mighty warrior and worthy to be our friend. [20]And so we have appointed you today to be the high priest of your nation; you are to be called the king's friend" (and he sent him a purple robe and a golden crown) "and you are to take our side and keep friendship with us."

Demetrius Writes to Jonathan

21 So Jonathan put on the holy garments in the seventh month of the one hundred and sixtieth year,[x] at the feast of tabernacles, and he recruited troops and equipped them with arms in abundance. [22]When Deme'trius heard of these things he was grieved and said, [23]"What is this that we have done? Alexander has gotten ahead of us in forming a friendship with the Jews to strengthen himself. [24]I also will write them words of encouragement and promise them honor and gifts, that I may have their help." [25]So he sent a message to them in the following words:

"King Deme'trius to the nation of the Jews, greeting. [26]Since you have kept your agreement with us and have continued your friendship with us, and have not sided with our enemies, we have heard of it and rejoiced. [27]And now continue still to keep faith with us, and we will repay you with good for what you do for us. [28]We will grant you many immunities and give you gifts.

29 "And now I free you and exempt all the Jews from payment of tribute and salt tax and crown levies, [30]and instead of collecting the third of the grain and the half of the fruit of the trees that I should receive, I release them from this day and henceforth. I will not collect them from the land of Judah or from the three districts added to it from Samar'ia and Galilee, from this day and for all time. [31]And let Jerusalem and her environs, her tithes and her revenues, be holy and free from tax. [32]I release also my control of the citadel in Jerusalem and give it to the high priest, that he may station in it men of his own choice to guard it. [33]And every one of the Jews taken as a captive from the land of Judah into any part of my kingdom, I set free without payment; and let all officials cancel also the taxes on their cattle.

34 "And all the feasts and sabbaths and new moons and appointed days, and the three days before a feast and the three after a feast—let them all be days of immunity and release for all the Jews who are in my kingdom. [35]No one shall have authority to exact anything from them or annoy any of them about any matter.

36 "Let Jews be enrolled in the king's forces to the number of thirty thousand men, and let the maintenance be given them that is due to all the forces of the king. [37]Let some of them be stationed in the great strongholds of the king, and let some of them be put in positions of trust in the kingdom. Let their officers and leaders be of their own number, and let them live by their own laws, just as the king has commanded in the land of Judah.

10:14 Beth-zur: See note on 4:29.

10:20 high priest of your nation: After the death of Alcimus (159 B.C.), there is no evidence of a high priest in Jerusalem for this seven-year period until Jonathan is given the appointment here (152 B.C.). High priests were traditionally chosen from the line of Zadok, which appears to have been broken with the appointment of Menelaus by Antiochus IV in 171 B.C. While not from the traditional high-priestly Oniad family, the Hasmoneans (who descend from Joarib) appear to have been Zadokites as well (cf. 1 Chron 24:7). **purple robe:** Friends of the king were allowed to wear purple, the royal color.

10:21 feast of tabernacles: One of Israel's great pilgrimage feasts, celebrated for seven days in connection with the autumn harvest, in which the people were to live in tents to remember their time in the wilderness. See Lev 23:33–43.

10:25–45 Demetrius' letter bears witness to the dramatically reversed political fortunes of the Jewish people, whose strength under the Maccabees has now made them a key ally for both claimants to the Seleucid crown. Here the Jews are addressed as a self-governing nation, no longer directly taxed, able to have their own officials, and promised control over nearby territories and even the citadel. The omission of Jonathan's name from Demetrius' letter may reflect fears that Jonathan has gone over to Alexander's side.

10:29 payment of tribute: See note on 1:4. **salt tax:** Imposed on the salt collected from the Dead Sea (referenced again in 11:35). **crown levies:** Gifts given to the king to honor him or gain his favor, which became expected whenever the king demanded them (e.g., accession, birthday, etc.).

10:30 third of the grain ... half of the fruit: A high rate of taxation, which may have been punitively imposed on the Jewish nation because of their revolt. See notes on 1:20, 29. **three districts:** Identified in 11:34 as Aphairema, Lydda, and Rathamin, areas north and west of Jerusalem. In 10:38, Demetrius declares them to be annexed from Samaria and added to Judea, which likely corresponds with traditional Jewish claims over these areas and Judas' prior victories within them.

10:33 cattle: According to Josephus, the tax on cattle refers to the empire's right to make use of Israel's beasts of burden.

10:34 three days before ... after: The journeying time for those outside of Judea.

[w]Gk *he.*
[x]152 B.C.

38 "As for the three districts that have been added to Judea from the country of Samar'ia, let them be so annexed to Judea that they are considered to be under one ruler and obey no other authority but the high priest. ³⁹Ptolema'is and the land adjoining it I have given as a gift to the sanctuary in Jerusalem, to meet the necessary expenses of the sanctuary. ⁴⁰I also grant fifteen thousand shekels of silver yearly out of the king's revenues from appropriate places. ⁴¹And all the additional funds which the government officials have not paid as they did in the first years,ʸ they shall give from now on for the service of the temple.ᶻ ⁴²Moreover, the five thousand shekels of silver which my officialsᵃ have received every year from the income of the services of the temple, this too is canceled, because it belongs to the priests who minister there. ⁴³And whoever takes refuge at the temple in Jerusalem, or in any of its precincts, because he owes money to the king or has any debt, let him be released and receive back all his property in my kingdom.

44 "Let the cost of rebuilding and restoring the structures of the sanctuary be paid from the revenues of the king. ⁴⁵And let the cost of rebuilding the walls of Jerusalem and fortifying it round about, and the cost of rebuilding the walls in Judea, also be paid from the revenues of the king."

Death of Demetrius

46 When Jonathan and the people heard these words, they did not believe or accept them, because they remembered the great wrongs which Deme'triusᵇ had done in Israel and how he had greatly oppressed them. ⁴⁷They favored Alexander, because he had been the first to speak peaceable words to them, and they remained his allies all his days.

48 Now Alexander the king assembled large forces and encamped opposite Deme'trius. ⁴⁹The two kings met in battle, and the army of Deme'trius fled, and Alexanderᶜ pursued him and defeated them. ⁵⁰He pressed the battle strongly until the sun set, and Deme'trius fell on that day.

Treaty of Ptolemy and Alexander

51 Then Alexander sent ambassadors to Ptol'emy king of Egypt with the following message: ⁵²"Since I have returned to my kingdom and have taken my seat on the throne of my fathers, and established my rule—for I crushed Deme'trius and gained control of our country; ⁵³I met him in battle, and he and his army were crushed by us, and we have taken our seat on the throne of his kingdom— ⁵⁴now therefore let us establish friendship with one another; give me now your daughter as my wife, and I will become your son-in-law, and will make gifts to you and to her in keeping with your position."

55 Ptol'emy the king replied and said, "Happy was the day on which you returned to the land of your fathers and took your seat on the throne of their kingdom. ⁵⁶And now I will do for you as you wrote, but meet me at Ptolema'is, so that we may see one another, and I will become your father-in-law, as you have said."

57 So Ptol'emy set out from Egypt, he and Cleopa'tra his daughter, and came to Ptolema'is in the one hundred and sixty-second year.ᵈ ⁵⁸Alexander the king met him, and Ptol'emyᵉ gave him Cleopa'tra his daughter in marriage, and celebrated her wedding at Ptolema'is with great pomp, as kings do.

59 Then Alexander the king wrote to Jonathan to come to meet him. ⁶⁰So he went with pomp to Ptolema'is and met the two kings; he gave them and their friends silver and gold and many gifts, and found favor with them. ⁶¹A group of pestilent men from Israel, lawless men, gathered together against him to accuse him; but the king paid no attention to them. ⁶²The king gave orders to take off Jonathan's garments and to clothe him in purple, and they did so. ⁶³The king also seated him at his side; and he said to his officers, "Go forth with him into the middle of the city and proclaim that no one is to bring charges against him about any matter, and let no one annoy him for any reason." ⁶⁴And when his accusers saw the honor that was paid him, in accordance with the proclamation, and saw him clothed in purple, they all fled. ⁶⁵Thus the king honored him and enrolled him among his chief friends, and made him general and governor of the province. ⁶⁶And Jonathan returned to Jerusalem in peace and gladness.

Apollonius Is Defeated by Jonathan

67 In the one hundred and sixty-fifth yearᶠ Deme'trius the son of Demetrius came from Crete to

---

10:38 three districts: See note on 10:30.

10:39 Ptolemais: May have been granted by Demetrius to encourage Jonathan to attack Alexander there. The relationship between the Jews and Ptolemais was not strong, and they would have resisted supporting the Jerusalem Temple. See note on 5:22.

10:51 Ptolemy: Ptolemy VI Philometor, whom Antiochus IV defeated in 1:18.

10:57 Cleopatra: A recurring name among Egyptian royalty, here referring to Ptolemy's daughter Cleopatra Thea (ca. 164–121 B.C.).

10:65 general ... governor: The first time one of the Maccabees is acknowledged as the leader of Judea and chief friend of the king, increasing Jonathan's rank among his friends. The titles of general and governor confer upon Jonathan both military and civil authority.

10:67 Demetrius the son of Demetrius: Demetrius II Nicator, the 14-year-old son of Demetrius I who appears in

ʸ The Greek text of this verse is uncertain.
ᶻ Gk *house.*
ᵃ Gk *they.*
ᵇ Gk *he.*
ᶜ Other authorities read *Alexander fled, and Demetrius.*
ᵈ 150 B.C.
ᵉ Gk *he.*
ᶠ 147 B.C.

the land of his fathers. ⁶⁸When Alexander the king heard of it, he was greatly grieved and returned to Antioch. ⁶⁹And Deme′trius appointed Apollo′nius the governor of Coe′le-syr′ia, and he assembled a large force and encamped against Jam′nia. Then he sent the following message to Jonathan the high priest:

70 "You are the only one to rise up against us, and I have become a laughingstock and reproach because of you. Why do you assume authority against us in the hill country? ⁷¹If you now have confidence in your forces, come down to the plain to meet us, and let us match strength with each other there, for I have with me the power of the cities. ⁷²Ask and learn who I am and who the others are that are helping us. Men will tell you that you cannot stand before us, for your fathers were twice put to flight in their own land. ⁷³And now you will not be able to withstand my cavalry and such an army in the plain, where there is no stone or pebble, or place to flee."

74 When Jonathan heard the words of Apollo′nius, his spirit was aroused. He chose ten thousand men and set out from Jerusalem, and Simon his brother met him to help him. ⁷⁵He encamped before Joppa, but the men of the city closed its gates, for Apollo′nius had a garrison in Joppa. ⁷⁶So they fought against it, and the men of the city became afraid and opened the gates, and Jonathan gained possession of Joppa.

77 When Apollo′nius heard of it, he mustered three thousand cavalry and a large army, and went to Azo′tus as though he were going farther. At the same time he advanced into the plain, for he had a large troop of cavalry and put confidence in it. ⁷⁸Jonathanᵍ pursued him to Azo′tus, and the armies engaged in battle. ⁷⁹Now Apollo′nius had secretly left a thousand cavalry behind them. ⁸⁰Jonathan learned that there was an ambush behind him, for they surrounded his army and shot arrows at his men from early morning till late afternoon. ⁸¹But his men stood fast, as Jonathan commanded, and the enemy'sʰ horses grew tired.

82 Then Simon brought forward his force and engaged the phalanx in battle (for the cavalry was exhausted); they were overwhelmed by him and fled, ⁸³and the cavalry was dispersed in the plain. They fled to Azo′tus and entered Beth-da′gon, the temple of their idol, for safety. ⁸⁴But Jonathan burned Azo′tus and the surrounding towns and plundered them; and the temple of Da′gon, and those who had taken refuge in it he burned with fire. ⁸⁵The number of those who fell by the sword, with those burned alive, came to eight thousand men.

86 Then Jonathan departed from there and encamped against Aska′lon, and the men of the city came out to meet him with great pomp. ⁸⁷And Jonathan and those with him returned to Jerusalem with much booty. ⁸⁸When Alexander the king heard of these things, he honored Jonathan still more; ⁸⁹and he sent to him a golden buckle, such as it is the custom to give to the kinsmen of kings. He also gave him Ek′ron and all its environs as his possession.

Ptolemy Invades Syria

11 Then the king of Egypt gathered great forces, like the sand by the seashore, and many ships; and he tried to get possession of Alexander's kingdom by trickery and add it to his own kingdom. ²He set out for Syria with peaceable words, and the people of the cities opened their gates to him and went to meet him, for Alexander the king

---

this narrative five years after the death of his father. He had been sent away for safety and returned via Crete with a mercenary force. Josephus records that he landed in Cilicia, a region northwest of Antioch.

10:69 Apollonius: The governor of Coele-syria (see note on 7:8), whom Josephus identifies as Apollonius Daus. Like Jonathan, Apollonius may have been a local ruler whom Alexander sought as an ally. His loyalties are somewhat unclear, as Josephus relates that he was first appointed by Alexander, and it is possible that this allegiance would have shifted with Demetrius II's arrival. **Jamnia:** See note on 4:15.

10:70–85 Apollonius challenges Jonathan to battle on the plain to negate the Maccabees' tactical advantages in mountain terrain, which they have utilized to defeat larger forces in the past (such as at Beth-horon in 3:16). • The battles against Apollonius in Philistine cities recall Israel's prior wars with their ancient enemies. Apollonius' reference to "your fathers" probably alludes to the Philistine victories over Israel in 1 Sam 4 and elsewhere. The word for "pebble" (*kochlax*) is found only twice in the Greek Bible: here (10:73) and 1 Sam 14:14 LXX, where it refers to the weapons Jonathan and his armor-bearer used to defeat the Philistines, and "stone" may also allude to David's weapon in his defeat of the Philistine Goliath in 1 Sam 17. Jonathan's destruction of Dagon's temple similarly evokes the Lord's defeat of Dagon when the Ark is captured by the Philistines in 1 Sam 5.

10:75 Joppa: A port city north of Jamnia and 40 miles northwest of Jerusalem, which served as the primary seaport for Judea.

10:77 Azotus: South of Jamnia. See note on 4:15.

10:84 the temple of Dagon: Dagon was a grain god worshiped by the Philistines. In 1 Sam 5, Dagon's temple in Azotus (Ashdod) is where the Philistines bring the Ark of the Covenant after capturing it from Israel.

10:86 Askalon: A coastal city ten miles south of Azotus.

10:88 Alexander ... honored Jonathan: If Apollonius has supported Demetrius II and turned his back on Alexander (see note on 10:69), Jonathan has now defeated one of Demetrius' key allies and preserved friendship with Alexander (cf. 10:47).

10:89 Ekron: An old Philistine city, about five miles inland from the coast from Azotus.

11:1–3 There are competing accounts of Ptolemy's original motives. Josephus recounts that Ptolemy was initially coming to Alexander's aid (before switching loyalties to Demetrius II), while 1 Mac identifies Ptolemy's designs as deceitful from the beginning.

ᵍ Gk *He.*
ʰ Gk *their.*

had commanded them to meet him, since he was Alexander's[i] father-in-law. ³But when Ptol'emy entered the cities he stationed forces as a garrison in each city.

4 When he[j] approached Azo'tus, they showed him the temple of Da'gon burned down, and Azotus and its suburbs destroyed, and the corpses lying about, and the charred bodies of those whom Jonathan[k] had burned in the war, for they had piled them in heaps along his route. ⁵They also told the king what Jonathan had done, to throw blame on him; but the king kept silent. ⁶Jonathan met the king at Joppa with pomp, and they greeted one another and spent the night there. ⁷And Jonathan went with the king as far as the river called Eleu'therus; then he returned to Jerusalem.

8 So King Ptol'emy gained control of the coastal cities as far as Seleu'cia by the sea, and he kept devising evil designs against Alexander. ⁹He sent envoys to Deme'trius the king, saying, "Come, let us make a covenant with each other, and I will give you in marriage my daughter who was Alexander's wife, and you shall reign over your father's kingdom. ¹⁰For I now regret that I gave him my daughter, for he has tried to kill me." ¹¹He threw blame on Alexander[l] because he coveted his kingdom. ¹²So he took his daughter away from him and gave her to Deme'trius. He was estranged from Alexander, and their enmity became manifest.

13 Then Ptol'emy entered Antioch and put on the crown of Asia. Thus he put two crowns upon his head, the crown of Egypt and that of Asia. ¹⁴Now Alexander the king was in Cili'cia at that time, because the people of that region were in revolt. ¹⁵And Alexander heard of it and came against him in battle. Ptol'emy marched out and met him with a

strong force, and put him to flight. ¹⁶So Alexander fled into Arabia to find protection there, and King Ptol'emy was exalted. ¹⁷And Zab'diel the Arab cut off the head of Alexander and sent it to Ptol'emy. ¹⁸But King Ptol'emy died three days later, and his troops in the strongholds were killed by the inhabitants of the strongholds. ¹⁹So Deme'trius became king in the one hundred and sixty-seventh year.[m]

Jonathan's Diplomacy

20 In those days Jonathan assembled the men of Judea to attack the citadel in Jerusalem, and he built many engines of war to use against it. ²¹But certain lawless men who hated their nation went to the king and reported to him that Jonathan was besieging the citadel. ²²When he heard this he was angry, and as soon as he heard it he set out and came to Ptolema'is; and he wrote Jonathan not to continue the siege, but to meet him for a conference at Ptolemais as quickly as possible.

23 When Jonathan heard this, he gave orders to continue the siege; and he chose some of the elders of Israel and some of the priests, and put himself in danger, ²⁴for he went to the king at Ptolema'is, taking silver and gold and clothing and numerous other gifts. And he won his favor. ²⁵Although certain lawless men of his nation kept making complaints against him, ²⁶the king treated him as his predecessors had treated him; he exalted him in the presence of all his friends. ²⁷He confirmed him in the high priesthood and in as many other honors as he had formerly had, and made him to be regarded as one of his chief friends. ²⁸Then Jonathan asked the king to free Judea and the three districts of Samar'ia[n] from tribute, and promised him three hundred talents. ²⁹The king consented, and wrote a

---

11:4 Azotus: See note on 4:15.
11:6 Joppa: See note on 10:75.
11:7 as far as ... Eleutherus: A long journey about 200 miles northward, around two-thirds of the way to Antioch.
11:8 Seleucia by the sea: Antioch's port city to the west on the coast of the Mediterranean.
11:9 Demetrius the king: Demetrius II Nicator. See note on 10:67. **my daughter:** See note on 10:57.
11:10-11 Josephus records an alleged murder plot by Alexander's friend Ammonius against Ptolemy on this expedition at Ptolemais. In Josephus' account, this conflict leads Ptolemy to abandon his support of Alexander in favor of Demetrius II.
11:13 Antioch: The Seleucid capital in Syria. Josephus relates that Ptolemy was made king by the people of Antioch, who had come to detest Alexander. After gaining both crowns, Ptolemy persuaded the people of Antioch to accept Demetrius II as king (whose father Demetrius they had also hated), knowing that the Romans would not tolerate his direct control over both kingdoms.

11:14 Cilicia: A region northwest of Antioch, where Demetrius II first landed and may have still remained. See note on 10:67.
11:16 Arabia: Historians in antiquity referred to Arabia, not just as the Arabian peninsula, but also as the interior desert regions east of Syria and Israel. This is likely the direction of Alexander's flight, which may also correspond with the area where Paul goes after his Baptism in Damascus (cf. Gal 1:17).
11:17 Zabdiel the Arab: Josephus identifies Zabdiel as an Arab prince. The Greek historian Diodorus describes Alexander's death as a result of collusion between Zabdiel (called by the Greek name Diocles) and Alexander's own disillusioned soldiers.
11:18 King Ptolemy died: Josephus records Ptolemy's death as a result of wounds he received in his battle with Alexander's forces.
11:24 Ptolemais: See note on 5:22.
11:28 three districts: The Samaritan territories promised by Demetrius I Soter, the father of the now-reigning Demetrius II Nicator, in the letter that Jonathan and the people rejected (see note on 10:30). By only requesting their release from tribute, Jonathan presumes to have them already in his possession. **three hundred talents:** Less than the 440 and 740 talents bid by Jason and Menelaus in their attempts to purchase the high priesthood from Antiochus Epiphanes in 2 Mac 4:8, 24.

---

[i] Gk *his*.
[j] Other ancient authorities read *they*.
[k] Gk *he*.
[l] Gk *him*.
[m] 145 B.C.
[n] Cn: Gk *the three districts and Samaria*.

letter to Jonathan about all these things; its contents were as follows:

30 "King Deme'trius to Jonathan his brother and to the nation of the Jews, greeting. [31]This copy of the letter which we wrote concerning you to Las'thenes our kinsman we have written to you also, so that you may know what it says. [32]King Deme'trius to Las'thenes his father, greeting. [33]To the nation of the Jews, who are our friends and fulfil their obligations to us, we have determined to do good, because of the good will they show toward us. [34]We have confirmed as their possession both the territory of Judea and the three districts of Aphai'rema and Lydda and Rath'amin; the latter, with all the region bordering them, were added to Judea from Samar'ia. To all those who offer sacrifice in Jerusalem, we have granted release from° the royal taxes which the king formerly received from them each year, from the crops of the land and the fruit of the trees. [35]And the other payments henceforth due to us of the tithes, and the taxes due to us, and the salt pits and the crown taxes due to us—from all these we shall grant them release. [36]And not one of these grants shall be canceled from this time forth for ever. [37]Now therefore take care to make a copy of this, and let it be given to Jonathan and put up in a conspicuous place on the holy mountain."

The Intrigue of Trypho

38 Now when Deme'trius the king saw that the land was quiet before him and that there was no opposition to him, he dismissed all his troops, each man to his own place, except the foreign troops which he had recruited from the islands of the nations. So all the troops who had served his fathers hated him. [39]Now Try'pho had formerly been one of Alexander's supporters. He saw that all the troops were murmuring against Deme'trius. So he went to Imal'kue the Arab, who was bringing up Anti'ochus, the young son of Alexander, [40]and insistently urged him to hand Anti'ochusᴾ over to

him, to become king in place of his father. He also reported to Imal'kueᴾ what Deme'trius had done and told of the hatred which the troops of Demetrius had for him; and he stayed there many days.

41 Now Jonathan sent to Deme'trius the king the request that he remove the troops of the citadel from Jerusalem, and the troops in the strongholds; for they kept fighting against Israel. [42]And Deme'trius sent this message to Jonathan, "Not only will I do these things for you and your nation, but I will confer great honor on you and your nation, if I find an opportunity. [43]Now then you will do well to send me men who will help me, for all my troops have revolted." [44]So Jonathan sent three thousand stalwart men to him at Antioch, and when they came to the king, the king rejoiced at their arrival.

45 Then the men of the city assembled within the city, to the number of a hundred and twenty thousand, and they wanted to kill the king. [46]But the king fled into the palace. Then the men of the city seized the main streets of the city and began to fight. [47]So the king called the Jews to his aid, and they all rallied about him and then spread out through the city; and they killed on that day as many as a hundred thousand men. [48]They set fire to the city and seized much spoil on that day, and they saved the king. [49]When the men of the city saw that the Jews had gained control of the city as they pleased, their courage failed and they cried out to the king with this entreaty, [50]"Grant us peace, and make the Jews stop fighting against us and our city." [51]And they threw down their arms and made peace. So the Jews gained glory in the eyes of the king and of all the people in his kingdom, and they returned to Jerusalem with much spoil.

52 So Deme'trius the king sat on the throne of his kingdom, and the land was quiet before him. [53]But he broke his word about all that he had promised; and he became estranged from Jonathan and did not repay the favors which Jonathanᵠ had done him, but oppressed him greatly.

11:32 Lasthenes: Originally the general of Demetrius' mercenary troops, who held considerable influence and power with the young king.

11:34–35 Promises made by Demetrius I in his appeal to the Jews (10:25–45) after Alexander's offer of friendship. The exemption from royal taxes would not have held for Samaritans, who offered sacrifices at Mount Gerizim rather than Jerusalem.

11:37 the holy mountain: The Temple Mount in Jerusalem.

11:38 foreign troops: The mercenary force of 10:67. Diodorus records that it was Lasthenes who convinced the king to disband his troops. Leaving his local forces without an income, and preferring his own private army, would prove to be a serious political mistake for Demetrius. See 11:43.

11:39 Trypho: A former soldier and now governor who had served under Demetrius I, Alexander Balas, and now Demetrius II. **Imalkue the Arab:** An otherwise unknown figure who may have had some relation to Zabdiel (cf. 11:17). **Antiochus:** Antiochus VI Dionysus, son of Alexander Balas, who would have been around four or five years old at this time.

11:47 as many as a hundred thousand: The testimony of Josephus and Diodorus fills in additional details: the king was protected by the Jewish forces, which, being overwhelmed by the more numerous rebels, resorted to firing arrows down from higher ground in the palace. This started fires that turned the tide in the battle, leaving the rebellious citizens defenseless against Demetrius' mercenaries and eventually leaving most of the city burned.

11:53 broke his word: Demetrius had promised to give Jonathan Judea, three districts from Samaria, and exemption from taxes and to evacuate the citadel and strongholds in Judea (11:30–37, 41–42). This lack of fidelity is in keeping with Demetrius' Seleucid predecessors (cf. 6:62; 7:18).

° Or *Samaria, for all those who offer sacrifice in Jerusalem, in place of.*
ᴾ Gk *him.*
ᵠ Gk *he.*

Trypho Seizes Power

54 After this Try'pho returned, and with him the young boy Anti'ochus who began to reign and put on the crown. ⁵⁵All the troops that Deme'trius had cast off gathered around him, and they fought against Demetrius,ʳ and he fled and was routed. ⁵⁶And Try'pho captured the elephantsˢ and gained control of Antioch. ⁵⁷Then the young Anti'ochus wrote to Jonathan, saying, "I confirm you in the high priesthood and set you over the four districts and make you one of the friends of the king." ⁵⁸And he sent him gold plate and a table service, and granted him the right to drink from gold cups and dress in purple and wear a gold buckle. ⁵⁹Simon his brother he made governor from the Ladder of Tyre to the borders of Egypt.

Campaigns of Jonathan and Simon

60 Then Jonathan set forth and traveled beyond the river and among the cities, and all the army of Syria gathered to him as allies. When he came to Aska'lon, the people of the city met him and paid him honor. ⁶¹From there he departed to Gaza, but the men of Gaza shut him out. So he besieged it and burned its suburbs with fire and plundered them. ⁶²Then the people of Gaza pleaded with Jonathan, and he made peace with them, and took the sons of their rulers as hostages and sent them to Jerusalem. And he passed through the country as far as Damascus.

63 Then Jonathan heard that the officers of Deme'trius had come to Ka'desh in Galilee with a large army, intending to remove him from office. ⁶⁴He went to meet them, but left his brother Simon in the country. ⁶⁵Simon encamped before Beth-zur and fought against it for many days and hemmed it in. ⁶⁶Then they asked him to grant them terms of peace, and he did so. He removed them from there, took possession of the city, and set a garrison over it.

67 Jonathan and his army encamped by the waters of Gennes'aret. Early in the morning they marched to the plain of Ha'zor, ⁶⁸and behold, the army of the foreigners met him in the plain; they had set an ambush against him in the mountains, but they themselves met him face to face. ⁶⁹Then the men in ambush emerged from their places and joined battle. ⁷⁰All the men with Jonathan fled; not one of them was left except Mattathi'as the son of Ab'salom and Judas the son of Chal'phi, commanders of the forces of the army. ⁷¹Jonathan tore his garments and put dust on his head, and prayed. ⁷²Then he turned back to the battle against the enemyᵗ and routed them, and they fled. ⁷³When his men who were fleeing saw this, they returned to him and joined him in the pursuit as far as Ka'desh, to their camp, and there they encamped. ⁷⁴As many as three thousand of the foreigners fell that day. And Jonathan returned to Jerusalem.

Alliances with Rome and Sparta

12 Now when Jonathan saw that the time was favorable for him, he chose men and sent them to Rome to confirm and renew the friendship with them. ²He also sent letters to the same effect to the Spartans and to other places. ³So they went to Rome and entered the senate chamber and said, "Jonathan the high priest and the Jewish nation have sent us to renew the former friendship and alliance with them." ⁴And the Romansᵘ gave them letters to the people in every place, asking them to provide for the envoysᵛ safe conduct to the land of Judah.

11:54–56 Demetrius fled and continued to rule from Seleucia on the coast, maintaining control over parts of the empire, including much of the coastal plain and Gaza (11:61).

11:56 elephants: Likely the war elephants left behind after Ptolemy Philometor's death (cf. 11:18).

11:57 wrote to Jonathan: Like their predecessors, Antiochus VI and Trypho recognize the importance of Jonathan as an ally. **four districts:** Judea and the three districts of Samaria (cf. 10:38; 11:34).

11:58 table service: Literally "service", which may refer to the servants who attend or to the table instruments themselves. Within the context of the verse (which next refers to drinking from gold cups), the second reading is more likely.

11:59 made governor: Simon, who had already been functioning as Jonathan's general in the area (cf. 5:20–23; 10:82), is now confirmed by the Seleucids as the official governor of the region, which now covers cities previously outside Jewish control. **Ladder of Tyre:** A natural boundary of cliffs extending from Galilee to the sea between Tyre to the north and Ptolemais to the south. This would have completed the Maccabean control of the coastal plain gained during their battles with Apollonius (10:75–89), in addition to Judas' control of Judea and the districts of Samaria.

11:60 beyond the river: Referring to the province by this name. See note on 7:8. **Askalon:** See note on 10:86.

11:61 Gaza: The old Philistine city closest to the Egyptian border along the Mediterranean coast.

11:62 Damascus: A major city 150 miles northeast of Jerusalem. Jonathan's expedition to a city this far away illustrates the extent of his jurisdiction.

11:63 Kadesh in Galilee: Just northwest of Lake Huleh, which lies to the north of Lake Gennesaret (Sea of Galilee).

11:65 Beth-zur: See note on 4:29.

11:67 Gennesaret: The Sea of Galilee. **plain of Hazor:** Ten miles north of the Sea of Galilee, just south of Lake Huleh.

11:68–74 While 1 Mac rarely speaks of divine interventions, in this case God's response to Jonathan's prayer seems to be the only explanation for how Jonathan and his two generals drive back a much larger force.

12:1 renew the friendship: By sending another envoy to the Romans, Jonathan seeks to strengthen the loyalties first established under Judas and to deter further Seleucid aggression. See 8:23.

12:2 Spartans: Sparta was a famous Greek city-state, which the historian Strabo identifies as the most prominent in Peloponnesus, the southern region of Greece. **other places:** May include the cities listed in 15:22–23.

ʳ Gk *him.*
ˢ Gk *beasts.*
ᵗ Gk *them.*
ᵘ Gk *they.*
ᵛ Gk *them.*

5 This is a copy of the letter which Jonathan wrote to the Spartans: [6]"Jonathan the high priest, the senate of the nation, the priests, and the rest of the Jewish people to their brethren the Spartans, greeting. [7]Already in time past a letter was sent to Oni'as the high priest from A'rius,[w] who was king among you, stating that you are our brethren, as the appended copy shows. [8]Oni'as welcomed the envoy with honor, and received the letter, which contained a clear declaration of alliance and friendship. [9]Therefore, though we have no need of these things, since we have as encouragement the holy books which are in our hands, [10]we have undertaken to send to renew our brotherhood and friendship with you, so that we may not become estranged from you, for considerable time has passed since you sent your letter to us. [11]We therefore remember you constantly on every occasion, both in our feasts and on other appropriate days, at the sacrifices which we offer and in our prayers, as it is right and proper to remember brethren. [12]And we rejoice in your glory. [13]But as for ourselves, many afflictions and many wars have encircled us; the kings round about us have waged war against us. [14]We were unwilling to annoy you and our other allies and friends with these wars, [15]for we have the help which comes from Heaven for our aid; and we were delivered from our enemies and our enemies were humbled. [16]We therefore have chosen Nume'nius the son of Anti'ochus and Antip'ater the son of Jason, and have sent them to Rome to renew our former friendship and alliance with them. [17]We have commanded them to go also to you and greet you and deliver to you this letter from us concerning the renewal of our brotherhood. [18]And now please send us a reply to this."

19 This is a copy of the letter which they sent to Oni'as: [20]"A'rius, king of the Spartans, to Oni'as the high priest, greeting. [21]It has been found in writing concerning the Spartans and the Jews that they are brethren and are of the family of Abraham. [22]And now that we have learned this, please write us concerning your welfare; [23]we on our part write to you that your cattle and your property belong to us, and ours belong to you. We therefore command that our envoys[x] report to you accordingly."

Further Campaigns of Jonathan and Simon

24 Now Jonathan heard that the commanders of Deme'trius had returned, with a larger force than before, to wage war against him. [25]So he marched away from Jerusalem and met them in the region of Ha'math, for he gave them no opportunity to invade his own country. [26]He sent spies to their camp, and they returned and reported to him that the enemy[y] were being drawn up in formation to fall upon the Jews[z] by night. [27]So when the sun set, Jonathan commanded his men to be alert and to keep their arms at hand so as to be ready all night for battle, and he stationed outposts around the camp. [28]When the enemy heard that Jonathan and his men were prepared for battle, they were afraid and were terrified at heart; so they kindled fires in their camp and withdrew.[a] [29]But Jonathan and his men did not know it until morning, for they saw the fires burning. [30]Then Jonathan pursued them, but he did not overtake them, for they had crossed the Eleu'therus river. [31]So Jonathan turned aside against the Arabs who are called Zabade'ans and he crushed them and plundered them. [32]Then he broke camp and went to Damascus, and marched through all that region.

33 Simon also went forth and marched through the country as far as Aska'lon and the neighboring strongholds. He turned aside to Joppa and took it

---

12:5–18 Here and in the correspondences found elsewhere in 1 Maccabees (cf. chaps. 8, 13–15), it is difficult to assess the degree to which these exchanges are paraphrased by the author or represent more-or-less verbatim transcriptions. In either case, such letters would likely have been originally written in Greek or Aramaic, then translated into Hebrew by the author, before finally being rendered from Hebrew into Greek by the translator of 1 Mac.

12:6 senate: The assembly of elders in Jerusalem, which came to be the Sanhedrin in New Testament times.

12:7 a letter was sent: A record of this letter to the Jews from Arius is given in 12:19–23, which is similarly reported by Josephus and asserts that both the Spartans and Jews are descendants of Abraham. The Jews' connection with Sparta is further illustrated in 2 Mac 5:9 by the high priest Jason's escape to Sparta on account of their nations' kinship. **Onias:** Either Onias I or Onias II, his grandson, who were both high priests during the long reign of Arius (309–265 B.C.).

12:9 holy books: Most likely the Jewish Scriptures. According to the prologue of Sirach, which dates to ca. 130 B.C., Jews recognized three groupings of books in the Old Testament: the Law of Moses, the books of the Prophets, and a variety of ancestral writings.

12:15 help which comes from Heaven: The reference to God's providential help makes sense in the context of the two nations' belief in their shared Abrahamic origins. See notes on 3:19 and 12:7.

12:16 Numenius ... Antipater: Josephus identifies them as members of the Jewish senate. The father of Antipater, Jason, may be the same ambassador sent to Rome in 8:17.

12:19–23 See note on 12:7.

12:24 Demetrius: Demetrius II Nicator. See note on 10:67.

12:25 Hamath: A city over 250 miles north of Jerusalem along the river Orontes, south of the Seleucid capital of Antioch.

12:30 Eleutherus river: See note on 11:7.

12:31 Zabadeans: A tribe of Arab peoples like the Nabateans, living northwest of Damascus and southwest of Hamath. Jonathan's reasons for attacking them are not stated, though one possibility is a relation to Zabdiel the Arab, who killed their ally Alexander Balas (cf. 11:17).

12:32 Damascus: See note on 11:62.

12:33 Askalon: See note on 10:86. **Joppa:** See note on 10:75.

---

[w] Vg Compare verse 20: Gk *Darius.*

[x] Gk *they.*

[y] Gk *they.*

[z] Gk *them.*

[a] Other ancient authorities omit *and withdrew.*

by surprise, [34]for he had heard that they were ready to hand over the stronghold to the men whom Deme'trius had sent. And he stationed a garrison there to guard it.

35 When Jonathan returned he convened the elders of the people and planned with them to build strongholds in Judea, [36]to build the walls of Jerusalem still higher, and to erect a high barrier between the citadel and the city to separate it from the city, in order to isolate it so that its garrison[b] could neither buy nor sell. [37]So they gathered together to build up the city; part of the wall on the valley to the east had fallen, and he repaired the section called Chaphen'atha. [38]And Simon built Ad'-ida in the Shephe'lah; he fortified it and installed gates with bolts.

Trypho Captures Jonathan

39 Then Try'pho attempted to become king of Asia and put on the crown, and to raise his hand against Anti'ochus the king. [40]He feared that Jonathan might not permit him to do so, but might make war on him, so he kept seeking to seize and kill him, and he marched forth and came to Beth-shan. [41]Jonathan went out to meet him with forty thousand picked fighting men, and he came to Beth-shan. [42]When Try'pho saw that he had come with a large army, he was afraid to raise his hand against him. [43]So he received him with honor and commended him to all his friends, and he gave him gifts and commanded his friends and his troops to obey him as they would himself. [44]Then he said to Jonathan, "Why have you wearied all these people when we are not at war? [45]Dismiss them now to their homes and choose for yourself a few men to stay with you, and come with me to Ptolema'is. I will hand it over to you as well as the other strongholds and the remaining troops and all the officials, and will turn round and go home. For that is why I am here."

46 Jonathan[c] trusted him and did as he said; he sent away the troops, and they returned to the land of Judah. [47]He kept with himself three thousand men, two thousand of whom he left in Galilee, while a thousand accompanied him. [48]But when Jonathan entered Ptolema'is, the men of Ptolemais closed the gates and seized him, and all who had entered with him they killed with the sword.

49 Then Try'pho sent troops and cavalry into Galilee and the Great Plain to destroy all Jonathan's soldiers. [50]But they realized that Jonathan[c] had been seized and had perished along with his men, and they encouraged one another and kept marching in close formation, ready for battle. [51]When their pursuers saw that they would fight for their lives, they turned back. [52]So they all reached the land of Judah safely, and they mourned for Jonathan and his companions and were in great fear; and all Israel mourned deeply. [53]And all the nations round about them tried to destroy them, for they said, "They have no leader or helper. Now therefore let us make war on them and blot out the memory of them from among men."

Simon Takes Command

13 Simon heard that Try'pho had assembled a large army to invade the land of Judah and destroy it, [2]and he saw that the people were trembling and fearful. So he went up to Jerusalem, and gathering the people together [3]he encouraged them, saying to them, "You yourselves know what great things I and my brothers and the house of my father have done for the laws and the sanctuary; you know also the wars and the difficulties which we have seen. [4]By reason of this all my brothers have perished for the sake of Israel, and I alone am left. [5]And now, far be it from me to spare my life in any time of distress, for I am not better than my brothers. [6]But I will avenge my nation and the sanctuary and your wives and children, for all the nations have gathered together out of hatred to destroy us."

7 The spirit of the people was rekindled when they heard these words, [8]and they answered in a loud voice, "You are our leader in place of Judas and Jonathan your brother. [9]Fight our battles, and all that you say to us we will do." [10]So he assembled all the warriors and hastened to complete the walls of Jerusalem, and he fortified it on every side. [11]He sent Jonathan the son of Ab'salom to Joppa, and with him a considerable army; he drove out its occupants and remained there.

12:37 Chaphenatha: Perhaps a quarter of Jerusalem, the location of which is uncertain.

12:38 Adida in the Shephelah: Also known as Hadid (Ezra 2:33), a fortified city in Lydda, one of the three districts of Samaria given to Jonathan by Demetrius II (11:34) and then Trypho (11:57). The city was about 25 miles northwest of Jerusalem in the Shephelah, the foothills between the Judean mountains and the coastal plain.

12:39–40 Trypho fears Jonathan's allegiance to Antiochus VI because of his loyalty to his father, Alexander Balas, who granted Jonathan the high priesthood and had not broken his word with him (cf. 10:47).

12:39 Trypho: The Seleucid general who had been ruling for the boy-king Antiochus VI. See note on 11:39.

12:40 Beth-shan: A city south of the Sea of Galilee. See note on 5:52.

12:45 Ptolemais: See note on 5:22.

12:49 Great Plain: The Jezreel Valley, southwest of the Sea of Galilee.

13:1–9 Simon's rise to power begins the fourth major section of the book.

13:11 Jonathan the son of Absalom: Possibly the brother of the commander Mattathias, the son of Absalom mentioned in 11:70. **Joppa:** See note on 10:75.

---

[b]Gk *they*.
[c]Gk *he*.

Deceit and Treachery of Trypho

12 Then Try'pho departed from Ptolema'is with a large army to invade the land of Judah, and Jonathan was with him under guard. ¹³And Simon encamped in Ad'ida, facing the plain. ¹⁴Try'pho learned that Simon had risen up in place of Jonathan his brother, and that he was about to join battle with him, so he sent envoys to him and said, ¹⁵"It is for the money that Jonathan your brother owed the royal treasury, in connection with the offices he held, that we are detaining him. ¹⁶Send now a hundred talents of silver and two of his sons as hostages, so that when released he will not revolt against us, and we will release him."

17 Simon knew that they were speaking deceitfully to him, but he sent to get the money and the sons, lest he arouse great hostility among the people, who might say, ¹⁸"Because Simon^d did not send him the money and the sons, he perished." ¹⁹So he sent the sons and the hundred talents, but Try'pho^e broke his word and did not release Jonathan.

20 After this Try'pho came to invade the country and destroy it, and he circled around by the way to Ado'ra. But Simon and his army kept marching along opposite him to every place he went. ²¹Now the men in the citadel kept sending envoys to Try'pho urging him to come to them by way of the wilderness and to send them food. ²²So Try'pho got all his cavalry ready to go, but that night a very heavy snow fell, and he did not go because of the snow. He marched off and went into the land of Gilead. ²³When he approached Bas'kama, he killed Jonathan, and he was buried there. ²⁴Then Try'pho turned back and departed to his own land.

Jonathan's Tomb

25 And Simon sent and took the bones of Jonathan his brother, and buried him in Mo'dein, the city of his fathers. ²⁶All Israel bewailed him with great lamentation, and mourned for him many days. ²⁷And Simon built a monument over the tomb of his father and his brothers; he made it high that it might be seen, with polished stone at the front and back. ²⁸He also erected seven pyramids, opposite one another, for his father and mother and four brothers. ²⁹And for the pyramids^f he devised an elaborate setting, erecting about them great columns, and upon the columns he put suits of armor for a permanent

---

13:12 Ptolemais: See note on 5:22.

13:13 Adida: See note on 12:38.

13:17–19 Simon is placed in a nearly impossible situation, having been made leader and now facing the deceitful Trypho's claims that Jonathan is alive as a hostage and can be purchased back. Simon's fear of the people's judgment forces him to send the money and put additional lives at risk, even though he suspects that Trypho will break his word like the previous Seleucid leaders.

13:20 Adora: Also known as Adoraim, five miles southwest of Hebron and 25 miles south of Jerusalem. Trypho employs the same approach against Jerusalem as Lysias, attempting to come around from the south (cf. 4:29).

13:21 citadel: See note on 1:33.

13:22 a very heavy snow: While not unheard of, heavy snow in the mountainous region south of Jerusalem is sufficiently rare that the Jews would have regarded the event as help from heaven (cf. 3:19; 12:15). **Gilead:** See note on 5:9.

13:23 Baskama: An unknown location along the route between Gilead and Antioch (cf. 13:23).

13:25 Modein: See note on 2:1.

13:27–30 Burial monuments were common around the Mediterranean. Josephus also attests to monuments with pyramids in Judea around this time (*Antiquities* 20, 95). The armor served as a memorial of the military victories of the Maccabean family, and ships likely commemorated their control of the coastal region. The memorial stood during the period when 1 Mac was written, and Josephus testifies to its existence in the first century A.D.

^d Gk *I*.
^e Gk *he*.
^f Gk *for these*.

WORD STUDY

Deceitfully (13:17)

dolos (Gk.): "deceit" or "treachery". If there were a single word to summarize the actions of the rulers of the Gentiles and their Hellenizing Jewish allies in 1 Maccabees, it would surely be *dolos*—deceit. It is the characteristic term used to describe the Maccabees' opponents and arises in a wide array of contexts. In 1 Mac 1:30, the peaceable words spoken in deceit precede the ravaging of Jerusalem by Antiochus IV's forces. Later on, Bacchides, Nicanor, and the Hellenizing priest Alcimus similarly attempt to capture Judas with their deceitful promises of friendship (1 Mac 7:10, 27–30). The Egyptian king Ptolemy uses deceit to acquire his son-in-law Alexander's kingdom (1 Mac 11:1), and the Selecuid usurper Tryphon employs it to extort Simon (1 Mac 13:17) and even kill the young king whom he is supposed to be serving (1 Mac 13:31). Finally, the book closes with the traitor Ptolemy deceitfully using a banquet to kill Simon and his sons, hoping to gain power for himself at the price of the nation's freedom (1 Mac 16:13–18). If deceit is a defining characteristic of the devil, who speaks his own native tongue when he lies (Jn 8:44), surely honesty is a hallmark of those who belong to God. Such, indeed, is the case with Mattathias and his sons, who never employ deceit or any such tactics in 1 Maccabees. The Maccabees thus bear witness to the God of Israel just as much by their simple integrity—which contrasts so strikingly with the world around them—as they do by their courage and fortitude in battle.

memorial, and beside the suits of armor carved ships, so that they could be seen by all who sail the sea. ³⁰This is the tomb which he built in Mo'dein; it remains to this day.

Judea Gains Independence

31 Try'pho dealt treacherously with the young king Anti'ochus; he killed him ³²and became king in his place, putting on the crown of Asia; and he brought great calamity upon the land. ³³But Simon built up the strongholds of Judea and walled them all around, with high towers and great walls and gates and bolts, and he stored food in the strongholds. ³⁴Simon also chose men and sent them to Deme'trius the king with a request to grant relief to the country, for all that Try'pho did was to plunder. ³⁵Deme'trius the king sent him a favorable reply to this request, and wrote him a letter as follows, ³⁶"King Deme'trius to Simon, the high priest and friend of kings, and to the elders and nation of the Jews, greeting. ³⁷We have received the gold crown and the palm branch which you*g* sent, and we are ready to make a general peace with you and to write to our officials to grant you release from tribute. ³⁸All the grants that we have made to you remain valid, and let the strongholds that you have built be your possession. ³⁹We pardon any errors and offenses committed to this day, and cancel the crown tax which you owe; and whatever other tax has been collected in Jerusalem shall be collected no longer. ⁴⁰And if any of you are qualified to be enrolled in our bodyguard,*h* let them be enrolled, and let there be peace between us."

41 In the one hundred and seventieth year*i* the yoke of the Gentiles was removed from Israel, ⁴²and the people began to write in their documents and contracts, "In the first year of Simon the great high priest and commander and leader of the Jews."

The Capture of Gazara by Simon

43 In those days Simon*j* encamped against Gaza'ra*k* and surrounded it with troops. He made a siege engine, brought it up to the city, and battered and captured one tower. ⁴⁴The men in the siege engine leaped out into the city, and a great tumult arose in the city. ⁴⁵The men in the city, with their wives and children, went up on the wall with their clothes torn, and they cried out with a loud voice, asking Simon to make peace with them; ⁴⁶they said, "Do not treat us according to our wicked acts but according to your mercy." ⁴⁷So Simon reached an agreement with them and stopped fighting against them. But he expelled them from the city and cleansed the houses in which the idols were, and then entered it with hymns and praise. ⁴⁸He cast out of it all uncleanness, and settled in it men who observed the law. He also strengthened its fortifications and built in it a house for himself.

Simon Regains the Citadel

49 The men in the citadel at Jerusalem were prevented from going out to the country and back to buy and sell. So they were very hungry, and many of them perished from famine. ⁵⁰Then they cried to Simon to make peace with them, and he did so. But he expelled them from there and cleansed the citadel from its pollutions. ⁵¹On the twenty-third day of the second month, in the one hundred and seventy-first year,*l* the Jews*m* entered it with praise and palm branches, and with harps and cymbals and stringed instruments, and with hymns and songs, because a great enemy had been crushed and removed from Israel. ⁵²And Simon*n* decreed that every year they should celebrate this day with rejoicing. He strengthened the fortifications of the temple hill alongside the citadel, and he and his men

---

13:31 young king Antiochus: Antiochus VI would have been around seven years old at the time of his death. See note on 11:39.

13:34 Demetrius the king: Demetrius II Nicator. Though he had broken his word with Jonathan after the Jewish forces rescued him in Antioch (11:41–53), Trypho now represents an even greater threat to the Jews and a common enemy to both. See note on 10:67.

13:36–42 Although Demetrius and Trypho were wrangling for control of the Seleucid empire at this time, Simon recognizes Demetrius' legitimacy and takes his release from taxation and the upholding of previous grants (perhaps the removal of Seleucid troops from the citadel and other strongholds; cf. 11:41–42) to mean freedom for Israel.

13:41–42 The Jews of Judea celebrate their independence from the foreign yoke by beginning their dating according to the rule of Simon. The description of Simon as "great high

priest and commander and leader" brings together language (*stratēgos*: commander or general) used previously to describe Jonathan and Onias (cf. 9:30; 10:20; 10:65; 12:20).

13:43 Gazara: Bacchides had fortified the city as a stronghold in 9:52 so that it remained (along with the citadel) as the last of the Seleucid garrisons in Judea. See note on 4:15. **siege engine:** In Greek, a "heleopolis" ("city-taker"), a mobile tower with battering rams and catapults used for attacking walled cities. The successful deployment of Hellenistic military technology illustrates the dramatic advances of the Hasmonean forces from their guerrilla roots.

13:45–47 Like the frequent contrast between the Maccabees' simple honesty and the deceit of Seleucid leaders and their allies, the siege of Gazara offers a contrast between Jewish and Gentile forces: while Trypho has just finished murdering 1,000 of Jonathan's men in ambush (12:47–48), Simon is willing to spare those who appeal to him for mercy.

13:51–52 Just as Israel rejoiced with praise and music when David reclaimed the ark and moved it to Zion in 2 Sam 6:5, so also Jerusalem rejoices in similar fashion with Simon's expulsion of their enemies and the return of the citadel to Israel.

13:52 every year: A rabbinic text from the first century A.D. attests that this day was preserved free from fasting or mourning as a memorial to the end of the citadel's occupation (*Meg Ta'an* 2).

---

g The word *you* in verses 37–40 is plural.
h Or *court*.
i 142 B.C.
j Gk *he*.
k Cn: Gk *Gaza*.
l 141 B.C.
m Gk *they*.
n Gk *he*.

dwelt there. 53 And Simon saw that John his son had
reached manhood, so he made him commander of all
the forces, and he dwelt in Gaza'ra.

Capture of Demetrius; and the Eulogy of Simon

14 In the one hundred and seventy-second year[o]
Deme'trius the king assembled his forces and
marched into Med'ia to secure help, so that he could
make war against Try'pho. 2 When Ar'saces the
king of Persia and Med'ia heard that Deme'trius had
invaded his territory, he sent one of his commanders
to take him alive. 3 And he went and defeated the
army of Deme'trius, and seized him and took him to
Ar'saces, who put him under guard.

4 The land[p] had rest all the days of Simon.
He sought the good of his nation;
his rule was pleasing to them,
as was the honor shown him, all his days.
5 To crown all his honors he took Joppa for a harbor,
and opened a way to the isles of the sea.
6 He extended the borders of his nation,
and gained full control of the country.
7 He gathered a host of captives;
he ruled over Gaza'ra and Beth-zur and the citadel,
and he removed its uncleanness from it;
and there was none to oppose him.
8 They tilled their land in peace;
the ground gave its increase,
and the trees of the plains their fruit.
9 Old men sat in the streets;
they all talked together of good things;
and the youths donned the glories and garments of war.
10 He supplied the cities with food,
and furnished them with the means of defense,
till his renown spread to the ends of the earth.
11 He established peace in the land,
and Israel rejoiced with great joy.
12 Each man sat under his vine and his fig tree,
and there was none to make them afraid.
13 No one was left in the land to fight them,
and the kings were crushed in those days.
14 He strengthened all the humble of his people;
he sought out the law,
and did away with every lawless and wicked man.
15 He made the sanctuary glorious,
and added to the vessels of the sanctuary.

Diplomacy with Rome and Sparta

16 It was heard in Rome, and as far away as
Sparta, that Jonathan had died, and they were
deeply grieved. 17 When they heard that Simon
his brother had become high priest in his place,
and that he was ruling over the country and the
cities in it, 18 they wrote to him on bronze tablets to
renew with him the friendship and alliance which
they had established with Judas and Jonathan
his brothers. 19 And these were read before the
assembly in Jerusalem.

20 This is a copy of the letter which the Spartans sent: "The rulers and the city of the Spartans
to Simon the high priest and to the elders and
the priests and the rest of the Jewish people, our
brethren, greeting. 21 The envoys who were sent
to our people have told us about your glory and
honor, and we rejoiced at their coming. 22 And what
they said we have recorded in our public decrees,
as follows, 'Nume'nius the son of Anti'ochus and
Antip'ater the son of Jason, envoys of the Jews,
have come to us to renew their friendship with us.
23 It has pleased our people to receive these men with
honor and to put a copy of their words in the public
archives, so that the people of the Spartans may
have a record of them. And they have sent a copy of
this to Simon the high priest.' "

24 After this Simon sent Nume'nius to Rome
with a large gold shield weighing a thousand minas,
to confirm the alliance with the Romans.[q]

13:53 John his son: John Hyrcanus, who is here placed in a position by his father, Simon, to take over when his time comes. We see in 16:3 that Simon is already advanced in age.

14:1 Media: See note on 8:8.

14:2 Arsaces: Mithridates I of the Arsaces dynasty, the king of the Parthian empire from 171 to 132 B.C. Jewish sources often referred to Parthia as Persia. The Parthians had conquered Persia and Media and had attacked Babylonia, all eastern parts of the Seleucid empire, and Demetrius' campaign for reinforcements was also meant to regain lost territory.

14:3 defeated ... Demetrius: The last appearance of Demetrius II in the book. King Arsaces would give him his daughter in marriage, and after nearly ten years as a Parthian hostage, he returned to Antioch for a short-lived (and similarly unpopular) second reign. His former wife, Cleopatra Thea, eventually betrayed him, leading to his death in 125 B.C.

14:4–15 A poem praising Simon's rule over a newly independent Israel. It represents a counterpoint to the poetic laments of 1:24–28 and 36–40, marking a reversal of the afflictions imposed by their former oppressors, the Seleucid king and the citadel.

14:5 Joppa: See note on 10:75.

14:7 Gazara: See note on 4:15. **Beth-zur:** See note on 4:29. **citadel:** See note on 1:33.

14:8 the ground gave its increase: This comment reflects the promised rewards for obedience noted in Lev 26:4.

14:12 his vine and his fig tree: A reference to Mic 4:4, which speaks of the blessings of peace that Israel will inherit for obedience in the latter days. This blessing corresponds with the faithfulness to God embodied in the four successive Maccabean leaders and may reflect a hope that this promised time is now at hand.

14:22 Numenius ... Antipater: See note on 12:16.

14:24 a thousand minas: Estimates vary on the weight of minas in ancient Israel, though this is likely to have weighed over 1,000 pounds.

---

[o] 140 B.C.

[p] Other authorities add *of Judah*.

[q] Gk *them*.

Official Honors for Simon

25 When the people heard these things they said, "How shall we thank Simon and his sons? [26]For he and his brothers and the house of his father have stood firm; they have fought and repulsed Israel's enemies and established its freedom." [27]So they made a record on bronze tablets and put it upon pillars on Mount Zion.

This is a copy of what they wrote: "On the eighteenth day of E'lul, in the one hundred and seventy-second year,[r] which is the third year of Simon the great high priest, [28]in Asar'amel,[s] in the great assembly of the priests and the people and the rulers of the nation and the elders of the country, the following was proclaimed to us:

29 "Since wars often occurred in the country, Simon the son of Mattathi'as, a priest of the sons[t] of Jo'arib, and his brothers, exposed themselves to danger and resisted the enemies of their nation, in order that their sanctuary and the law might be perserved; and they brought great glory to their nation. [30]Jonathan rallied the[u] nation, and became their high priest, and was gathered to his people. [31]And when their enemies decided to invade their country and lay hands on their sanctuary, [32]then Simon rose up and fought for his nation. He spent great sums of his own money; he armed the men of his nation's forces and paid them wages. [33]He fortified the cities of Judea, and Beth-zur on the borders of Judea, where formerly the arms of the enemy had been stored, and he placed there a garrison of Jews. [34]He also fortified Joppa, which is by the sea, and Gaza'ra, which is on the borders of Azo'tus, where the enemy formerly dwelt. He settled Jews there, and provided in those cities[v] whatever was necessary for their restoration.

35 "The people saw Simon's faithfulness[w] and the glory which he had resolved to win for his nation, and they made him their leader and high priest, because he had done all these things and because of the justice and loyalty which he had maintained toward his nation. He sought in every way to exalt his people. [36]And in his days things prospered in his hands, so that the Gentiles were put out of the[x] country, as were also the men in the city of David in Jerusalem, who had built themselves a citadel from which they used to sally forth and defile the environs of the sanctuary and do great damage to its purity. [37]He settled Jews in it, and fortified it for the safety of the country and of the city, and built the walls of Jerusalem higher.

38 "In view of these things King Deme'trius confirmed him in the high priesthood, [39]and he made him one of the king's[y] friends and paid him high honors. [40]For he had heard that the Jews were addressed by the Romans as friends and allies and brethren, and that the Romans[z] had received the envoys of Simon with honor.

41 "And[a] the Jews and their priests decided that Simon should be their leader and high priest for ever, until a trustworthy prophet should arise, [42]and that he should be governor over them and that he should take charge of the sanctuary and appoint men over its tasks and over the country and the weapons and the strongholds, and that he should take charge of the sanctuary, [43]and that he should be obeyed by all, and that all contracts in the country should be written in his name, and that he should be clothed in purple and wear gold.

44 "And none of the people or priests shall be permitted to nullify any of these decisions or to oppose what he says, or to convene an assembly in the country without his permission, or to be clothed in purple or put on a gold buckle. [45]Whoever acts contrary to these decisions or nullifies any of them shall be liable to punishment."

14:25–49 This section is especially important as the primary historical witness to the establishment of the Hasmonean dynasty in Israel, which also provides the terms for the religious and political leadership of subsequent generations of Jewish high priests.

14:27 Mount Zion: The elevation of Jerusalem. **Elul:** August–September.

14:28 Asaramel: Reference obscure. Some conjectures based on similar Hebrew words take the referent to be Simon as the prince of the People of God, while others regard the referent as a location, the court of the People of God.

14:34 Azotus: See note on 4:15.

14:41 leader and high priest: Simon is invested with both religious and political authority, a development that, while prefigured by the increasing political importance of earlier high priests and especially his brother Jonathan, nevertheless has never been official policy in Israel. This novelty may be the reason for the lengthy praise of Simon's deeds, which serve as justification for the combined leadership role. **until a trustworthy prophet:** The authority granted to Simon and his sons is presented as continuing until the arrival of a faithful prophet, who would ostensibly carry authority to pass judgment on the leadership arrangement. On the expectation of a coming prophet, see 4:46.

14:43–44 clothed in purple and wear gold: The traditional signs of a king. Though neither Simon nor his son John claimed this title for himself, Simon's grandson Alexander Janneus would do so 40 years later. In the midst of the nation's celebration of Simon, this text presents two subtle points of caution in relation to the book's affirmations elsewhere. The first is the affirmation that David's throne is eternal in 2:57, which complicates any potential kingship of the Hasmonean family, who do not arise from David's line. The second is the author's praise of the Roman leaders in 8:14 for their refusal to wear royal purple, which sits in tension with the directive here that the color be worn by Simon and forbidden to all others.

---

[r] 140 B.C.
[s] This word resembles the Hebrew words for *the court of the people of God* or *the prince of the people of God*.
[t] The Greek text of this phrase is uncertain.
[u] Gk *their*.
[v] Gk *them*.
[w] Other authorities read *conduct*.
[x] Gk *their*.
[y] Gk *his*.
[z] Gk *they*.
[a] Gk *honor; and that*.

Paul and the Maccabees

How would the Apostle Paul have viewed the Maccabees after his encounter with Christ on the Damascus road?

On the one hand, there are striking parallels between Mattathias and his sons and how Paul describes himself within his "former life in Judaism". Both Saul the Pharisee and the Maccabees were devoted to the Jewish faith and zealous for the traditions of their fathers (Gal 1:14; Acts 22:3; 1 Mac 2:17, 27-28). Both sought to preserve and enforce the Mosaic Law within Jerusalem and beyond and were willing to employ violent measures to do so (Acts 9:1-2, 21; 1 Mac 2:44-48; 3:5). Indeed, since the Pharisees' own origins are usually traced to the Hasideans, who joined with the Maccabees in 1 Mac 2:42-44 (and have Judas identified as their leader in 2 Mac 14:6), Saul may have been self-consciously imitating the Maccabean movement by his actions. If Paul regarded his former life as Saul the Pharisee to be rubbish compared with knowing Christ, would he have consigned the Maccabees to the rubbish heap as well?

On the other hand, we have clues that the case may not be so simple. For one, the New Testament book with the clearest allusions to the Maccabees is the Letter to the Hebrews, which modern scholars suggest was written by a disciple or associate of the apostle and which most in the early Church believed to have been written by Paul himself. Within Hebrews 11's lengthy tribute to the faith of Israel's heroes, commentators identify Heb 11:35 as a reference to the events of 2 Maccabees 7, and patristic readers like St. John Chrysostom connected those praised in 11:38 who hid "in dens and caves of the earth" with Mattathias and his sons, who are described with similar language in the Maccabean books (1 Mac 1:53; 2:28-31; cf. 2 Mac 5:27; 6:11; 10:6). Further, one of the closest Old Testament parallels to Hebrews 11 is the speech of Mattathias in 1 Maccabees, where the father similarly recounts the fidelity of Israel's heroes for his sons (2:51-61), which may have served as a model for the Hebrews passage. Whether indirectly bearing his influence or Pauline in a direct sense, the evidence from Hebrews would suggest that Paul viewed the Maccabees like other heroes in this passage, such as Gideon or Samson, who were valiant (if not necessarily impeccable) examples of faith in Israel's history.

Other clues are provided within the book of 1 Maccabees itself. At two key points in the narrative—the rededication of the altar (1 Mac 4:46) and the establishment of Simon as high priest and leader (1 Mac 14:41)—the Maccabees' arrangements are presented as provisional until a faithful prophet should arise. Like Deuteronomy's foretelling of a prophet like Moses (Deut 18:15-18), these passages in 1 Maccabees contributed to the Jewish expectation of a promised figure that would appear to guide and lead Israel. From a historical perspective, the influence of the 1 Maccabees passages in particular helps to explain why the Jewish leadership in Christ's time, whose authority was inherited from Simon Maccabees' arrangement, felt such a threat from Jesus. Acclaimed by the crowds as "the prophet" at his triumphal entry into Jerusalem (Mt 21:11, 46), Jesus carried the title of the one whose authority over Israel's altar, priesthood, and leadership would be greater than their own.

This identification of Jesus as Israel's promised prophet continued after his Resurrection, both by Peter in his first sermon in the Temple (Acts 3:22-24) and by Stephen before the high priest (Acts 7:37), with the authorities responding to this perceived threat by imprisoning the former and stoning the latter. Paul similarly echoes this testimony after his conversion, declaring before Agrippa that his message of this promised leader who would "proclaim light both to the nation and to the Gentiles" is "nothing but what the prophets and Moses said would come to pass" (Acts 26:22-23). This is the point where Paul finds fault with his countrymen and his former self—not with their religion or zeal, but that their zeal for God is not according to knowledge (Rom 10:2), ignorant that the goal to which Israel's faith pointed has now arrived (Rom 10:4; 15:8). And just as this prophet and his follower Stephen embodied a righteousness more perfect than that of Moses, praying for their enemies even as they were put to death by them, so too would Paul testify that those in Christ are now empowered by him to bless even their enemies and to conquer evil with good (Rom 12:14-21).

How, then, would Paul have viewed the Maccabees after he encountered Christ on the Damascus road? The testimony in Hebrews, which at the least bears Paul's influence, would suggest he believed Mattathias and his sons were faithfully obeying God by resisting Antiochus, who wished to make his earthly kingdom into one people by abolishing Judaism and imposing Greek religion and culture. At the same time, with the arrival of the faithful prophet to whom Deuteronomy and 1 Maccabees attest, Paul came to recognize that God was mysteriously bringing about a unity of Jew and Greek within his own kingdom, making all nations into one people by grafting the Greeks into the rich root of Israel (Rom 11:13-24). Having cleansed the Gentiles by Christ's blood, God's astonishing action broke down even the Law's barriers that had kept Israel separated from the other nations and left these nations alienated from Israel's commonwealth (Eph 2:11-16). And a yet greater mystery, unsearchable for Paul and the Maccabees alike: that the promised figure's arrival would not only be good news for both Jews and Greeks, but that these hated enemies' conversion would become God's means of drawing fallen Israel back to himself (Rom 11:11, 25-33).

In short, the distinction between Paul and the Maccabean resistance is a matter of neither religion nor zeal but, rather, of their respective places within the larger story of salvation history. While the Maccabees belong among Israel's heroes of faith for giving their lives to preserve God's covenant and promises, Paul stands at the fulfillment of these promises and the New Covenant's inauguration, having heard the voice of Israel's true leader and eternal high priest, who sets up a new altar to sanctify those of every nation by his own blood (Heb 13:10-12). For Paul, while everything is rubbish in comparison to knowing Christ, each of God's promises—including the allusive but real foreshadowing in 1 Maccabees—finds its Yes in him (2 Cor 1:20).

46 And all the people agreed to grant Simon the right to act in accord with these decisions. ⁴⁷So Simon accepted and agreed to be high priest, to be commander and ethnarch of the Jews and priests, and to be protector of them all.ᵇ ⁴⁸And they gave orders to inscribe this decree upon bronze tablets, to put them up in a conspicuous place in the precincts of the sanctuary, ⁴⁹and to deposit copies of them in the treasury, so that Simon and his sons might have them.

Letter of Antiochus VII

15 Anti′ochus, the son of Deme′trius the king, sent a letter from the islands of the sea to Simon, the priest and ethnarch of the Jews, and to all the nation; ²its contents were as follows: "King Anti′ochus to Simon the high priest and ethnarch and to the nation of the Jews, greeting. ³Whereas certain pestilent men have gained control of the kingdom of our fathers, and I intend to lay claim to the kingdom so that I may restore it as it formerly was, and have recruited a host of mercenary troops and have equipped warships, ⁴and intend to make a landing in the country so that I may proceed against those who have destroyed our country and those who have devastated many cities in my kingdom, ⁵now therefore I confirm to you all the tax remissions that the kings before me have granted you, and release from all the other payments from which they have released you. ⁶I permit you to mint your own coinage as money for your country, ⁷and I grant freedom to Jerusalem and the sanctuary. All the weapons which you have prepared and the strongholds which you have built and now hold shall remain yours. ⁸Every debt you owe to the royal treasury and any such future debts shall be canceled for you from now on and for all time. ⁹When we gain control of our kingdom, we will bestow great honor upon you and your nation and the temple, so that your glory will become manifest in all the earth."

10 In the one hundred and seventy-fourth yearᶜ Anti′ochus set out and invaded the land of his fathers. All the troops rallied to him, so that there were few with Try′pho. ¹¹Anti′ochus pursued him, and he came in his flight to Dor, which is by the sea; ¹²for he knew that troubles had converged upon him, and his troops had deserted him. ¹³So Anti′ochus encamped against Dor, and with him were a hundred and twenty thousand warriors and eight thousand cavalry. ¹⁴He surrounded the city, and the ships joined battle from the sea; he pressed the city hard from land and sea, and permitted no one to leave or enter it.

Rome Supports the Jews

15 Then Nume′nius and his companions arrived from Rome, with letters to the kings and countries, in which the following was written: ¹⁶"Lucius, consul of the Romans, to King Ptol′emy, greeting. ¹⁷The envoys of the Jews have come to us as our friends and allies to renew our ancient friendship and alliance. They had been sent by Simon the high priest and by the people of the Jews, ¹⁸and have brought a gold shield weighing a thousand minas. ¹⁹We therefore have decided to write to the kings and countries that they should not seek their harm or make war against them and their cities and their country, or make alliance with those who war against them. ²⁰And it has seemed good to us to accept the shield from them. ²¹Therefore if any pestilent men have fled to you from their country, hand them over to Simon the high priest, that he may punish them according to their law."

22 The consulᵈ wrote the same thing to Deme′trius the king and to At′talus and A″riara′thes and Ar′saces, ²³and to all the countries, and to Samp′sames,ᵉ and to the Spartans, and to De′los, and to Myn′dos, and to Sic′yon, and to Ca′ria, and to Sa′mos, and to Pamphyl′ia, and to Ly′cia, and to Hal″icarnas′sus, and to Rhodes, and to Phase′lis, and to Cos, and to Si′de, and to Ar′adus and Gorty′na and Cni′dus and Cyprus and Cyre′ne. ²⁴They also sent a copy of these things to Simon the high priest.

14:47 high priest . . . commander and ethnarch: Simon is given the three roles of high priest, commander of the army, and civil magistrate, centralizing religious, military, and political authority under Hasmonean leadership.

15:1 Antiochus: Antiochus VII Sidetes (or Euergetes), the son of Demetrius I and younger brother of the recently captured Demetrius II.

15:3 pestilent men: Trypho and those who supported him.

15:6 mint your own coinage: This grants formal economic independence to the Jews.

15:9 bestow great honor upon you: The same promise made by Antiochus' brother Demetrius II in 11:42, who soon

after broke his word. Like Jonathan, Simon finds himself in the favorable position of being a powerful potential ally to competing claimants for the Seleucid throne, which elicits promises of honors and exemptions for the Jewish people.

15:11 Dor: A Mediterranean port south of Ptolemais and north of Joppa.

15:15 Numenius: See note on 12:16.

15:16 Lucius: Either Lucius Caecilius Metellus (Roman consul in 142 B.C.) or Lucius Calpernius Piso (consul in 140–139 B.C.). **Ptolemy:** The Egyptian king Ptolemy VIII Euergetes II, the brother of Ptolemy VI Philometor, who ruled over Egypt during most of the Maccabean period until his death (cf. 11:18).

15:22 Demetrius . . . Attalus . . . Ariarathes . . . Arsaces: Respectively, the Seleucid, Pergamon, Cappadocian, and Parthian kings.

15:23 Sampsames . . . Cyrene: Independent city-states in the eastern Mediterranean.

ᵇ Or *to preside over them all.*
ᶜ 138 B.C.
ᵈ Gk *He.*
ᵉ The name is uncertain.

Antiochus VII Threatens Simon

25 Anti'ochus the king besieged Dor anew,[f] continually throwing his forces against it and making engines of war; and he shut Try'pho up and kept him from going out or in. [26]And Simon sent to Anti'ochus[g] two thousand picked men, to fight for him, and silver and gold and much military equipment. [27]But he refused to receive them, and he broke all the agreements he formerly had made with Simon,[g] and became estranged from him. [28]He sent to him Ath"eno'bius, one of his friends, to confer with him, saying, "You hold control of Joppa and Gaza'ra and the citadel in Jerusalem; they are cities of my kingdom. [29]You have devastated their territory, you have done great damage in the land, and you have taken possession of many places in my kingdom. [30]Now then, hand over the cities which you have seized and the tribute money of the places which you have conquered outside the borders of Judea; [31]or else give me for them five hundred talents of silver, and for the destruction that you have caused and the tribute money of the cities, five hundred talents more. Otherwise we will come and conquer you."

32 So Ath"eno'bius the friend of the king came to Jerusalem, and when he saw the splendor of Simon, and the sideboard with its gold and silver plate, and his great magnificence, he was amazed. He reported to him the words of the king, [33]but Simon gave him this reply: "We have neither taken foreign land nor seized foreign property, but only the inheritance of our fathers, which at one time had been unjustly taken by our enemies. [34]Now that we have the opportunity, we are firmly holding the inheritance of our fathers. [35]As for Joppa and Gaza'ra, which you demand, they were causing great damage among the people and to our land; for them we will give you a hundred talents." Ath"eno'bius[h] did not answer him a word, [36]but returned in wrath to the king and reported to him these words and the splendor of Simon and all that he had seen. And the king was greatly angered.

Victory over Cendebeus

37 Now Try'pho embarked on a ship and escaped to Orthosi'a. [38]Then the king made Cendebe'us commander-in-chief of the coastal country, and gave him troops of infantry and cavalry. [39]He commanded him to encamp against Judea, and commanded him to build up Ked'ron and fortify its gates, and to make war on the people; but the king pursued Try'pho. [40]So Cendebe'us came to Jam'nia and began to provoke the people and invade Judea and take the people captive and kill them. [41]He built up Ked'ron and stationed there horsemen and troops, so that they might go out and make raids along the highways of Judea, as the king had ordered him.

16 John went up from Gaza'ra and reported to Simon his father what Cendebe'us had done. [2]And Simon called in his two older sons Judas and John, and said to them: "I and my brothers and the house of my father have fought the wars of Israel from our youth until this day, and things have prospered in our hands so that we have delivered Israel many times. [3]But now I have grown old, and you by His mercy are mature in years. Take my place and my brother's, and go out and fight for our nation, and may the help which comes from Heaven be with you."

4 So John[i] chose out of the country twenty thousand warriors and horsemen, and they marched against Cendebe'us and camped for the night in Mo'dein. [5]Early in the morning they arose and marched into the plain, and behold, a large force of infantry and horsemen was coming to meet them; and a stream lay between them. [6]Then he and his army lined up against them. And he saw

---

15:27 broke all the agreements: With his opposition subdued, Antiochus VII follows his brother's example in reneging on his promises (cf. 11:53).

15:28 Athenobius: An associate of Antiochus VII who is otherwise unknown. **Joppa … Gazara:** See 4:15. **citadel:** See note on 1:33. Antiochus regarded the citadel and these cities as Seleucid possessions, and they are not mentioned in his initial letter to Simon (cf. 15:7).

15:29 many places: Antiochus could be referring to those places taken on the coastal plain and Beth-zur on the border of Idumea.

15:31 five hundred … five hundred: A combined 1,000 talents. By comparison, this is a far larger amount than the 300 talents promised by Jonathan to Demetrius II in return for release from tribute in 11:28.

15:33–35 Simon appeals to Hellenistic law, which permits taking back ancestral land.

15:37 Orthosia: A port north of Dor near the Eleutherus River (see note on 11:7). From Orthosia, Trypho went to Apamea near Antioch, where he was eventually killed by Antiochus.

15:38 Cendebeus: Identified by Josephus as a friend of Antiochus VII, whose title of commander-in-chief would have granted him authority over other governors in the area.

15:39 Kedron: A city on the coastal plain, four miles southeast from Jamnia.

15:40 Jamnia: See note on 4:15.

16:1 Gazara: See note on 4:15.

16:2–3 Simon commissions John and Judas to fight for the nation as those who will inherit the help that comes from heaven (cf. 3:19; 12:15). Thirty years have now passed since Mattathias' initial revolt, so that Simon would likely have been over fifty years old at this point.

16:4 Modein: See note on 2:1.

16:6–10 This passage shows John to be a worthy successor to his grandfather, uncles, and father. John returns to Modein, meets a large army, crosses first over a stream, gives confidence to his soldiers by his example, and arranges his army as Judas did (cf. 3:55, 58–60; 5:40–43).

---

[f] Or *on the second day.*
[g] Gk *him.*
[h] Gk *He.*
[i] Other authorities read *he.*

that the soldiers were afraid to cross the stream, so he crossed over first; and when his men saw him, they crossed over after him. [7]Then he divided the army and placed the horsemen in the midst of the infantry, for the cavalry of the enemy were very numerous. [8]And they sounded the trumpets, and Cendebe′us and his army were put to flight, and many of them were wounded and fell; the rest fled into the stronghold. [9]At that time Judas the brother of John was wounded, but John pursued them until Cendebe′us[j] reached Ked′ron, which he had built. [10]They also fled into the towers that were in the fields of Azo′tus, and John[j] burned it with fire, and about two thousand of them fell. And he returned to Judea safely.

Murder of Simon and His Sons

11 Now Ptol′emy the son of Abu′bus had been appointed governor over the plain of Jericho, and he had much silver and gold, [12]for he was son-in-law of the high priest. [13]His heart was lifted up; he determined to get control of the country, and made treacherous plans against Simon and his sons, to do away with them. [14]Now Simon was visiting the cities of the country and attending to their needs, and he went down to Jericho with Mattathi′as and Judas his sons, in the one hundred and seventy-seventh year,[k] in the eleventh month, which is the month of Shebat′. [15]The son of Abu′bus received them treacherously in the little stronghold called

Dok, which he had built; he gave them a great banquet, and hid men there. [16]When Simon and his sons were drunk, Ptol′emy and his men rose up, took their weapons, and rushed in against Simon in the banquet hall, and they killed him and his two sons and some of his servants. [17]So he committed an act of great treachery and returned evil for good.

John Succeeds Simon

18 Then Ptol′emy wrote a report about these things and sent it to the king, asking him to send troops to aid him and to turn over to him the cities and the country. [19]He sent other men to Gaza′ra to do away with John; he sent letters to the captains asking them to come to him so that he might give them silver and gold and gifts; [20]and he sent other men to take possession of Jerusalem and the temple hill. [21]But some one ran ahead and reported to John at Gaza′ra that his father and brothers had perished, and that "he has sent men to kill you also." [22]When he heard this, he was greatly shocked; and he seized the men who came to destroy him and killed them, for he had found out that they were seeking to destroy him.

[23]The rest of the acts of John and his wars and the brave deeds which he did, and the building of the walls which he built, and his achievements, [24]behold, they are written in the chronicles of his high priesthood, from the time that he became high priest after his father.

16:9 **Kedron:** See note on 15:39.
16:10 **Azotus:** See note on 4:15.
16:11 **Ptolemy the son of Abubus:** A governor over the region of Jericho who married one of Simon's daughters.
16:14 **eleventh month:** Falls in January–February.

16:15 **treacherously:** The murderous deception of Ptolemy recalls the deceit of earlier faithless Jews who sought power from the Seleucids, such as Alcimus in 7:16. **Dok:** Three miles northwest of Jericho.
16:23–24 This brief summary assures the reader that John did not succumb to the plot of his brother-in-law but went on to act in the manner of his predecessors in their leadership of Israel. The reference to the chronicles of John's high priesthood recalls the language used for the chronicles of Israel's kings in 1 and 2 Kings.

---

[j] Gk *he.*
[k] 134 B.C.

STUDY QUESTIONS
1 Maccabees

Chapter 1

For understanding
1. **1:11.** Who were the "lawless men" and what were they commonly called? In light of the divine instructions given to Israel, what warning do these words serve to give the reader? While the covenant prohibition is specific to Israel's conquest of the land, how is the rationale against them also illustrated in 1 Maccabees?
2. **1:14.** What was the gymnasium? How was removing the marks of one's circumcision seen?
3. **1:24–28.** As the first of many poetic sections in 1 Maccabees, when was this lament composed? What does the allusion to Joel's call to repentance, along with the nation being "clothed in shame", show about the author's viewpoint?
4. **1:54.** How was the "desolating sacrilege" also known? To what does it refer? What does 2 Mac 6:2 record about it? Where else is the abomination of desolation mentioned? To what does it refer there? What does Jesus use this act of Antiochus to describe?

For application
1. **1:1–8.** How does history validate Lord Acton's saying that "power tends to corrupt, and absolute power corrupts absolutely"? What examples can you think of that might disprove the saying? What virtues would be necessary for one in power to resist its corrupting influence?
2. **1:11–15.** Why do religious people living in a secular culture tend to accommodate themselves to it? What happens to their religious commitments as a result? How is this accommodating tendency reflected in the life of the Catholic Church in our country?
3. **1:41–50.** How do appeals for national unity ring in the ears of a population that is forced to abandon its culture and conform to that of the occupying power? Why is the practice of religion a threat to power?
4. **1:62–64.** In Robert Bolt's play *A Man for All Seasons*, Thomas More says of himself, "This is not the stuff of which martyrs are made." What changed his mind? What conditions would bring you to the point of choosing to accept martyrdom rather than submit to evil?

Chapter 2

For understanding
1. **2:23–26.** On whose zeal is that of Mattathias modeled? As a leader in the community, what responsibility does Mattathias have? Like Phinehas, who was given a perpetual priesthood (cf. 2:54), what will the line of Mattathias eventually form? What does the likening of Mattathias to Phinehas serve to show, and in contrast with what? While Christ's New Covenant differs from the Mosaic Law regarding punishment for apostasy, what responsibility do both affirm? What Christian teaching does Mattathias' defensive war to protect the innocent and restore justice anticipate?
2. **2:27–28.** How does Mattathias' summons echo the call of Moses and the violent zeal of the sons of Levi? What does the analogy with the Levites, who received the priesthood for their willingness to prioritize God over tribal or familial ties, here foreshadow?
3. **2:39–41.** Since war on the Sabbath was seen as violating the biblical commandment of rest, what justification for Mattathias' defensive warfare does the author present? What precedent was there for warfare on the Sabbath? How did Patristic readers such as Tertullian understand the Maccabees' example?
4. **Word Study: Show Zeal (2:50).** By itself, what is the moral value of zeal? How does an analogy like being "fired up" illustrate its meaning, both positively and negatively? How does Scripture thus present both negative and positive examples of zealousness? How does 1 Maccabees show heroes who are zealous in the positive sense? How have Christians throughout the centuries rightly regarded zealous figures like the Maccabees as heroes of the faith? How does zeal apply to Christ's disciples and even to Christ himself?

For application
1. **2:7.** How do you regard the age in which you live? In what other age would you prefer to have been born? Why do you think the Lord wants you where you are?
2. **2:22.** How do you discern when a law is unjust? What is the obligation of a Christian to obey such a law, and where does refusal to obey find its justification (cf. CCC 2242)?
2. **2:39–41.** What right does a person have to defend his life, even to the point of killing an attacker? When does engaging in legitimate defense become a grave obligation (CCC 2263–65)?
4. **2:50.** At what point in Jesus' ministry did his disciples recall of him that "zeal for your house will consume me" (Jn 2:17)? To what kind of zeal does Christ call his disciples? Have you ever had the opportunity to show zeal for God's house? If so, how have you shown it?

Chapter 3

For understanding
1. **3:10–26.** What does the absence of mention in 2 Maccabees of the battles against Apollonius and Seron possibly suggest? Why would such battles also necessitate the taking of spoils?
2. **3:19.** Of what is the use of "Heaven" with reference to God an indirect way of speaking in 1 Maccabees?

3.   **3:27-31.** What does the author set as the primary reasons for Antiochus' expedition into Persia? What do other reasons, derived from ancient sources, include? What does the author's focus on Antiochus' actions as they relate to Israel show?
4.   **3:46-53.** Why does Judas take the people to Mizpah? What do they consult there and ask for in prayer? As St. John Chrysostom writes regarding their fasting and petitions, of what did the Maccabees remind the people?

For application
1.   **3:19.** What expressions does English have to refer to God without mentioning his name? How careful are you to avoid taking the name of God in vain, even casually?
2.   **3:29.** Many in our country have overextended their financial resources. What is your attitude to buying on credit or being in debt? What options do you have for handling debt? What do you think God wants of you regarding your indebtedness?
3.   **3:47.** In times of national emergency, what is the value of taking time to fast and pray? What does the act of fasting from food add to prayer? What are some occasions on which you have been asked to fast and pray?
4.   **3:50-57.** Following their time of prayer for direction, the army prepared for action immediately. In their case, what prompted them not to wait before making a decision? When you are under time constraints and have several options, how do you decide what is the Lord's will if you have not received a clear answer?

Chapter 4

For understanding
1.   **4:15.** What is another name for Gazara, and where is it? Where is Idumea, and how far do its plains extend? Where are Azotus and Jamnia? For what is Azotus, also known as Ashdod, remembered?
2.   **4:30-33.** How does Judas' prayer recall the two examples of David (1 Sam 17) and Jonathan (1 Sam 14:1-14)?
3.   **4:46.** To what Jewish expectation does this brief comment allude?
4.   **4:52-59.** Three years after the abomination of desolation was erected in 167 B.C., what did Judas complete and institute? From what is the name Hanukkah derived? How is Hanukkah like the feasts of the Temple's dedication under Solomon (1 Kings 8:65-66) and Hezekiah (2 Chron 29:17)?

For application
1.   **4:17.** Although his soldiers needed weapons and armor, why did Judas urge them to wait before plundering the enemy's camp? What is delayed gratification? How might a premature celebration over an early victory be dangerous when a larger one looms?
2.   **4:24.** What is the most recent personal victory for which you have given thanks? Do your prayers of thanks make use of Scripture (e.g., by quoting verses that come to mind)? How important is Scripture in your daily prayer?
3.   **4:30-33.** Read carefully Judas' prayer before a battle where he is vastly outnumbered. What is his level of confidence as he prays? What does he wish upon the enemy? How can his prayer inspire yours as you face an enemy whose strength is greater than yours?
4.   **4:52-59.** How long is the Christmas season? How do you and your family celebrate it throughout that period? Why celebrate it for such a long time?

Chapter 5

For understanding
1.   **5:1-8.** By what circumstances are Judas' campaigns in this chapter spurred, and what may have occasioned them? Though Judas assumes the role of a second Joshua, how is the motivation for his battles presented?
2.   **5:30.** What war machines did Hellenistic warfare include? How do the Maccabean forces fare with them?
3.   **5:46.** What and where is Ephron? What are the reasons for its hostility? On what are Judas' actions here modeled?
4.   **5:61-62.** What is the significance of these verses? What are the twofold errors of Joseph and Azariah that brought them and those who followed them to destruction?

For application
1.   **5:18-19.** Think of a time when you had to delegate responsibility to a subordinate, whether an employee or even a child in the family. What was the situation? What qualities did you look for? What limitations did you place on the subordinate's role? How did you ensure that the subordinate did as instructed?
2.   **5:33.** Recall the tactic of Gideon attacking Midian (Judg 7:18-20). Why would a smaller force attack while crying out with loud trumpets and prayer? Why do attacking soldiers shout as they fight?
3.   **5:55-62.** As a child, if you were punished for doing something you were told not to do, what were the consequences? Have you ever been told by the Lord not to do something you had in mind? If so, how well did you obey?

Chapter 6

For understanding
1.   **6:1-17.** While First Maccabees records the death of Antiochus after the restoration of the Temple in 164 B.C., when do 2 Mac and a Babylonian king list place it? For the author of 1 Mac, to whom does Antiochus serve as a counterexample?
2.   **6:28-31.** What forces and what strategy do the king (and Lysias, cf. 6:55) bring to bear? Because the use of elephants by the Seleucid army was banned by Rome in the treaty of Apamea in 188 B.C., what does their violation of this agreement lead the Romans to do, leading to what result?
3.   **6:43-46.** Who is the first of the Maccabees to die? How does the author record this event? Whose resolve is evoked by Eleazar's breaking straight through the phalanx to go directly to the enemy's heart? What does St. Ambrose, writing on fortitude, infer about Eleazar's valor?

4. **6:55–61.** Despite its defeats and weakened condition, to what did the nation's faithful observance of the Sabbath year eventually contribute, and how? What are the Seleucids thus forced to grant, corresponding with what promises in Lev 26:7–8?

For application
1. **6:3–9.** Have you experienced setbacks that caused you grief? If so, on hindsight, how significant were they, and how severely did they affect you emotionally? How have you surrendered them to the Lord?
2. **6:12–16.** What is the difference between remorse and repentance? Which of these does Antiochus show? What should be the outcome of real repentance?
3. **6:49.** According to Lev 25:2–7, what is supposed to happen to the land during the sabbatical year? What was the rationale for letting the land lie fallow, according to Leviticus? What goal might a person have in mind who decides to take a sabbatical year for himself?

Chapter 7

For understanding
1. **7:5.** Who is Alcimus, and how does he win the support of the Hasideans? Where has the last of the line of the Oniad family (which traditionally held the high priesthood) gone? Under whom do the Hasmoneans take the high priestly office?
2. **7:26.** Why was Nicanor forced to abandon the covenant he made with Judas? Since the account in 1 Mac passes over this, into what attempt does it go? Where is a longer account of the relationship between Nicanor and Judas given?
3. **7:40.** Where is Adasa situated? How many men is Judas recorded as having here, as compared to the number in 5:20? After the near defeat by Lysias, what has Judas managed to do with his small remaining army?
4. **7:50.** Of what does the phrase "rest for a few days" speak? What did the defeat of Nicanor in 160 or 161 B.C. mean in terms of coming conflict with Bacchides?

For application
1. **7:5.** Would you characterize Alcimus' desire to become high priest as a noble or an ignoble ambition? What in your opinion turns ambition itself one way or the other? What is your chief ambition in life?
2. **7:11.** Have you ever been approached by someone offering a large prize for a minimal investment? How does such a person try to gain your trust? What should alert you to the possibility of deceit?
3. **7:23.** Look up the articles in the *Catechism* on scandal, referred to in the note for this verse. Why would the conduct of Alcimus be considered scandal? Why is scandal never a private affair? Why is it that, according to some confessors, people will confess sins against every commandment but never the sin of scandal?
4. **7:50.** Why is it that in this life there is never a final victory? In the spiritual life, what victories have you had, and how quickly have they led to further spiritual warfare? What hope is there of final victory?

Chapter 8

For understanding
1. **8:1–16.** What does this positive portrayal of the Romans suggest about the time when 1 Mac was written? By the time of the New Testament, what had Rome become for the Jews? What contrasts between the Romans and the Seleucids were attractive to the Jews? At the same time, with whose expansive tendencies do the Romans' tendencies share parallels, and how would they prove ominous a century later?
2. **8:17–21.** How is Judas' finding it to be lawful to make an alliance with the Romans like what Joshua did with the Gibeonites?
3. **8:23–30.** What is an example of how this treaty closely parallels others between Rome and much smaller powers in this period? What do the similar features include?

For application
1. **8:4.** This verse mentions the patience of the Romans. In the context of the preceding verses, what form would their patience have taken? When you face a long-term goal, what benefit will the virtue of patience be to you?
2. **8:5–12.** How does the expansionism of Rome in this period of its history resemble the expansionism of modern superpowers? What do these superpowers claim as motives for occupying countries remote from their own territory? What limitations does Christian teaching place on the use of military force, according to the *Catechism* (CCC 2308–9)?
3. **8:17–21.** Given his military situation, what benefit does Judas see in creating an alliance with a power so far distant from himself? What influence would he expect an alliance with Rome to have on his enemies? By analogy, what influence would you expect a letter from an attorney threatening legal action to have on a personal adversary?

Chapter 9

For understanding
1. **9:5–6.** What is the state of mind of Judas' troops, even though previously they have won battles against greater odds? Though the text does not provide an explicit cause, what is one proposal?
2. **9:21–22.** What does the death of Judas recall? From what is "How are the mighty fallen" a refrain, and in which book of Scripture do references to a "savior" or "deliverer" commonly appear? Unlike the records of the kings of Judah, which are written in the annals, where are those of Judas recorded?
3. **9:35–42.** What do Jonathan and Simon do in revenge for their brother's capture? What further details does Josephus' recounting of these bleak events provide? With what number does this then correspond, and what law does it fulfill? With the death of John, who are the only remaining sons of Mattathias?

4. **9:54.** What wall does Alcimus set out to tear down, acting in line with whose aims? How were the two courts noted in Scripture, and how was the division marked in Herod's temple? In Acts 21:27–36, why is Paul nearly killed because of it? To which prophets is "work of the prophets" likely a reference? What are two examples of the surprising pattern in Scripture of Satan leading people toward pursuing ends that are similar to God's own, but with impure motives and means that are contrary to God's ways? Nevertheless, what does Alcimus' misguided attempt paradoxically foreshadow?

For application
1. **9:7–10.** Faced by such great odds (800 against 22,000), would you have sided with Judas or with his soldiers? How would you evaluate Judas' determination to fight rather than retreat? In the note for verses 7–22, would you agree or disagree with St. Ambrose's assessment of Judas' fortitude?
2. **9:22.** Even if a biographer is an eyewitness to the life of his subject, why must he select which deeds of the subject to record? How do the writers of the four Gospels select which of Jesus' deeds and sayings to report?
3. **9:27.** Read the note for this verse. What would be the value of prophecy for the Jews at this juncture in their history? What would be the value of prophecy in our own day? What do you think the Lord would say to us in our situation?
4. **9:54.** The note for this verse refers to Eph 2:11–22, which describes how Jesus broke the dividing wall between Jew and Gentile by his own blood. According to the *Catechism*, what are the links between Jews and Christians both then and now (CCC 839)? Despite that, what accounts for the hostility some Christians manifest toward Jews?

Chapter 10

For understanding
1. **10:3–5.** Despite Jonathan's residence being in Michmash rather than Jerusalem, what does Demetrius recognize about Jonathan? What twofold reversal does this mark?
2. **10:20.** After the death of Alcimus (159 B.C.), what evidence is there of a high priest in Jerusalem for this seven-year period? From whose line were high priests traditionally chosen? While not from the traditional high-priestly Oniad family, from which tribe do the Hasmoneans appear to have originated? Who were allowed to wear purple, the royal color?
3. **10:25–45.** To what does Demetrius' letter bear witness? How are the Jews addressed here? What fear might the omission of Jonathan's name from Demetrius' letter reflect?
4. **10:30.** Why might the high rate of taxation have been punitively imposed on the Jewish nation? Which three districts are referred to here? When Demetrius declares them to be annexed from Samaria and added to Judea, with what claim does his decree likely correspond?

For application
1. **10:3–6.** If you were in Jonathan's position, what would you think of Demetrius' offer? Even if you distrusted it, how would you take advantage of it?
2. **10:18–21.** What was there about Alexander's offer that might have caused Jonathan to accept it? Since he was already acting as a civil governor, what did the high priesthood add to his role?
3. **10:25–45.** Demetrius' second offer appears to give the Jews everything they could ever want. How do you weigh the benefits and drawbacks of two competing offers such as these? How do you decide whether an offer is too good to be true?
4. **10:60.** Why would Jonathan go to meet two kings "with pomp"? What may he have hoped to gain by doing so? If you were to face an uncertain reception by an authority figure, how would you present yourself so as to communicate yourself to advantage?

Chapter 11

For understanding
1. **11:13.** Of what importance was Antioch in Syria? What does Josephus relate that the people of Antioch, who had come to detest Alexander, did? After gaining both crowns, what did Ptolemy persuade the people of Antioch to do, and why?
2. **11:16.** How did historians in antiquity refer to Arabia? Of whose flight is this likely the direction, and how may it also correspond with a direction that Paul took?
3. **11:38.** As Diodorus records, who convinced the king to disband his troops? Why would this prove to be a serious political mistake for Demetrius?
4. **11:59.** Who is now confirmed by the Seleucids as the region's official governor? What is the Ladder of Tyre? Of which areas would it have completed Maccabean control?

For application
1. **11:9–12.** Of what value to Ptolemy is a woman like his daughter Cleopatra? What say as to her fate might she have had? What does Ptolemy's offer of his daughter's marriage to Demetrius II say about ancient attitudes toward the institution of marriage itself?
2. **11:23–24.** What was the risk that Jonathan faced by meeting with Demetrius II? What risks do diplomats often face when they meet with dictators or hostile rulers?
3. **11:38.** Why would the soldiers whom Demetrius dismissed from service become hostile to him? Even though the kingdom was at peace, what would the rationale be for maintaining a standing army? What danger would a trained group of soldiers without an income pose to the kingdom?

Chapter 12

For understanding
1. **12:5–18.** What is difficult to assess about this letter and the correspondences found elsewhere in 1 Maccabees (cf. chaps. 8, 13–15)? In either case, how would such letters likely have been originally written?

2. **12:7.** Where is a record of this letter to the Jews from Arius given, and what does it assert? How is the Jews' connection with Sparta further illustrated in 2 Mac 5:9? To which Onias is the high priestly reference?
3. **12:9.** To which holy books does the letter most likely refer? According to the prologue of Sirach, what three groupings of books in the Old Testament did Jews recognize?
4. **12:31.** Who were the Zabadeans? What were Jonathan's reasons for attacking them?

For application
1. **12:6.** What opening address were you taught to be correct when you compose a letter to a relative or friend? Why address someone as "Dear" if the person has no relationship with you? How would you begin a business letter when you did not know who was to read it?
2. **12:11.** When you assure others of your prayers on their behalf, how often do you actually pray for them? When others say they are praying for you, do you accept their assurance as fact, or do you dismiss it as a pious thought? Why does the Lord wish us to pray for one another?
3. **12:14-17.** Since the Jews state in their letter that they have been unwilling to trouble their allies for military assistance because they have received divine aid, what is the point of renewing historic treaties of friendship with Rome and Sparta? Why remind an important friend that he is still a friend?
4. **12:43-46.** When discussing offenses against the truth, what does the *Catechism* say about flattery and adulation (CCC 2480)? As illustrated in these verses, how can there be indirect flattery? What is the lie involved here?

Chapter 13

For understanding
1. **13:17-19.** In what way is Simon placed in a nearly impossible situation? What does Simon's fear of the people's judgment force him to do?
2. **Word Study: Deceitfully (13:17).** What does the Greek word *dolos* mean? What does it summarize in 1 Maccabees? In what wide array of contexts does it arise? If deceit is a defining characteristic of the devil, who speaks his own native tongue when he lies, of whom is honesty a hallmark? How is such, indeed, the case with Mattathias and his sons? To what do the Maccabees thus bear witness?
3. **13:27-30.** Who attests to monuments with pyramids in Judea? What purpose do the armor and the carved ships placed on the monuments serve? During what period did the memorial stand?
4. **13:45-47.** How does the siege of Gazara offer a contrast between Jewish and Gentile forces?

For application
1. **13:1-6.** Have you ever faced a situation where you had to assume leadership because no one else would do it? If so, what were the circumstances? What prompted your decision to step into the leader's role?
2. **13:14-19.** Consider Simon's dilemma. What were the issues? What would you have done in the situation? Have you ever had to make no-win decisions, and, if so, what was your rationale for what you did?
3. **13:25-30.** What is the most elaborate burial monument you have ever seen? Why do you think it was built? Why do people build elaborate monuments for themselves and family members? If you had the resources, how would you memorialize your parents and siblings at their grave sites?
4. **13:41-42.** On what did the Romans base their calendars? On what do Christians base theirs? Although Jews, Muslims, and others do not hold the birth of Jesus with the same regard as Christians, why do they use it as the basis of their calendars?

Chapter 14

For understanding
1. **14:12.** Of what does Mic 4:4 speak? With what does this blessing correspond, and what hope may it reflect?
2. **14:41.** With what authority is Simon invested, and what is the significance of this development? Why may this novelty be the reason for the lengthy praise of Simon's deeds? For how long is the authority granted to Simon and his sons presented as continuing?
3. **Topical Essay: Paul and the Maccabees.** On the one hand, what are some striking parallels between Mattathias and his sons and how Paul describes himself within his "former life in Judaism"? On the other hand, what clues do we have that the case may not be so simple? What other clues are provided within the book of 1 Maccabees itself? How does the identification of Jesus as Israel's promised prophet continue after his Resurrection, and how does Paul echo the testimony? How, then, might we deduce that Paul would have viewed the Maccabees after he encountered Christ on the Damascus road? In short, on what does the distinction between Paul and the Maccabean resistance rest?
4. **14:43-44.** Of what are the wearing of purple and gold signs? Though neither Simon nor his son John claimed this title for themselves, who did? In the midst of the nation's celebration of Simon, what two subtle points of caution does this text present?

For application
1. **14:9.** What is the difference between what old and young men treasure in peacetime? For example, why do old men talk of good things, and young men celebrate the glory of war when the land is at peace? In our day, how do the aged and the youth differ in their views of society?
2. **14:25-26.** What is the value for a community of publicly honoring its chief citizens? In our culture, how is honor customarily shown?
3. **14:41.** The note for this verse says that combining religious and political authority in the high priest had not been official policy in Israel. What are the advantages of combining civil and religious authority in such a personage? What are the dangers, both to religion and to political needs? How are these advantages and disadvantages reflected in Church history?

Study Questions

4. **14:48–49.** Where are the founding documents of our central government stored? Although we have the ability to make numerous copies of our constitution, why is it important for us to preserve the original? Since we have no original manuscripts of the Bible, how do we know we have a trustworthy version of the Scriptures?

Chapter 15

For understanding
1. **15:6.** What advantage does the privilege of minting their own coinage grant the Jews?
2. **15:27.** With his opposition subdued, what example does Antiochus VII follow?
3. **15:31.** How much money does Antiochus demand? How does this amount compare with the 300 talents promised by Jonathan to Demetrius II in return for release from tribute?
4. **15:33–35.** To what law does Simon appeal?

For application
1. **15:1–9.** The note for verse 9 says that Antiochus' promise is the same as one made to the Jews by his brother Demetrius II, which was broken. What does the expression "once burned, twice shy" mean to you? If you received a guarantee from a person or an organization that had previously reneged, how would you regard it?
2. **15:16–24.** What seems to have been the purpose of this communication from the Roman consul? Since the letter addresses King Demetrius, and Antiochus is the king's brother, what attention does Antiochus appear to have paid to it? What role might it have played in turning Antiochus against Simon (v. 27)?
3. **15:33–35.** To what does the Church's Code of Canon Law apply? To what does civil law apply? If you were defending the Church in a dispute with the civil government, to which code of law would you appeal? If the latter, how would you use the law to protect the Church's interests?

Chapter 16

For understanding
1. **16:2–3.** Whom does Simon commission to fight for the nation? How many years have now passed since Mattathias' initial revolt, and how old would Simon be?
2. **16:6–10.** What does this passage show about John? How does John show it?
3. **16:23–24.** Of what does this brief summary assure the reader regarding John? What does the reference to the chronicles of John's high priesthood recall?

For application
1. **16:2–3.** When did you first realize that, as an adult, you were responsible for not only your own life but that of your family? How did that realization strike you? What were some of the responsibilities you took upon yourself?
2. **16:6.** What is your philosophy of leadership? As a leader, what are some of the best ways you can use to encourage subordinates to follow your directions? What is "servant leadership"?
3. **16:23–24.** If you have ever thought of writing an autobiography, what would be its purpose? How, for example, might it be of use to your children or other family members? What sort of information would you put in it, and how would you decide which details to omit?

INTRODUCTION TO THE SECOND BOOK OF THE MACCABEES

Author and Date Like 1 Maccabees, the Book of 2 Maccabees originates from the period of the Seleucid empire's control over the land of Israel (198–142 B.C.). While 1 Maccabees begins with the first offenses of the Seleucid ruler Antiochus IV and continues with the leadership of the three Hasmonean brothers (169–134 B.C.), 2 Maccabees begins slightly earlier, in 176 B.C., describing the events that led up to Antiochus' sacrilege and taking the story down to the time of Judas Maccabeus in 161 B.C. The author, who never reveals his name, attests to be writing an edifying account of the events of this period, drawing largely upon a five-volume history of Jason of Cyrene, a source that has not survived on its own (2:23). In contrast with the historiographic style of 1 Maccabees, the author's stated aim in 2 Maccabees is to make the source material pleasing to read and easy to memorize (2:25; cf. 15:39), which he does by presenting selections from the mass of historical details (2:28–31) and offering direct theological commentary on specific events from the Seleucid oppression and Maccabean revolt. The book's striking descriptions of divine and angelic appearances and its clear articulation of belief in the resurrection suggest that the author may have been aligned with the Pharisees (whose theology is later attested to share similar emphases), and the book's sophisticated Greek style would identify the author as a highly literate Jew with an impressive Hellenistic education. While the larger work of Jason of Cyrene was evidently penned in North Africa, scholars are uncertain whether 2 Maccabees was written in the land of Israel or elsewhere in the Mediterranean world.

Second Maccabees is usually dated between 124 and 63 B.C. These endpoints are set by two passages in the book: the first letter appended to the book in 1:1–9 is usually dated to 124 B.C., meaning the canonical form of the book could not have appeared before this date; and the remark in 15:37 that Jerusalem was still in possession of the Hebrews at the time of writing suggests the book appeared before the Roman conquest of Judea in 63 B.C. This dating scheme is widely accepted, although some manuscript evidence suggests that the letter preserved in 1:1–9 was written in 143 B.C. rather than 124 B.C. (see notes on 1:7 and 1:9). If so, then 2 Maccabees could have been a complete book by the late 140s B.C.

Title As with 1 Maccabees, the title of 2 Maccabees is derived from the nickname of Judas, the leader of the Jewish resistance (see Introduction to the First Book of the Maccabees: *Title*). While the Maccabean books are transmitted in the manuscript tradition as "first" and "second", this does not reflect a chronological ordering: the narrative of 2 Maccabees actually begins a few years prior to the inciting events of 1 Maccabees, and the book may have reached its final form earlier than 1 Maccabees as well.

Place in the Canon On the canonicity of the Maccabean books among Christians and Jews in ancient times, see Introduction to the First Book of the Maccabees: *Place in the Canon*. Second Maccabees follows the same path to canonical acceptance as 1 Maccabees, save that the book is cited by Christians with greater frequency than 1 Maccabees, which is in part due to its distinctive doctrinal content. For example, Origen of Alexandria presents the speech of the martyred woman in 7:28 as the scriptural basis for the doctrine of creation "out of nothing" (*On First Principles* 2, 1), and St. Cyprian explains Paul's statement in Rom 8:18 that our future glory outweighs our present sufferings by making five references to the resurrection in chapters 6–7 (*Testimonies Against the Jews* 3, 17). As St. Augustine writes, the Maccabean books "are held as canonical, not by the Jews, but by the Church, on account of the extreme and wonderful sufferings of certain martyrs, who, before Christ had come in the flesh, contended for the law of God even unto death, and endured most grievous and horrible evils" (*City of God* 18, 36).

The early Church's frequent appeals to 2 Maccabees stands in contrast to the relative absence of such usage by Jewish sources in this period. Indeed, beyond the retelling of the martyr stories in chapters 6–7 by the author of the non-canonical *4 Maccabees*, which dates to the first century A.D., we have no direct citations of the book by Jews in the centuries after it was written, with neither of the parallel narratives in 1 Maccabees or in Josephus' *Antiquities of the Jews* showing clear evidence of reliance on 2 Maccabees. However, praise of the martyred mother and her seven sons is often found in the early rabbinic writings, which, considering the book's prior inclusion among the writings of the Greek Septuagint, seems likely to have been kept in memory by 2 Maccabees.

Like other books included in the Greek Septuagint but not in the rabbinic canon of Scripture, the canonicity of 2 Maccabees was called into question by the Protestant Reformers in the sixteenth century. However, while books like 1 Maccabees inspired little controversy in this period, the same cannot be said for 2 Maccabees: indeed, because it helped to support the Church's theology of Purgatory and indulgences, 2 Maccabees became the most controversial of the deuterocanonical books in this period. In a famous debate between Martin Luther and Johannes Eck at Leipzig in 1519, Luther responded to Eck's assertion that Purgatory was demonstrated in 2 Mac 12 by stating that the book was not authoritative for the Jews and Jerome and, thus, could not form an adequate basis for Church teaching. The reformer's dislike of 2 Maccabees continued in the following decades, with Luther describing it as Scripture's most despised book in 1521 and later identifying himself as a great enemy of it (along with Esther!) in his *Table Talk*. While Luther still appreciated sections like the martyrdoms in chapters 6–7, his overall antagonism toward the book was emulated by other reformers like Calvin, who similarly recognized the basis for beliefs like Purgatory and intercession for the dead in 2 Mac 12. Nevertheless, early Anabaptists (such as the Mennonites) continued regarding 2 Maccabees as Scripture for centuries after the Reformation, with these groups regarding the martyrs of chapters 6–7 as an inspiration for their nonviolent response to persecution. For more on this topic, see essay: *2 Maccabees and the Canon of Scripture* at 12:43.

Structure Scholars have proposed a number of different possible structures for 2 Maccabees. Since the book was composed using various historical accounts (especially the five volumes of Jason of Cyrene, 2:23), the author's structuring of the narrative likely incorporates preexisting structural elements preserved in his sources, giving the final narrative a complex texture that can be plausibly outlined in more than one way. Popular divisions for the main narrative include a structure based on the reign of four kings (Seleucus IV, 3:1—4:6; Antiochus IV, 4:7—10:9; Antiochus V, 10:10—13:26; Demetrius I, 14:1—15:37), or five sections that each conclude with a summary statement by the author (see 3:40; 7:42; 10:9; 13:26; and 15:37). The strongest case can be made for a structure that divides the book into two major parts, with each section explaining the backstory to a feast that is instituted at the section's end (Hanukkah in 10:9; Nicanor's Day in 15:36). These two major sections are prefaced by two historically significant festal letters (1:1–9; 1:10—2:18) and the author's introduction (2:19–32), and they are followed by a brief concluding note from the author (15:37–39). See *Outline*.

Literary Background In contrast with 1 Maccabees, 2 Maccabees was originally written in Greek rather than Hebrew. Rather than mirroring Hebrew compositional style, 2 Maccabees possesses a literary Greek style that is so elevated that it occasionally eludes translation. The author employs an impressive array of vocabulary, with one count estimating that there are twenty-six words used in the book that are unattested elsewhere in Greek literature. We might distinguish the styles of 1 and 2 Maccabees with a musical analogy: while both are playing largely the same melody, 1 Maccabees does so in a manner that resembles a simple medieval plainchant, while 2 Maccabees is more like a highly ornamented composition from the baroque period. While the author of 2 Maccabees makes clear that his genre is popular history rather than technical historiography (see 2:24–31; 15:39), the past century of scholarship has confirmed the book's value as a historical witness, particularly with respect to the controversial process of Hellenization among Jews that led up to Antiochus' persecution.

Themes and Characteristics The key themes of 2 Maccabees can be most clearly identified by listening to the voice of the author, who pauses his narrative at three points to address the reader regarding the main message to be learned from the events. **(1)** In 4:16–17, the author reflects on the *consequences for sin*. In this context, while the Jews who deserted the Mosaic Law in favor of Greek customs paid no heed to the divine repercussions, they did not foresee that the sinful people they wished to imitate would become their enemies and God's instrument of punishment. **(2)** In 5:17–20, the author builds on this theme by explaining how *obedience affects history*. The author illustrates this principle by drawing a contrast regarding the fate of the Temple: while the nation's obedience in chapter 3 led to God's miraculous protection of the Temple from Heliodorus, the disobedience of the people in chapter 5 causes even God's own holy sanctuary to share in the nation's misfortunes and become defiled. **(3)** In 6:12–17, the author precedes his account of the Jewish martyrdoms with a reflection on how *discipline is a sign of God's kindness*. While unthinkable calamities came upon the nation for its disobedience, these misfortunes were intended as discipline to draw the nation back to God. In fact, the paradoxical reality of God's election of Israel means that it is punished *more* quickly for its sins than any other nation, which is not a sign of disfavor but, rather, of the unbreakable bond between God and his people.

Taken together, one can regard 2 Maccabees as an extensive reflection on the nature and reality of God's justice as illustrated through the events of the Seleucid persecution and Maccabean revolt. It is easy to fall into the error of imposing an "either-or" paradigm upon the theology of biblical books—i.e., either that a given book presents God's justice as entirely manifest in this life or that this justice is reserved for a future, post-mortem judgment that is only hinted at in the present. The Book of 2 Maccabees shows us that the correct paradigm is a "both-and": while God will indeed set all things right at the future judgment, which serves as the basis for the martyrs' hope in chapter 7, the rest of the book is filled with examples of God's justice being revealed in the present life as well (such as the rescue, judgment, and restoration of Jerusalem's Temple in chapters 3, 5, and 8–10, and the punishments of Antiochus IV and Nicanor in chapters 9 and 15). Theologically, the presence of God's justice both now and in the future reminds the reader that amidst the complexities of history, God providentially manifests his judgments in this life as a sign of his righteousness and mercy so as to prepare us for the final judgment at the resurrection.

In addition to these recurring themes, 2 Maccabees carries a number of theological characteristics that make it distinctive in relation to other Old Testament books and a particularly valuable resource for Christian doctrine. For example, in contrast with the tendency in much Hebrew historiography (such as 1 Maccabees) to portray God's Providence in implicit rather than explicit terms, 2 Maccabees is full of *vivid epiphanies* that openly manifest God's power to his people (3:24–26; 10:29–30; 11:8; 12:22; 15:13, 27). While most Old Testament books have little to say regarding *bodily resurrection*, 2 Maccabees is a clear exception to this rule, as the dramatic events of chapter 7 hinge upon the martyrs' explicit hope in God's resurrecting power (see essay: *Resurrection in the Old Testament* at 2 Mac 7). The doctrine of *creation out of nothing*, which is traced to the description of God's creative action in Genesis 1, is also given its clearest biblical articulation in chapter 7, where it serves as the basis for the martyrs' hope that their disintegrated bodies can be restored (see note on 7:28). The idea of *substitutionary atonement*, prophetically described in passages like Isaiah 53, is given its clearest embodied example in the Old Testament in 2 Mac 7, where the righteous martyrs attest that their suffering will serve to turn away God's wrath from Israel (see note on 7:38). The practice of *praying for the dead* is most clearly attested in chapter 12, where Judas takes up a collection for sacrifices to be offered for his fallen soldiers who were entangled in forbidden practices (see note on 12:44–45). Along with this, the idea that *saints intercede for us* is similarly described in this Old Testament book, as the prayers of Onias and Jeremiah are revealed to be the strength of the Jewish forces in chapter 15 (see note on 15:14).

Christian Perspective As noted above, the distinctive characteristics of 2 Maccabees have made it a rich source for Christian theological reflection in a wide range of areas. Christian history has by far given most attention to the Maccabean martyrs and their dramatic witness to the resurrection. The earliest Christian usage of 2 Maccabees is found in Hebrews 11, where the author's tribute to the faith of Israel's heroes includes an allusion—typically recognized even by Protestant commentators—to the martyrs of chapters 6–7, who refused release so they might attain a better resurrection (Heb 11:35). Early Christian stories about the martyrs consciously evoked the accounts of Eleazar, the mother, and her seven sons, who were regarded as models for how Christians are called to suffer and die before their persecutors. For example, the second-century bishop Polycarp, after being dragged before the proconsul, rejects his offer to escape death by echoing the seventh brother's reply to Antiochus: "What are you waiting for?" (compare *Martyrdom of Polycarp* 11, 2, with 7:30). Later in the second century, the records of the martyrs of Lyon emphasize their parallels with their Maccabean predecessors. For example, the martyred woman Blandina is described in terms that evoke the Maccabean mother: after the younger martyrs' deaths, "Blandina, last of all, having, as a noble mother, encouraged her children and sent them before her victorious to the King, endured herself all their conflicts and hastened after them" (compare Eusebius, *Ecclesiastical History* 5, 2, 55, with 7:5–41). The account of the martyrs of Lyon similarly includes a subtle parallel between Eleazar and the aged bishop Pothinus, who, like his Maccabean forebear, was put to death by the authorities at the age of ninety (compare Eusebius, *Ecclesiastical History* 5, 5, 8, with 6:24). In the midst of violent persecution in the third century, Origen instructs Christians facing death for their faith to look to the Maccabean martyrs as their guide. Having recounted the story of the seven brothers and their mother, Origen commends them as an example of how the harshest sufferings and tortures can be overcome by the spell of love for God, "which is exceedingly more powerful than any other love spell" (*Exhortation to Martyrdom* 27). Origen's counsel appears to have been followed in the persecutions under Valerian in the late 250s: the mother of the martyr Marian is said to have "rejoiced like the mother of the Maccabees", and the martyr Flavian's eager mother is likewise praised as "a mother of the race of Maccabees" (*Martyrdom of Marian and James* 13, 1; cf. *Martyrdom of Montanus and Lucius* 16, 4).

As the forerunners of Christian martyrdom, the martyrs of 2 Maccabees were naturally celebrated within the early Church's liturgy and preaching as well. Evidence of a feast of the Maccabean martyrs goes back to the fourth century A.D., first aligning with Hanukkah in December before being moved to August 1, where the date still stands. The degree to which the Maccabean martyrs were revered as Christian saints is well illustrated by the fate of their relics: first preserved at their own basilica in Antioch, portions of the martyrs' bodies are now attested to be held at churches in Istanbul, Cyprus, Rome, and as far off as Cologne, Germany! The uniqueness of the Maccabean martyrs continued to be marked in the succeeding centuries, with St. Bernard of Clairvaux writing a letter in the twelfth century explaining why only the Maccabees, among all the Old Testament saints, are celebrated with a solemnity equal to that of the Christian martyrs (*Letter XLIV*).

The martyrs' remarkable stories were also a popular topic in the Church's preaching; Theophilus of Antioch in A.D. 404 describes the Maccabean martyrs as praised in the churches of Christ throughout the entire world. Three homilies from St. John Chrysostom on the Maccabean martyrs have been preserved, which were preached near the end of the fourth century to coincide with their feast day. According to Chrysostom, the martyrs of 2 Maccabees were even more glorious than later Christian ones, because they overcame their fear of suffering at a time before Christ had broken the power of death and exhibited no fear of death when Abraham, Moses, Elijah, and even Peter fled from it. As Chrysostom teaches, this can have been done only by the power of Christ's coming advent: for just as the sun, before it dawns, still begins to illumine the earth by its coming rays, so too did the Maccabean martyrs serve as early rays of the Sun of Righteousness who was soon to arise (cf. Mal 4:2). In dying for the Law, Chrysostom teaches, these martyrs truly died for the Law's author, Christ, the giver of both the Old Covenant and the New (*On Eleazar and the Seven Boys* 5–6). St. Augustine makes similar points in a homily on the Maccabean martyrs, using the analogy of a king's procession, in which some attendants march in front of the king's chariot and others behind. In the same way, the Maccabean martyrs died for Christ veiled in the Law before his advent, while later Christian martyrs died for Christ unveiled in the Gospel. As Augustine beautifully testifies, "Christ possesses both; Christ helped both in their struggle; Christ has crowned both" (*Sermon 300*).

OUTLINE OF THE SECOND BOOK OF THE MACCABEES

1. Introduction (1:1—2:32)
A. First festal letter to Jews in Egypt, 124/143 B.C. (1:1–9)
B. Second festal letter from the senate and Judas to Aristobulus, ca. 164 B.C. (1:10—2:18)
C. Author's introduction (2:19–32)

2. The First Feast Cycle: Hanukkah (3:1—10:9)
A. Heliodorus and God's protection of the Temple (3:1–40)
B. Priestly corruption and Antiochus Epiphanes' suppression of Judaism (4:1—6:11)
C. Redeeming martyrdoms of the righteous (6:12—7:42)
D. Rise of Judas and God's deliverance (8:1–36)
E. Defeat of Antiochus and establishment of Hanukkah (9:1—10:9)

3. The Second Feast Cycle: Nicanor's Day (10:10—15:36)
A. Judas repels Antiochus Eupator's counterattacks (10:10—13:26)
B. Nicanor's friendship and betrayal (14:1–46)
C. Defeat of Nicanor and establishment of Nicanor's Day (15:1–36)

4. Conclusion (15:37–39)
A. Author's concluding remarks (15:37–39)

THE SECOND BOOK OF THE

MACCABEES

A Letter to the Jews in Egypt

1 The Jewish brethren in Jerusalem and those in the land of Judea,

To their Jewish brethren in Egypt,

Greeting, and good peace.

2 May God do good to you, and may he remember his covenant with Abraham and Isaac and Jacob, his faithful servants. ³May he give you all a heart to worship him and to do his will with a strong heart and a willing spirit. ⁴May he open your heart to his law and his commandments, and may he bring peace. ⁵May he hear your prayers and be reconciled to you, and may he not forsake you in time of evil. ⁶We are now praying for you here.

7 In the reign of Deme′trius, in the one hundred and sixty-ninth year,ᵃ we Jews wrote to you, in the critical distress which came upon us in those years after Jason and his company revolted from the holy land and the kingdom ⁸and burned the gate and shed innocent blood. We begged the Lord and we were heard, and we offered sacrifice and cereal offering, and we lighted the lamps and we set out the loaves. ⁹And now see that you keep the feast of booths in the month of Chis′lev, in the one hundred and eighty-eighth year.ᵇ

A Letter to Aristobulus

10 Those in Jerusalem and those in Judea and the senate and Judas,

To Aristob′ulus, who is of the family of the anointed priests, teacher of Ptol′emy the king, and to the Jews in Egypt,

Greeting, and good health.

11 Having been saved by God out of grave dangers we thank him greatly for taking our side against the king.ᶜ ¹²For he drove out those who fought against the holy city. ¹³For when the leader reached Persia with a force that seemed

---

1:1—2:18 The narrative of 2 Maccabees is prefaced by two letters written by Jews in Jerusalem and Judea to their brethren in Egypt. Like the letters preserved in Esther 9:20–22, 29–32, that instruct Jews to celebrate the feast of Purim, the letters in 2 Maccabees are written to encourage the celebration of a new Feast of Booths (known to us as Hanukkah) in honor of the Temple's purification (see 1:9, 18; 2:16). There are interpretative questions regarding the dating and division of these letters, but most regard the first as reaching from 1:1–9 and originating in either 124 or 143 B.C., with the second covering 1:10–2:18 and being written shortly after the Temple's rededication in 164 B.C. and before Judas' death in 160 B.C.

1:1 in Egypt: A Jewish population had been living in Egypt from at least the time of the Babylonian Exile in 586 B.C. (cf. Jer 43:4–7), with more migrating in 160s B.C. under the leadership of Onias IV, the heir of the Jerusalem high priesthood.

1:2–5 A prayer for the Jews in Egypt that God would uphold his covenant promises with them and open their hearts to obey his Law. If written around 124 B.C., the time of evil may refer to the persecution of Egyptian Jews under Ptolemy VIII, which the Jewish historian Josephus recounts in *Against Apion* 2, 5.

1:7 Demetrius: Demetrius II Nicator, king of the Seleucid empire. **in the one hundred and sixty-ninth year:** 143 B.C., when the Jews gained full independence from the Seleucid empire under Simon Maccabee (cf. 1 Mac 13:31–42). **we Jews wrote to you:** The Greek text reads "we have written", which can be interpreted in either a past or present sense. If past ("we wrote"), this would be a reference to an earlier letter from the Judeans that has not been preserved. If present ("we are writing"), this would be a reference to the present letter, which would be written on the occasion of Jewish independence in 143 B.C. **Jason:** The brother of the high priest Onias III. For the story of his revolt, see 4:7–22.

1:9 feast of booths ... month of Chislev: In accordance with Lev 23, the Feast of Booths (or Tabernacles) was celebrated for eight days beginning on the 15th of Tishri, the seventh month (September–October). This was a harvest celebration that also became a great commemoration of the Temple and was renewed under Nehemiah's leadership after the Temple was rebuilt (Neh 8:13–18). This celebration becomes the model for the feast of the Temple's rededication (Hanukkah) under the Maccabees, which is similarly celebrated for eight days, beginning with the date of Judas' purification of the sanctuary on the 25th of Chislev (December). See also 10:5–6. **one hundred and eighty-eighth year:** 124 B.C. While this is the most common reading, some variants record "one hundred and forty-eighth year", i.e., 164 B.C. By this reading, the reference to 164 B.C. commemorates the date of the first Hanukkah, with the reference in 1:7 to 143 B.C. indicating the date of the present letter, which is written to mark the beginning of Jewish independence in the postexilic period.

1:10 senate: The assembly of elders in Jerusalem, which came to be the Sanhedrin in New Testament times. See word study: *Senate* at Jud 4:8. **Judas:** Judas Maccabeus, the first of Mattathias' sons to continue the campaign to gain freedom for the Jewish nation and after whose nickname ("the hammer") the two books are titled. The dating of this second letter, otherwise unstated, would be between the first feast of purification (164 B.C.) and the death of Judas (160 B.C.). **Aristobulus:** Aristobulus the Peripatetic, a well-known Jewish philosopher in Alexandria. Aristobulus' works were addressed to the Egyptian king Ptolemy VI Philometor and were intended to show that Greek learning was derived from the earlier wisdom of the Hebrews.

1:11 the king: The Seleucid king Antiochus IV Epiphanes. Additional details on Antiochus' raid and subsequent death are found in chap. 9, 1 Mac 6, and in Greek historians such as Polybius (*Histories* 31, 9).

1:13 temple of Nanea: A temple of a Mesopotamian goddess, which the Greeks identified with Artemis or Aphrodite.

ᵃ 143 B.C.
ᵇ 124 B.C.
ᶜ Cn: Gk *as those who array themselves against a king.*

irresistible, they were cut to pieces in the temple of Nane′a by a deception employed by the priests of Nanea. [14]For under pretext of intending to marry her, Anti′ochus came to the place together with his friends, to secure most of its treasures as a dowry. [15]When the priests of the temple of Nane′a had set out the treasures and Anti′ochus had come with a few men inside the wall of the sacred precinct, they closed the temple as soon as he entered it. [16]Opening the secret door in the ceiling, they threw stones and struck down the leader and his men, and dismembered them and cut off their heads and threw them to the people outside. [17]Blessed in every way be our God, who has brought judgment upon those who have behaved impiously.

Fire Consumes Nehemiah's Sacrifice

18 Since on the twenty-fifth day of Chis′lev we shall celebrate the purification of the temple, we thought it necessary to notify you, in order that you also may celebrate the feast of booths and the feast of the fire given when Nehemi′ah, who built the temple and the altar, offered sacrifices.

19 For when our fathers were being led captive to Persia, the pious priests of that time took some of the fire of the altar and secretly hid it in the hollow of a dry cistern, where they took such precautions that the place was unknown to any one. [20]But after many years had passed, when it pleased God, Nehemi′ah, having been commissioned by the king of Persia, sent the descendants of the priests who had hidden the fire to get it. And when they reported to us that they had not found fire but thick liquid, he ordered them to dip it out and bring it. [21]And when the materials for the sacrifices were presented, Nehemi′ah ordered the priests to sprinkle the liquid on the wood and what was laid upon it. [22]When this was done and some time had passed and the sun, which had been clouded over, shone out, a great fire blazed up, so that all marveled. [23]And while the sacrifice was being consumed, the priests offered prayer—the priests and every one. Jonathan led, and the rest responded, as did Nehemi′ah. [24]The prayer was to this effect:

"O Lord, Lord God, Creator of all things, who are awe-inspiring and strong and just and merciful, who alone are King and are kind, [25]who alone are bountiful, who alone are just and almighty and eternal, who rescue Israel from every evil, who chose the fathers and consecrated them, [26]accept this sacrifice on behalf of all your people Israel and preserve your portion and make it holy. [27]Gather together our scattered people, set free those who are slaves among the Gentiles, look upon those who are rejected and despised, and let the Gentiles know that you are our God. [28]Afflict those who oppress and are insolent with pride. [29]Plant your people in your holy place, as Moses said."

1:14 intending to marry her: The marriage of a king to a goddess was an ancient ritual performed to ensure the land's fertility. The Latin historian Granius Licinianus records that Antiochus IV had previously performed this rite in Syria at the temple of Atargatis (Diana) as a pretext for robbing its treasures (*Annals* 28), and Polybius writes that Antiochus had similarly despoiled most of the temples of Egypt (*Histories* 30, 26).

1:16 cut off their heads: The testimony later in chap. 9 (as well as in Polybius and 1 Mac 6) suggests that only Antiochus' soldiers lose their heads in this encounter, with Antiochus dying in agony shortly after his retreat.

1:18—2:15 This lengthy portion of the letter recounts various wonders that God has worked in Israel's history to provide and preserve the sacrificial fire. The appeal to an array of scriptural figures—Nehemiah, Jeremiah, Solomon, Moses—is essential for establishing the heritage and rationale for a new feast, Hanukkah, which does not have the advantage of having been prescribed in the Torah.

1:18 feast of booths: See note on 1:9. **the feast of the fire:** The Greek text literally reads "and of the fire", making it likely that this refers to the same feast. The fire refers to the following story where a liquid remnant of the fire from Solomon's Temple ignites and burns the sacrifice upon the altar under Nehemiah, providing a sign of continuity between the two Temples and a signal that the sacrifices of both are acceptable to God (cf. Judg 6:21; 1 Kings 18:33–38). This memory is then foundational for Judas' rededication. See note on 1:31. **Nehemiah, who built the temple and the altar:** Commentators speculate as to why the author of 2 Maccabees credits Nehemiah with constructing the Temple and altar, since Ezra records that these were built by Zerubbabel (Ezra 5–6) prior to Nehemiah's arrival in Jerusalem in 445 B.C. (Neh 2:11). Similar identifications of Nehemiah as the Temple's builder are found in other early Jewish sources, e.g., Josephus recounts how Nehemiah received permission from Artaxerxes to finish building the Temple (*Antiquities* 11, 165–66; cf. Neh 2:8), and one rabbinic text even identifies Zerubbabel and Nehemiah as the same person (Babylonian Talmud, *Sanhedrin* 38a). Within the context of 2 Maccabees, it would seem that Nehemiah's role as a builder is emphasized because of the analogy it provides with Judas, under whose leadership the Temple's altar is rebuilt (2:19; 10:3). This is added to other parallels: both men free the city from foreign influence, and both celebrate the Feast of Booths to commemorate God's deliverance.

1:19 Persia: The Jewish nation was originally exiled to Babylon, which Persia later annexed (cf. 2 Chron 36:15–21).

1:20 thick liquid: Identified in 1:36 as naphtha, a highly flammable petroleum substance. Naphtha is attested elsewhere in antiquity by the historians Strabo and Plutarch, who recount how a fascinated Alexander the Great set a servant on fire with the mysterious substance, which similarly broke into flames before being lit (Strabo, *Geography* 16, 1; Plutarch, *Alexander* 35).

1:23 Jonathan: An otherwise unidentified figure who may correspond with the Jonathan in Neh 12:11 or be an alternate name for the prayer leader Mattaniah in Neh 11:17 (as both carry the meaning of "the Lord's gift").

1:29 as Moses said: An allusion to the Song of the Sea, sung after the Israelites escaped Egypt through the miraculously parted waters: "You will bring them in, and plant them on your own mountain, the place, O LORD, which you have made for your abode, the sanctuary, O LORD, which your hands have established" (Ex 15:17). This reference is particularly meaningful in the present context, when Jews in Jerusalem are writing to their dispersed brethren in Egypt in the hope that God will bring them back once again.

[30]Then the priests sang the hymns. [31]And when the materials of the sacrifice were consumed, Nehemi'ah ordered that the liquid that was left should be poured upon large stones. [32]When this was done, a flame blazed up; but when the light from the altar shone back, it went out. [33]When this matter became known, and it was reported to the king of the Persians that, in the place where the exiled priests had hidden the fire, the liquid had appeared with which Nehemi'ah and his associates had burned the materials of the sacrifice, [34]the king investigated the matter, and enclosed the place and made it sacred. [35]And with those persons whom the king favored he exchanged many excellent gifts. [36]Nehemi'ah and his associates called this "nephthar," which means purification, but by most people it is called naphtha.[d]

Jeremiah Hides the Tent, Ark, and Altar

2 One finds in the records that Jeremi'ah the prophet ordered those who were being deported to take some of the fire, as has been told, [2]and that the prophet after giving them the law instructed those who were being deported not to forget the commandments of the Lord, nor to be led astray in their thoughts upon seeing the gold and silver statues and their adornment. [3]And with other similar words he exhorted them that the law should not depart from their hearts.

4 It was also in the writing that the prophet, having received an oracle, ordered that the tent and the ark should follow with him, and that he went out to the mountain where Moses had gone up and had seen the inheritance of God. [5]And Jeremi'ah came and found a cave, and he brought there the tent and the ark and the altar of incense, and he sealed up the entrance. [6]Some of those who followed him came up to mark the way, but could not find it. [7]When Jeremi'ah learned of it, he rebuked them and declared: "The place shall be unknown until God gathers his people together again and shows his mercy. [8]And then the Lord will disclose these things, and the glory of the Lord and the cloud will appear, as they were shown in the case of Moses, and as Solomon asked that the place should be specially consecrated."

9 It was also made clear that being possessed of wisdom Solomon[e] offered sacrifice for the

---

1:31 upon large stones: Though not explicitly stated, these would seem to be the same stones that Judas ignites and draws fire from when the Temple is rededicated (see 10:3). This provides the rationale for recounting Nehemiah's story: the same stones upon which Nehemiah poured the liquid, after it astonishingly rekindled Solomon's original fire at the Temple's rededication, have given their purifying fire once more under Judas. Such a reading also explains why the subsequent celebration is called the feast of fire; cf. 1:18.

1:31–33 Christian interpretation sees this mysterious fire-water as a symbol of the Holy Spirit, which comes upon the baptized both to cleanse and burn away sin • "What else can this mean—namely, that fire became water and water called forth fire—but that spiritual grace burns out our sins through fire and through water cleanses them? We know now that this is in truth the sacred fire that then, as a type of the future remission of sins, came down upon the sacrifice. This fire is hidden in the time of captivity, during which sin reigns, but in the time of liberty it is brought forth. And though it is changed into the appearance of water, yet it preserves its nature as fire so as to consume the sacrifice.... You are that victim. Contemplate in silence each single point. The breath of the Holy Spirit descends on you; he seems to burn you when he consumes your sins. The sacrifice that was consumed in the time of Moses was a sacrifice for sin, wherefore Moses said, as is written in the book of the Maccabees: 'Because the sacrifice for sin was not to be eaten, it was consumed' (2 Mac 2:11). Does it not seem to be consumed for you when, in the sacrament of Baptism, the whole outer man perishes?" (St. Ambrose, *On the Duties of the Clergy* 3, 18, 105, and 107).

1:34 the king investigated the matter: The importance of sacred fire within Zoroastrianism, the religious system of the Persians, accounts for the king's interest in the wonders taking place in Jerusalem.

1:36 nephthar ... naphtha: See note on 1:20. **purification:** The term used for the feast of Hanukkah in this letter (1:18; 2:16). Josephus calls this feast the "festival of lights" (though he himself does not seem to know the reason for the name), which may be connected with the renewed naphtha fire under Judas (see 1:18, 32). Surprisingly, the traditional Hanukkah story regarding the single vial of oil that miraculously burns for eight days is first found in the Babylonian Talmud, written centuries after these events.

2:1 records ... Jeremiah the prophet: This narrative is not present in the canonical book of Jeremiah, though several early Jewish sources discuss the hiding of the Temple's vessels by Jeremiah/Baruch (e.g., *2 Baruch* 6, *4 Baruch* 3). Eupolemus, a Jewish historian contemporary with the Maccabees (and likely the same Eupolemus noted in 4:11 and 1 Mac 8:17) similarly comments on Jeremiah's relocation of the ark at the time of the Exile. Jeremiah held a distinct significance for Jews in Egypt, since the prophet had gone there into exile after the Temple was destroyed in 586 B.C. (cf. Jer 43–44).

2:2–3 For these exhortations, see the Epistle of Jeremiah in Baruch 6.

2:4 mountain: Mount Nebo (see Deut 34:1). This was also the area where Moses' burial site was hidden (Deut 34:6).

2:7 gathers his people: The hope that God would again gather his dispersed people is a focal point of the second letter (also 1:27, 29 and 2:18), which is linked together with observing the new feast. In 2:7–8, the inclusion of Jeremiah's testimony about the future reappearance of the ark and God's glory serves as an encouragement to observe this new feast, a celebration of God's mercy in re-gathering his people that would hopefully precede these reappearances. These "gathering" references may indicate a desire that Egyptian Jews treat Hanukkah as a pilgrimage feast, just like the Feast of Booths upon which it is modeled (cf. 1:18). While little testimony survives from this period, we know that Jesus observed Hanukkah, making the pilgrimage to Jerusalem from Galilee (Jn 10:22–23).

2:9–11 The author recounts the wonders that accompanied the newly dedicated sacrifices under Moses and Solomon (Lev 9:22–24; 2 Chron 7:1), perhaps in hope of similar wonders that would accompany God's most recent deliverance of

---

[d]Gk *nephthai.*
[e]Gk *he.*

dedication and completion of the temple. [10]Just as Moses prayed to the Lord, and fire came down from heaven and devoured the sacrifices, so also Solomon prayed, and the fire came down and consumed the whole burnt offerings. [11]And Moses said, "They were consumed because the sin offering had not been eaten." [12]Likewise Solomon also kept the eight days.

13 The same things are reported in the records and in the memoirs of Nehemi'ah, and also that he founded a library and collected the books about the kings and prophets, and the writings of David, and letters of kings about votive offerings. [14]In the same way Judas also collected all the books that had been lost on account of the war which had come upon us, and they are in our possession. [15]So if you have need of them, send people to get them for you.

16 Since, therefore, we are about to celebrate the purification, we write to you. Will you therefore please keep the days? [17]It is God who has saved all his people, and has returned the inheritance to all, and the kingship and priesthood and consecration, [18]as he promised through the law. For we have hope in God that he will soon have mercy upon us and will gather us from everywhere under heaven into his holy place, for he has rescued us from great evils and has purified the place.

The Compiler's Preface

19 The story of Judas Mac"cabe'us and his brothers, and the purification of the great temple, and the dedication of the altar, [20]and further the wars against Anti'ochus Epiph'anes and his son Eu'pator, [21]and the appearances which came from heaven to those who strove zealously on behalf of Judaism, so that though few in number they seized the whole land and pursued the barbarian hordes, [22]and recovered the temple famous throughout the world and freed the city and restored the laws that were about to be abolished, while the Lord with great kindness became gracious to them—[23]all this, which has been set forth by Jason of Cyre'ne in five volumes, we shall attempt to condense into a single book. [24]For considering the flood of numbers involved and the difficulty there is for those who wish to enter upon the narratives of history because of the mass of material, [25]we have aimed to please those who wish to read, to make it easy for those who are

---

the rededicated Temple (2:17). Moses' statement in 2:11 does not have a precise parallel in the Old Testament, and commentators suspect it interprets the events of Lev 9 or relates to the surrounding episodes in Lev 8 and 10. In either case, the point drawn in the letter is that the sacrifice being consumed by heavenly fire signals its acceptability to God (cf. 1 Kings 18:37–39).

2:14 In the same way Judas: Showing continuity between the Maccabean leader and Nehemiah, who guided the nation the last time the Temple's worship was fully restored.

2:18 as he promised through the law: An allusion to Ex 19:6, where God promises to make the people of Israel "a kingdom of priests and a holy nation." **gather us:** See note on 2:7.

2:20 Antiochus: See note on 1:11. **Eupator:** Antiochus V Eupator (meaning "of a good father"), the young king who reigned with his regent Lysias for two years until his death by order of Demetrius I.

2:23–32 The closest scriptural parallel to the author's account of his own writing comes from the preface to the Gospel of Luke, where Luke recounts how he, following many other writers, labored to put together an orderly account of Christ's ministry for Theophilus (Lk 1:1–4). Just as God's inspiration did not negate Luke's efforts, but provided them with divine guidance and vision, so too God inspired the author in 2 Maccabees (CCC 106). • Vatican II reaffirmed the Church's teaching that when God selected human authors to compose the Scriptures, he acted in them and by them, making full use of their individual faculties and powers to produce the biblical books (*Dei Verbum* 11).

2:23 Jason of Cyrene: An otherwise unknown historian. Cyrene was an important Greek city in North Africa, located about 500 miles west of Alexandria. **five volumes:** These volumes are no longer extant, making it impossible to know the precise relationship between Jason's original work and our author's synthesis in 2 Maccabees.

WORD STUDY

Appearances (2:21)

Epiphaneia (Gk.) means "appearance" or "apparition" and is the source for our English word "epiphany". This term can be used to describe either the ordinary appearing of a human being or a divine manifestation, such as Christ's First and Second Comings in the NT (1 Tim 6:14; 2 Tim 1:10). This second sense of *epiphaneia* is common in 2 Maccabees and is employed in 2:21 as a word play to set up a contrast between Antiochus "Epiphanes" and the heavenly apparitions sent by the God of Israel. Antiochus, of course, had given himself the nickname Epiphanes as a claim that he was the presence of God upon the earth, stamping his coins with the phrase "King Antiochus, God Manifest" (*epiphanous*). Throughout 2 Maccabees, the wicked plans of this "God Manifest" are countered by heavenly manifestations from the one true God, who makes his power visible and protects his people when they turn to him (3:24–26; 10:29–30; 11:8; 12:22; 15:13, 27). This theme in 2 Maccabees is further developed in the Gospel of John, when Jesus attends the festival of Hanukkah in Jerusalem. While the Jews seek to stone Jesus—since, like Antiochus Epiphanes, he stands in the Temple as a man who declares himself to be God—they do not recognize that their Hanukkah feast has astonishingly been visited by God's genuine *epiphaneia*, in whom the Father truly dwells (Jn 10:38).

inclined to memorize, and to profit all readers. [26]For us who have undertaken the toil of abbreviating, it is no light matter but calls for sweat and loss of sleep, [27]just as it is not easy for one who prepares a banquet and seeks the benefit of others. However, to secure the gratitude of many we will gladly endure the uncomfortable toil, [28]leaving the responsibility for exact details to the compiler, while devoting our effort to arriving at the outlines of the condensation. [29]For as the master builder of a new house must be concerned with the whole construction, while the one who undertakes its painting and decoration has to consider only what is suitable for its adornment, such in my judgment is the case with us. [30]It is the duty of the original historian to occupy the ground and to discuss matters from every side and to take trouble with details, [31]but the one who recasts the narrative should be allowed to strive for brevity of expression and to forego exhaustive treatment. [32]At this point therefore let us begin our narrative, adding only so much to what has already been said; for it is foolish to lengthen the preface while cutting short the history itself.

Arrival of Heliodorus in Jerusalem

3 While the holy city was inhabited in unbroken peace and the laws were very well observed because of the piety of the high priest Oni'as and his hatred of wickedness, [2]it came about that the kings themselves honored the place and glorified the temple with the finest presents, [3]so that even Seleu'cus, the king of Asia, defrayed from his own revenues all the expenses connected with the service of the sacrifices. [4]But a man named Simon, of the tribe of Benjamin, who had been made captain of the temple, had a disagreement with the high priest about the administration of the city market; [5]and when he could not prevail over Oni'as he went to Apollo'nius of Tarsus,[f] who at that time was governor of Coe'le-syr'ia and Phoeni'cia. [6]He reported to him that the treasury in Jerusalem was full of untold sums of money, so that the amount of the funds could not be reckoned, and that they did not belong to the account of the sacrifices, but that it was possible for them to fall under the control of the king. [7]When Apollo'nius met the king, he told him of the money about which he had been informed. The king[g] chose He"liodo'rus, who was in charge of his affairs, and sent him with commands to effect the removal of the aforesaid money. [8]He"liodo'rus at once set out on his journey, ostensibly to make a tour of inspection of the cities of Coe'le-syr'ia and Phoeni'cia, but in fact to carry out the king's purpose.

9 When he had arrived at Jerusalem and had been kindly welcomed by the high priest of[h] the city, he told about the disclosure that had been made and stated why he had come, and he inquired whether this really was the situation. [10]The high priest explained that there were some deposits belonging to widows and orphans, [11]and also some money of Hyrca'nus, son of Tobi'as, a man of very prominent position, and that it totaled in all four hundred talents of silver and two hundred of gold. To such an extent the impious Simon had misrepresented the facts. [12]And he said that it was utterly impossible that wrong should be done to those people who had trusted in the holiness of the place and in the sanctity and inviolability of the temple which is honored throughout the whole world. [13]But He"liodo'rus, because of the king's commands which he had, said that this money must in any case be confiscated for the king's treasury. [14]So he set a day and went in to direct the inspection of these funds.

There was no little distress throughout the whole city. [15]The priests prostrated themselves before the altar in their priestly garments and called toward heaven upon him who had given the law about

---

3:1 **Onias:** Onias III, high priest in Jerusalem from 196 to 175 B.C., who plays an important role in 2 Mac as the last of the traditional Oniad line to serve faithfully in the priestly office.

3:3 **Seleucus:** King Seleucus IV Philopator, who reigned from 187 to 175 B.C. and was the older brother of Antiochus Epiphanes.

3:4 **Simon, of the tribe of Benjamin:** Other manuscript variants state that Simon is of the priestly tribe of Bilgah (Neh 12:5, 18; 1 Chron 24:14), which is of importance for tracing the heritage of Simon's brother Menelaus. See note on 4:23–25.

3:5 **Apollonius of Tarsus:** An otherwise unknown governor, who is likely the predecessor to the better-known Apollonius in 2 Mac 4 rather than the same person. **governor of Coele-syria and Phoenicia:** Also known as the "province Beyond the River" (1 Mac 7:8), an area that included all the land west of the Euphrates River out to the Mediterranean Sea. The term Coele-syria is also used more narrowly to describe

the land north of Palestine, encompassing modern Lebanon and Syria.

3:7 **Heliodorus:** A royal official of Seleucus IV Philopator, who is identified by the Greek historian Appian as eventually conspiring in the king's assassination. Apart from his appearance as the villain in 2 Mac 3, little was known about Heliodorus before 2007, when archaeologists at Tell Maresha in Judea discovered a stele that preserves Heliodorus' correspondence with King Seleucus. Bearing the date of 178 B.C., the stele details the king's orders for the oversight of temples in Coele-syria and Phoenicia, which appears to serve as a precursor for the attempted robbery described in 2 Maccabees.

3:11 **Hyrcanus, son of Tobias:** Known from the Jewish historian Josephus as the youngest son of Joseph from the Tobiad family, which had become wealthy collecting taxes for the Ptolemies under their rule and lived east of the Jordan. **four hundred talents ... two hundred:** For context, a drachma was often reckoned as a day's wage (Tob 5:14), and 6,000 drachmas made one talent. This means if one worked every day, one talent would be equivalent to over 16 years' wages.

3:15 **law about deposits:** See, for example, the laws regarding deposits in Lev 6:1–7.

---

[f] Gk *Apollonius son of Tharseas.*
[g] Gk *He.*
[h] Some authorities read *and.*

deposits, that he should keep them safe for those who had deposited them. [16]To see the appearance of the high priest was to be wounded at heart, for his face and the change in his color disclosed the anguish of his soul. [17]For terror and bodily trembling had come over the man, which plainly showed to those who looked at him the pain lodged in his heart. [18]People also hurried out of their houses in crowds to make a general supplication because the holy place was about to be brought into contempt. [19]Women, clothed with sackcloth under their breasts, thronged the streets. Some of the maidens who were kept indoors ran together to the gates, and some to the walls, while others peered out of the windows. [20]And holding up their hands to heaven, they all made entreaty. [21]There was something pitiable in the prostration of the whole populace and the anxiety of the high priest in his great anguish.

The Lord Protects His Temple

22 While they were calling upon the Almighty Lord that he would keep what had been entrusted safe and secure for those who had entrusted it, [23]He"liodo'rus went on with what had been decided. [24]But when he arrived at the treasury with his bodyguard, then and there the Sovereign of spirits and of all authority caused so great a manifestation that all who had been so bold as to accompany him were astounded by the power of God, and became faint with terror. [25]For there appeared to them a magnificently caparisoned horse, with a rider of frightening mien, and it rushed furiously at He"liodo'rus and struck at him with its front hoofs. Its rider was seen to have armor and weapons of gold. [26]Two young men also appeared to him, remarkably strong, gloriously beautiful and splendidly dressed, who stood on each side of him and scourged him continuously, inflicting many blows on him. [27]When he suddenly fell to the ground and deep darkness came over him, his men took him up and put him on a stretcher [28]and carried him away, this man who had just entered the aforesaid treasury with a great retinue and all his bodyguard but was now unable to help himself; and they recognized clearly the sovereign power of God. [29]While he lay prostrate, speechless because of the divine intervention and deprived of any hope of recovery, [30]they praised the Lord who had acted marvelously for his own place. And the temple, which a little while before was full

of fear and disturbance, was filled with joy and gladness, now that the Almighty Lord had appeared.

Onias Prays for Heliodorus

31 Quickly some of He"liodo'rus' friends asked Oni'as to call upon the Most High and to grant life to one who was lying quite at his last breath. [32]And the high priest, fearing that the king might get the notion that some foul play had been perpetrated by the Jews with regard to He"liodo'rus, offered sacrifice for the man's recovery. [33]While the high priest was making the offering of atonement, the same young men appeared again to He"liodo'rus dressed in the same clothing, and they stood and said, "Be very grateful to Oni'as the high priest, since for his sake the Lord has granted you your life. [34]And see that you, who have been scourged by heaven, report to all men the majestic power of God." Having said this they vanished.

The Conversion of Heliodorus

35 Then He"liodo'rus offered sacrifice to the Lord and made very great vows to the Savior of his life, and having bidden Oni'as farewell, he marched off with his forces to the king. [36]And he bore testimony to all men of the deeds of the supreme God, which he had seen with his own eyes. [37]When the king asked He"liodo'rus what sort of person would be suitable to send on another mission to Jerusalem, he replied, [38]"If you have any enemy or plotter against your government, send him there, for you will get him back thoroughly scourged, if he escapes at all, for there certainly is about the place some power of God. [39]For he who has his dwelling in heaven watches over that place himself and brings it aid, and he strikes and destroys those who come to do it injury." [40]This was the outcome of the episode of He"liodo'rus and the protection of the treasury.

Simon Accuses Onias

4 The previously mentioned Simon, who had informed about the money against[i] his own country, slandered Oni'as, saying that it was he who had incited He"liodo'rus and had been the real cause of the misfortune. [2]He dared to designate as a plotter against the government the man who was the benefactor of the city, the protector of his fellow countrymen, and a zealot for the laws. [3]When his hatred progressed to such a degree that even murders were committed by one of Simon's approved agents, [4]Oni'as recognized that the rivalry

---

3:24 so great a manifestation: This is the first of the heavenly apparitions noted by the author in the preface. For similar visions of horsemen elsewhere in Scripture, see Zech 1:7–17; Rev 6:1–8. See word study: *Appearances* at 2:21.

3:39 he who has his dwelling ... do it injury: A key thematic statement that prefigures the events that follow in 2 Maccabees. Heliodorus' unsuccessful invasion establishes

that God protects his Temple when the nation and its leaders faithfully obey his covenant, so that the Temple's later desecration under Antiochus can only be the result of the people's disobedience.

4:4 Apollonius, the son of Menestheus: A Seleucid governor known from ancient Greek sources. The author distinguishes him from the previous Apollonius in 3:5. Both of these governors supported Simon in his attempts to undermine the leadership of Onias.

---

[i] Gk *and.*

was serious and that Apollo′nius, the son of Menes′theus [j] and governor of Coe′le-syr′ia and Phoeni′cia, was intensifying the malice of Simon. [5]So he betook himself to the king, not accusing his fellow citizens but having in view the welfare, both public and private, of all the people. [6]For he saw that without the king's attention public affairs could not again reach a peaceful settlement, and that Simon would not stop his folly.

Jason's Reforms

7 When Seleu′cus died and Anti′ochus who was called Epiph′anes succeeded to the kingdom, Jason the brother of Oni′as obtained the high priesthood by corruption, [8]promising the king at an interview[k] three hundred and sixty talents of silver and, from another source of revenue, eighty talents. [9]In addition to this he promised to pay one hundred and fifty more if permission were given to establish by his authority a gymnasium and a body of youth for it, and to enroll the men of Jerusalem as citizens of Antioch. [10]When the king assented and Jason[l] came to office, he at once shifted his countrymen over to the Greek way of life. [11]He set aside the existing royal concessions to the Jews, secured through John the father of Eupol′emus, who went on the mission to establish friendship and alliance with the Romans; and he destroyed the lawful ways of living and introduced new customs contrary to the law. [12]For with alacrity he founded a gymnasium right under the citadel, and he induced the noblest of the young men[m] to wear the Greek hat. [13]There was such an extreme of Hellenization and increase in the adoption of foreign ways because of the surpassing wickedness of Jason, who was ungodly and no high priest, [14]that the priests were no longer intent upon their service at the altar. Despising the sanctuary and neglecting the sacrifices, they hastened to take part in the unlawful proceedings in the wrestling arena after the call to the discus, [15]disdaining the honors prized by their fathers and putting the highest value upon Greek forms of prestige. [16]For this reason heavy disaster overtook them, and those whose ways of living they admired and wished to imitate completely became their enemies and punished them. [17]For it is no light thing to show irreverence to the divine laws—a fact which later events will make clear.

Jason Introduces Greek Customs

18 When the quadrennial games were being held at Tyre and the king was present, [19]the vile Jason sent envoys, chosen as being An″tio′chian citizens from Jerusalem, to carry three hundred silver drachmas for the sacrifice to Hercules. Those who carried the money, however, thought best not to use it for sacrifice, because that was inappropriate, but to expend it for another purpose. [20]So this money was intended by the sender for the sacrifice to Hercules, but by the decision of its carriers it was applied to the construction of triremes.

21 When Apollo′nius the son of Menes′theus was sent to Egypt for the coronation[n] of Phil″ome′tor as king, Anti′ochus learned that Philometor[o] had become hostile to his government, and he took measures for his own security. Therefore upon

---

4:7 **Antiochus:** Antiochus IV Epiphanes, the brother of Seleucus IV, seized the throne upon Seleucus' death. **Jason:** As a brother of Onias, Jason would have been of the traditional high-priestly family, but the manner in which he obtains the position reveals much about what his rule will look like.

4:8 **three hundred and sixty talents:** On the value of talents, see note on 3:11.

4:9 **citizens of Antioch:** Rather than enrolling the men of Jerusalem as citizens in the far-off Seleucid capital, this proposal would have meant turning Jerusalem into an Antioch-in-Jerusalem, adding it to the numerous other Seleucid cities that had adopted the name. Jerusalem would thus have been made into a Greek city, allowing the citizens to follow Greek law and abandon the Torah.

4:11 **John the father of Eupolemus:** Also known from 1 Mac 8:17. He is here credited with obtaining privileges for the Jews from Antiochus III to allow them to follow the Torah rather than Greek laws. John's son Eupolemus later became the Jews' envoy to the Romans and is likely to be identified with the Jewish historian Eupolemus from the same era. See note on 2:1.

4:12 **gymnasium:** A Greek institution where sporting activities were performed naked, which was especially offensive to Jewish moral sensibilities. **citadel:** A fortress in Jerusalem that the Seleucids built up and fortified for their occupation of the area. **Greek hat:** A brimmed hat modeled on the one worn by the Greek god Hermes, which was worn while training and served as a symbol of Greek culture.

4:13 **Hellenization:** The adoption of the Greek (Hellenistic) way of life.

4:16 **heavy disaster:** As the Book of Wisdom states, Israel is disciplined in this manner "that they might learn that one is punished by the very things by which he sins" (Wis 11:16).

4:18 **quadrennial games:** Literally "quinquennial games". The Greek system of counting years, which includes counting the first year, makes this equivalent to four years and what would now be called quadrennial. The games were inaugurated by Alexander after his conquest of Tyre in 332 B.C. **Tyre:** A port city northwest of Judea.

4:19 **Hercules:** Melqart, the traditional god of Tyre, whom the Greeks identified with Hercules.

4:20 **triremes:** An ancient warship with three levels of oars, which was used to sail the Mediterranean by the Phoenicians, Greeks, and Romans.

4:21 **Philometor:** Ptolemy VI, who began ruling in 172 B.C. at the age of 14 and whose advisors were hoping to take Palestine from Seleucid rule. **Joppa:** A port city 40 miles northwest of Jerusalem, which served as the primary seaport for Judea.

---

[j] Vg Compare verse 21: Gk uncertain.

[k] Or *by a petition.*

[l] Gk *he.*

[m] Some authorities add *subjecting them.*

[n] The exact meaning of the Greek word is uncertain.

[o] Gk *he.*

arriving at Joppa he proceeded to Jerusalem. ²²He was welcomed magnificently by Jason and the city, and ushered in with a blaze of torches and with shouts. Then he marched into Phoeni'cia.

Menelaus Becomes High Priest

23 After a period of three years Jason sent Menela'us, the brother of the previously mentioned Simon, to carry the money to the king and to complete the records of essential business. ²⁴But he, when presented to the king, extolled him with an air of authority, and secured the high priesthood for himself, outbidding Jason by three hundred talents of silver. ²⁵After receiving the king's orders he returned, possessing no qualification for the high priesthood, but having the hot temper of a cruel tyrant and the rage of a savage wild beast. ²⁶So Jason, who after supplanting his own brother was supplanted by another man, was driven as a fugitive into the land of Am'mon. ²⁷And Menela'us held the office, but he did not pay regularly any of the money promised to the king. ²⁸When Sos'tratus the captain of the citadel kept requesting payment, for the collection of the revenue was his responsibility, the two of them were summoned by the king on account of this issue. ²⁹Menela'us left his own brother Lysim'achus as deputy in the high priesthood, while Sos'tratus left Cra'tes, the commander of the Cyprian troops.*

The Murder of Onias; and the Punishment of Andronicus

30 While such was the state of affairs, it happened that the people of Tarsus and of Mallus revolted because their cities had been given as a present to Anti'ochis, the king's concubine. ³¹So the king went hastily to settle the trouble, leaving Andron'icus, a man of high rank, to act as his deputy. ³²But Menela'us, thinking he had obtained a suitable opportunity, stole some of the gold vessels of the temple and gave them to Andron'icus; other vessels, as it happened, he had sold to Tyre and the neighboring cities. ³³When Oni'as became fully aware of these acts he publicly exposed them, having first withdrawn to a place of sanctuary at Daphne near Antioch. ³⁴Therefore

---

4:22 Phoenicia: The coastal region northwest of Palestine, whose main cities included Tyre and Sidon.

---

*4:29: Vulgate reads: "And Menelaus was removed from the priesthood, Lysimachus his brother succeeding: and Sostratus was made governor of the Cyprians."

CITIES IN JUDEA AND SELEUCID TERRITORY

4:23–25 The genealogy of Menelaus presents a number of complications. Menelaus is here presented as the brother of the aforementioned Simon, who is of the tribe of Benjamin (3:4), a lineage that would make him unqualified for the high priesthood (cf. 4:25). However, some manuscripts of 3:4 offer a form of "Bilgah" in place of Benjamin, a tribe that is later disparaged in the Babylonian Talmud for enthusiastically embracing Hellenization and that may have presented at least some qualification for the office (cf. Neh 12:5, 18). Josephus' later testimony complicates the issue even more by identifying Menelaus as the brother of Jason—and thus qualified for the high priesthood as a member of the Oniad family—which most scholars suspect to be due to Josephus' confusing of Menelaus' brother Simon with an earlier Oniad Simon. While a conclusive solution is not possible at present, the Septuagint's reading of "Benjamin" is here taken as most likely to be original.

4:23 three years: Probably referring to the time since the appointment of Jason, and not the events of 4:21–22. **Menelaus:** The brother of Simon and likewise a usurper of the high priesthood. See note on 4:23–25.

4:24 by three hundred talents: Nearly double the previous tribute amount of 360 talents under Jason.

4:26 land of Ammon: The region east of the Jordan River.

4:28 Sostratus: The commander of the Seleucid forces stationed in Jerusalem at the citadel.

4:29 Lysimachus: A brother of Menelaus who proves to be of similar character. **Crates:** A commander of mercenary troops from Cyprus.

4:30 Tarsus . . . Mallus: Seleucid cities in the region of Cilicia, northwest of Antioch. **Antiochis:** A mistress of the king, holding a place within the household but not given the full status of a wife. It was common for kings to give cities to a wife or concubine so that she could draw revenue from the taxes.

4:31 Andronicus: Possibly Andronicus the Macedonian, attested by the historian Livy as the commander who successfully protected Ephesus when attacked by the Romans (190 B.C.).

4:33 place of sanctuary: A place protected by law or custom to which one could go when fearing an attack. **Daphne:** A city five miles from Antioch that had a sanctuary dedicated to Apollo and Artemis.

Menela'us, taking Andron'icus aside, urged him to kill Oni'as. Andronicus[p] came to Onias, and resorting to treachery offered him sworn pledges and gave him his right hand, and in spite of his suspicion persuaded Onias[q] to come out from the place of sanctuary; then, with no regard for justice, he immediately put him out of the way.* ³⁵For this reason not only Jews, but many also of other nations, were grieved and displeased at the unjust murder of the man. ³⁶When the king returned from the region of Cili'cia, the Jews in the city[r] appealed to him with regard to the unreasonable murder of Oni'as, and the Greeks shared their hatred of the crime. ³⁷Therefore Anti'ochus was grieved at heart and filled with pity, and wept because of the moderation and good conduct of the deceased; ³⁸and inflamed with anger, he immediately stripped off the purple robe from Andron'icus, tore off his garments, and led him about the whole city to that very place where he had committed the outrage against Oni'as, and there he dispatched the bloodthirsty fellow. The Lord thus repaid him with the punishment he deserved.

Unpopularity of Lysimachus and Menelaus

39 When many acts of sacrilege had been committed in the city by Lysim'achus with the connivance of Menela'us, and when report of them had spread abroad, the populace gathered against Lysimachus, because many of the gold vessels had already been stolen. ⁴⁰And since the crowds were becoming aroused and filled with anger, Lysim'achus armed about three thousand men and launched an unjust attack, under the leadership of a certain Aura'nus,† a man advanced in years and no less advanced in folly. ⁴¹But when the Jews[s] became aware of Lysim'achus' attack, some picked up stones, some blocks of wood, and others took handfuls of the ashes that were lying about, and threw them in wild confusion at Lysimachus and his men. ⁴²As a result, they wounded many of them, and killed some, and put them all to flight; and the temple robber himself they killed close by the treasury.

43 Charges were brought against Menela'us about this incident. ⁴⁴When the king came to Tyre, three men sent by the senate presented the case before him. ⁴⁵But Menela'us, already as good as beaten, promised a substantial bribe to Ptol'emy son of Dorym'enes to win over the king. ⁴⁶Therefore Ptol'emy, taking the king aside into a colonnade as if for refreshment, induced the king to change his mind. ⁴⁷Menela'us, the cause of all the evil, he acquitted of the charges against him, while he sentenced to death those unfortunate men, who would have been freed uncondemned if they had pleaded even before Scyth'ians. ⁴⁸And so those who had spoken for the city and the villages[t] and the holy vessels quickly suffered the unjust penalty. ⁴⁹Therefore even the Ty'rians, showing their hatred of the crime, provided magnificently for their funeral. ⁵⁰But Menela'us, because of the cupidity of those in power, remained in office, growing in wickedness, having become the chief plotter against his fellow citizens.

Jason Tries to Regain Control

5 About this time Anti'ochus made his second invasion of Egypt. ²And it happened that over all the city, for almost forty days, there appeared golden-clad horsemen charging through the air, in companies fully armed with lances and drawn swords—³troops of horsemen drawn up, attacks and counterattacks made on this side and on that, brandishing of shields, massing of spears, hurling of missiles, the flash of golden trappings, and armor of all sorts. ⁴Therefore all men prayed that the apparition might prove to have been a good omen.

5 When a false rumor arose that Anti'ochus was dead, Jason took no less than a thousand men and suddenly made an assault upon the city. When the troops upon the wall had been forced back and at last the city was being taken, Menela'us took refuge in the citadel. ⁶But Jason kept relentlessly slaughtering his fellow citizens, not realizing that success at the cost of one's kindred is the greatest misfortune, but imagining that he was setting up trophies of victory over enemies and not over fellow countrymen. ⁷He did not gain control of the government, however; and in the end got only

---

4:36 Cilicia: A region within Seleucid control to the northwest of Antioch.

4:39–42 The crowd's revolt against the leadership of Menelaus and Lysimachus illustrates the continued strength of the opposition to Hellenization in Jerusalem.

4:40 Auranus: Otherwise unknown.

4:44 senate: See note on 1:10.

4:45 Ptolemy son of Dorymenes: Another of Antiochus' generals. This is likely the same Ptolemy who shows hostility

to the Jews in 6:8 and 8:8–9 and evidently distinguished from Ptolemy Macron in 10:12, who is favorable toward the Jews.

4:47 Scythians: A nomadic people with a particular reputation for cruelty in the ancient world.

4:49 Tyrians: Citizens of Tyre.

5:1 second invasion of Egypt: The first invasion, passed over here, is described in 1 Mac 1:16–19. See also Dan 11:15–20, which similarly describes two invasions by the "king of the north". Since 2 Maccabees gives a synopsis of a larger history (see 2:23), events from both of Antiochus' appearances in Jerusalem may be synthesized in the account that follows.

5:2–3 The second of the heavenly visions spoken of in 2:21, though one that signals Jerusalem's impending judgment due to its repeated violations of the covenant.

5:5 Jason: See note on 4:7.

5:7 Ammonites: See note on 4:26.

---

*4:34, *put him out of the way*: Vulgate has "slew him."
†4:40, *Auranus*: Vulgate has "Tyrannus."
[p]Gk *He.*
[q]Gk *him.*
[r]Or *in each city.*
[s]Gk *they.*
[t]Other authorities read *the people.*

disgrace from his conspiracy, and fled again into the country of the Am'monites. [8]Finally he met a miserable end. Accused[u] before Ar'etas the ruler of the Arabs, fleeing from city to city, pursued by all men, hated as a rebel against the laws, and abhorred as the executioner of his country and his fellow citizens, he was cast ashore in Egypt; [9]and he who had driven many from their own country into exile died in exile, having embarked to go to the Lac"edaemo'nians in hope of finding protection because of their kinship. [10]He who had cast out many to lie unburied had no one to mourn for him; he had no funeral of any sort and no place in the tomb of his fathers.

11 When news of what had happened reached the king, he took it to mean that Judea was in revolt. So, raging inwardly, he left Egypt and took the city by storm. [12]And he commanded his soldiers to cut down relentlessly every one they met and to slay those who went into the houses. [13]Then there was killing of young and old, destruction of boys, women, and children, and slaughter of virgins and infants. [14]Within the total of three days eighty thousand were destroyed, forty thousand in hand-to-hand fighting; and as many were sold into slavery as were slain.

Pillage of the Temple

15 Not content with this, Anti'ochus[v] dared to enter the most holy temple in all the world, guided by Menela'us, who had become a traitor both to the laws and to his country. [16]He took the holy vessels with his polluted hands, and swept away with profane hands the votive offerings which other kings had made to enhance the glory and honor of the place. [17]Anti'ochus was elated in spirit, and did not perceive that the Lord was angered for a little while because of the sins of those who dwelt in the city, and that therefore he was disregarding the holy place. [18]But if it had not happened that they were involved in many sins, this man would have been scourged and turned back from his rash act as soon as he came forward, just as He"liodo'rus was, whom Seleu'cus the king sent to inspect the treasury. [19]But the Lord did not choose the nation for the sake of the holy place, but the place for the sake of the nation. [20]Therefore the place itself shared in the misfortunes that befell the nation and afterward participated in its benefits; and what was forsaken in the wrath of the Almighty was restored again in all its glory when the great Lord became reconciled.

21 So Anti'ochus carried off eighteen hundred talents from the temple, and hurried away to Antioch, thinking in his arrogance that he could sail on the land and walk on the sea, because his mind was elated. [22]And he left governors to afflict the people: at Jerusalem, Philip, by birth a Phryg'ian and in character more barbarous than the man who appointed him; [23]and at Ger'izim, Andron'icus; and besides these Menela'us, who lorded it over his fellow citizens worse than the others did. In his malice toward the Jewish citizens,[w] [24]Anti'ochus[x] sent Apollo'nius, the captain of the Mysians, with an army of twenty-two thousand, and commanded him to slay all the grown men and to sell the women and boys as slaves. [25]When this man arrived in Jerusalem, he pretended to be peaceably disposed and waited until the holy sabbath day; then, finding the Jews not at work, he ordered his men to parade under arms. [26]He put to the sword all those who came out to see them, then rushed into the city with his armed men and killed great numbers of people.

27 But Judas Mac"cabe'us, with about nine others, got away to the wilderness, and kept himself and his

---

5:8 Aretas: Aretas I, a Nabatean king in Arabia, southeast of the Dead Sea.

5:9 Lacedaemonians: The region of the Spartans in southern Greece, with whom the Jews believed to hold kinship (cf. 1 Mac 12:19–23).

5:19 for the sake of the nation: Christ similarly teaches that God does not create people simply for the sake of his institutes but, rather, gives institutes for the good of his people. Just as the Sabbath is created for man, rather than man for the Sabbath (Mk 2:27), so too is the Temple made for the nation of Israel, rather than the nation made for the Temple.

5:21 eighteen hundred talents: A tremendous sum, likely a combination of the previously mentioned deposits (3:11) and the Temple's sacred 'vessels. **sail on the land and walk on the sea:** An allusion to the Persian king Xerxes I (513–465 B.C.), who out of pride made a navigable canal around Athens and bridged the river Strymon, only to be repelled and made to flee in a single boat (Herodotus, *Histories* 7, 24; Josephus, *Jewish War* 2, 358). In a famous passage, Xerxes' uncle warns

him that his efforts will only cause God to strike him down for his pride, which the author's allusion shows will apply equally to Antiochus (Herodotus, *Histories* 7, 10).

5:22 governors to afflict the people: Antiochus' actions are described in the same terms as Pharaoh's, who similarly appointed "governors" (LXX: *epistatai*) to afflict the Hebrews in Ex 1:11. **Philip ... a Phrygian:** A mercenary from Asia Minor whom Antiochus appoints to punish those who sought to continue Sabbath observance (6:11) and who appeals for help when Judas begins his campaigns (8:8).

5:23 Gerizim: The mountain near Shechem that was regarded by Samaritans as the sacred place of worship (cf. Jn 4:20). **Andronicus:** Different from the Andronicus of 4:31 (whom Antiochus killed) and otherwise unknown.

5:24 Apollonius: The leader of Antiochus' mercenary army from Mysia (northwest Asia Minor) and likely the same person as the unnamed commander in 1 Mac 1:29.

5:27 got away to the wilderness: Judas and his companions take refuge in the wilderness, following the pattern of righteous leaders like Moses (Ex 3:1), David (1 Sam 23:14), and Elijah (1 Kings 19:3–9). **live on what grew wild:** Literally "grassy food". Rather than eat unclean food, Judas and his friends sustain themselves on wild herbs so as to not violate the Torah's food laws.

---

[u]Cn: Gk *Imprisoned.*
[v]Gk *he.*
[w]Or *worse than the others did in his malice toward the Jewish citizens.*
[x]Gk *he.*

companions alive in the mountains as wild animals do; they continued to live on what grew wild, so that they might not share in the defilement.

The Suppression of Judaism

6 Not long after this, the king sent an Athenian[y] senator[z] to compel the Jews to forsake the laws of their fathers and cease to live by the laws of God, [2]and also to pollute the temple in Jerusalem and call it the temple of Olympian Zeus, and to call the one in Ger'izim the temple of Zeus the Friend of Strangers, as did the people who dwelt in that place.

3 Harsh and utterly grievous was the onslaught of evil. [4]For the temple was filled with debauchery and reveling by the Gentiles, who dallied with harlots and had intercourse with women within the sacred precincts, and besides brought in things for sacrifice that were unfit. [5]The altar was covered with abominable offerings which were forbidden by the laws. [6]A man could neither keep the sabbath, nor observe the feasts of his fathers, nor so much as confess himself to be a Jew.

7 On the monthly celebration of the king's birthday, the Jews[a] were taken, under bitter constraint, to partake of the sacrifices; and when the feast of Diony'sus came, they were compelled to walk in the procession in honor of Dionysus, wearing wreaths of ivy. [8]At the suggestion of Ptol'emy a decree was issued to the neighboring Greek cities, that they should adopt the same policy toward the Jews and make them partake of the sacrifices, [9]and should slay those who did not choose to change over to Greek customs. One could see, therefore, the misery that had come upon them. [10]For example, two women were brought in for having circumcised their children. These women they publicly paraded about the city, with their babies hung at their breasts, then hurled them down headlong from the wall. [11]Others who had assembled in the caves near by, to observe the seventh day secretly, were betrayed to Philip and were all burned together, because their piety kept them from defending themselves, in view of their regard for that most holy day.

Providential Significance of the Persecution

12 Now I urge those who read this book not to be depressed by such calamities, but to recognize that these punishments were designed not to destroy but to discipline our people. [13]In fact, not to let the impious alone for long, but to punish them immediately, is a sign of great kindness. [14]For in the case of the other nations the Lord waits patiently to punish them until they have reached the full measure of their sins; but he does not deal in this way with us, [15]in order that he may not take vengeance on us afterward when our sins have reached their height. [16]Therefore he never withdraws his mercy from us. Though he disciplines us with calamities, he does not forsake his own people. [17]Let what we have said serve as a reminder; we must go on briefly with the story.

The Martyrdom of Eleazar

18 Elea'zar, one of the scribes in high position, a man now advanced in age and of noble presence, was being forced to open his mouth to eat swine's flesh. [19]But he, welcoming death with honor rather than life with pollution, went up to the rack of his own accord, spitting out the flesh, [20]as men ought to go who have the courage to refuse things that it is not right to taste, even for the natural love of life.

21 Those who were in charge of that unlawful sacrifice took the man aside, because of their long acquaintance with him, and privately urged him to bring meat of his own providing, proper for him to use, and pretend that he was eating the flesh of the sacrificial meal which had been commanded by the king, [22]so that by doing this he might be saved from death, and be treated kindly on account of his old friendship with them. [23]But making a high resolve, worthy of his years and the dignity of his old age and the gray hairs which he had reached

---

•

6:1 Athenian senator: A leader from Athens who was either a senator or named Geron (a proper name that also means "senator"). **laws of their fathers:** The laws of Moses. Antiochus' compulsion to suppress the Jewish way of life was unusual, as conquering kings typically left ancestral laws in place. Antiochus likely saw Torah observance as undermining his own authority.

6:2 Olympian Zeus: The chief among the Greek gods, Zeus is often referred to as an Olympian after Mt. Olympus, the place where he was believed to reside. **the Friend of Strangers:** The Greek in this passage is ambiguous and may mean that the Samaritans requested their temple be called by this name or that the temple was so named in honor of the Samaritans' hospitality to the Greeks.

6:7 Dionysus: The Greek god of wine, often depicted with a wreath of ivy on his head, whose feast was celebrated once or twice a year.

6:8 Ptolemy: See note on 4:45.

6:11 betrayed: Suggests that those observing the Sabbath were given over by their own kin. **Philip:** See note on 5:22.

6:12–17 The author makes explicit one of the book's central themes: that those whom the Lord has chosen are quick to receive his discipline. This biblical principle appears elsewhere in Amos 3:2, 1 Cor 11:32, and Rev 3:19.

6:18 Eleazar: A Jewish scribe who serves as the hero of the following section by his refusal to violate the Torah's food laws.

6:19 the rack: A torture device that stretched one's limbs in opposite directions, often accompanied with floggings. Hebrews 11:35 alludes to this by using the rare Greek verb *tympanizō*, calling to mind the rack (the Greek noun *tympanos*) described in this passage.

---

[y] Some authorities read *Antiochian*.
[z] Or *Geron an Athenian*.
[a] Gk *they*.

2 Maccabees 6, 7

with distinction and his excellent life even from childhood, and moreover according to the holy God-given law, he declared himself quickly, telling them to send him to Hades.

24 "Such pretense is not worthy of our time of life," he said, "lest many of the young should suppose that Elea′zar in his ninetieth year has gone over to an alien religion, 25and through my pretense, for the sake of living a brief moment longer, they should be led astray because of me, while I defile and disgrace my old age. 26For even if for the present I should avoid the punishment of men, yet whether I live or die I shall not escape the hands of the Almighty. 27Therefore, by manfully giving up my life now, I will show myself worthy of my old age 28and leave to the young a noble example of how to die a good death willingly and nobly for the revered and holy laws."

When he had said this, he went[b] at once to the rack. 29And those who a little before had acted toward him with good will now changed to ill will, because the words he had uttered were in their opinion sheer madness.[c] 30When he was about to die under the blows, he groaned aloud and said: "It is clear to the Lord in his holy knowledge that, though I might have been saved from death, I am enduring terrible sufferings in my body under this beating, but in my soul I am glad to suffer these things because I fear him."

31 So in this way he died, leaving in his death an example of nobility and a memorial of courage, not only to the young but to the great body of his nation.

The Martyrdom of the Seven Brothers

7 It happened also that seven brothers and their mother were arrested and were being compelled by the king, under torture with whips and cords, to partake of unlawful swine's flesh. 2One of them, acting as their spokesman, said, "What do you intend to ask and learn from us? For we are ready to die rather than transgress the laws of our fathers."

3 The king fell into a rage, and gave orders that pans and caldrons be heated. 4These were heated immediately, and he commanded that the tongue of their spokesman be cut out and that they scalp him and cut off his hands and feet, while the rest of the brothers and the mother looked on. 5When he was utterly helpless, the king[d] ordered them to take him to the fire, still breathing, and to fry him in a pan. The smoke from the pan spread widely, but the brothers[e] and their mother encouraged one another to die nobly, saying, 6"The Lord God is watching over us and in truth has compassion on us, as Moses declared in his song which bore witness against the

---

6:24 ninetieth year: Eleazar's testimony became an example for early Christian martyrs such as Polycarp, who, when threatened with public tortures and death by the Roman proconsul, declares with strikingly similar language: "Eighty and six years have I served him, and he never did me any injury: How then can I blaspheme my King and my Savior?" (*Martyrdom of Polycarp* 9).

6:28 the young a noble example: The following martyrdoms of the seven young brothers, which serve to turn away God's wrath from Israel (7:38), are here traced back to Eleazar's fidelity, showing the power of one faithful individual to influence the fate of a whole nation.

7:1–42 The martyrdom of the mother and her seven sons is the most famous passage in 2 Maccabees. It is alluded to in Heb 11:35 and (together with Eleazar's martyrdom) serves as the basis for *4 Maccabees*, a later theological reflection on these events that is included as an appendix in some Russian Orthodox Bibles. • Augustine describes how the martyrs' zeal to preserve God's former sacraments should inspire Christians for the new: "If we feel the strongest admiration for the Maccabees, who refused to touch food that Christians lawfully use, how much more should a Christian in our day be ready to suffer all things for Christ's Baptism, for Christ's Eucharist, for Christ's sacred sign, since these are proofs of the accomplishment of what the former sacraments only pointed forward to in the future!" (*Against Faustus* 19, 14). • St. Gregory Nazianzen's fourth-century homily on the Maccabean martyrs' feast day commemorates them as worthy of universal recognition and as examples of the saints in the

Old Testament who were "pure in mind" and knew the Word before his advent (*Oration* 15, 1). These martyrs were "a living sacrifice, holy and acceptable to God" (Rom 12:1), which was purer and more splendid than any sacrifices prescribed by the law (*Oration* 15, 3).

7:1 and their mother: No mention is made of the martyrs' father, a fact that some Christian readers found significant. • "Martyrs who witness themselves as the sons of God in suffering are now no more counted as of any father but God, as in the Gospel the Lord teaches, saying, 'Call no man your father upon earth; for one is your Father, which is in heaven'" (St. Cyprian, *Exhortation to Martyrdom* 11). **compelled by the king:** The text does not identify the location of these events, but evidence from early reception suggests they took place in Antioch, the seat of King Antiochus. **swine's flesh:** The Torah lists pigs among foods that are unclean and thus unlawful for Israelites to eat (Lev 11:7). While *4 Maccabees* 8, 25, testifies that the Law of Moses would not have condemned the brothers to death for this violation, they choose to lose their lives rather than to violate God's commandments.

7:6 compassion on his servants: The figures here encourage one another with a promise from the Song of Moses in Deut 32, in which Moses foretells that though Israel will turn away from God and incur severe chastisement, God will once again restore his people and "have compassion on his servants" when their strength has run out (Deut 32:36). As the context of the passage makes clear, this restoration is understood in terms of life after death, which provides them with hope even as the first brother burns to death (7:5). • Writing amidst the violent persecutions of the third century A.D., Origen commends Christians to recite the Maccabean martyrs' words—"The Lord God is watching over us and in truth has compassion on us"—before their torturers (*Exhortation to Martyrdom*, 23).

---

[b] Other authorities read *was dragged.*
[c] The Greek text of this verse is uncertain.
[d] Gk *he.*
[e] Gk *they.*

people to their faces, when he said, 'And he will have compassion on his servants.'"

7 After the first brother had died in this way, they brought forward the second for their sport. They tore off the skin of his head with the hair, and asked him, "Will you eat rather than have your body punished limb by limb?" ⁸He replied in the language of his fathers, and said to them, "No." Therefore he in turn underwent tortures as the first brother had done. ⁹And when he was at his last breath, he said, "You accursed wretch, you dismiss us from this present life, but the King of the universe will raise us up to an everlasting renewal of life,* because we have died for his laws."

10 After him, the third was the victim of their sport. When it was demanded, he quickly put out his tongue and courageously stretched forth his hands, ¹¹and said nobly, "I got these from Heaven, and because of his laws I disdain them, and from him I hope to get them back again." ¹²As a result the king himself and those with him were astonished at the young man's spirit, for he regarded his sufferings as nothing.

13 When he too had died, they maltreated and tortured the fourth in the same way. ¹⁴And when he was near death, he said, "One cannot but choose to die at the hands of men and to cherish the hope that God gives of being raised again by him. But for you there will be no resurrection to life!"

7:9 everlasting renewal of life: See essay, *Resurrection in the Old Testament*.

---

*7:9, *to an everlasting renewal of life*: Vulgate has: "in the resurrection of eternal life."

Resurrection in the Old Testament

It is sometimes said that the Old Testament presents no clear vision of life after death, and there is much to support this claim. Those who have died are described as being gathered to their "fathers" (Gen 15:15; 2 Kings 22:20) or going down to "the Pit" or "Sheol", where the dead can no longer praise God (Ps 6:5; 30:9; cf. Job 10:21–22; Is 38:18). God's justice is often described in terms of consequences that extend to future generations (Ex 20:5–6; Num 14:18), but without reference to individual judgment after death. To be sure, certain passages seem to suggest possibilities beyond silence in the grave, such as Enoch "walking with God" (Gen 5:24), Job's anticipation of seeing his Redeemer after his flesh is destroyed (Job 19:25–27), Samuel being summoned from the dead by the Witch of Endor (1 Sam 28), and Elijah being taken up in a chariot (2 Kings 2:11). Nevertheless, in contrast with the testimony of Christ and the apostles, clear expressions of what happens to human beings after death are seldom found in the writings of the Old Testament.

There are definite exceptions to this rule, however, and none is more striking than 2 Mac 7. Within this chapter, we find repeated articulations of a resurrection to life and to death (7:9, 11, 14, 23, 29, 36) that are so clear that one may suspect he has accidentally opened to the New Testament! This idea is not simply stated but, indeed, serves as the theological linchpin of the entire narrative, as the reality of resurrection is what drives the mother and her sons to serve God faithfully to the point of death and, thus, redeem Israel by their fidelity (cf. 2 Mac 7:38). This passage aligns closely with the testimony of Dan 12, which similarly describes how the dead will rise to everlasting life or judgment (Dan 12:1–3). The prophets Ezekiel and Isaiah likewise contain references to physical resurrection, with Ezekiel witnessing God's reconstitution of Israel's dead in the vision of the Valley of Dry Bones (Ezek 37:1–14) and Isaiah testifying that the bodies of the deceased will rise and the earth give birth to the dead (Is 26:19).

While commentators rightly point out that some resurrection passages, particularly those in Ezekiel and Isaiah, serve as analogies for what will happen when the nation of Israel is restored from exile, this very point serves to demonstrate the existence of some notion of physical resurrection in these contexts. Analogies make use of things that are familiar in order to describe things that are unfamiliar. As such, individual resurrection works as an analogy only if it is more familiar to the audience than national restoration. An analogy that explained an unknown term by an even more unknown term would be a useless analogy: it would be like answering the question of "What's a dinosaur?" by saying "It's like a Stegosaurus!" Indeed, considering that the Hebrews dwelt for centuries among the Egyptians, whose religious system was fixated upon preparation for the afterlife, it would be extraordinary if the people of Israel had no conception at all of future life after death—even if what precisely this life might be like was not yet clear.

In sum, we can regard the Old Testament's testimony on the resurrection as well represented by the conflict between the Sadducees and Pharisees in Acts 23:6–8. The Sadducees regarded only the Bible's first five books (the Pentateuch) as authoritative, which they took as an insufficient basis for belief in the resurrection and, thus, denied the idea. By contrast, the Pharisees' acceptance of the wider canon, including the Prophets and other writings, gave them a great deal more evidence for the resurrection and led to their insistence upon it as a future reality. Second Maccabees offers the fullest and clearest statement of this Jewish expectation, which nevertheless still remains only a vague hope for the future—that is, until it becomes an event in Israel's history, with the resurrection of the Messiah as the first-born from the dead (Col 1:18; Rev 1:5).

15 Next they brought forward the fifth and maltreated him. [16]But he looked at the king,[f] and said, "Because you have authority among men, mortal though you are, you do what you please. But do not think that God has forsaken our people. [17]Keep on, and see how his mighty power will torture you and your descendants!"

18 After him they brought forward the sixth. And when he was about to die, he said, "Do not deceive yourself in vain. For we are suffering these things on our own account, because of our sins against our own God. Therefore[g] astounding things have happened. [19]But do not think that you will go unpunished for having tried to fight against God!"

20 The mother was especially admirable and worthy of honorable memory. Though she saw her seven sons perish within a single day, she bore it with good courage because of her hope in the Lord. [21]She encouraged each of them in the language of their fathers. Filled with a noble spirit, she fired her woman's reasoning with a man's courage, and said to them, [22]"I do not know how you came into being in my womb. It was not I who gave you life and breath, nor I who set in order the elements within each of you. [23]Therefore the Creator of the world, who shaped the beginning of man and devised the origin of all things, will in his mercy give life and breath back to you again, since you now forget yourselves for the sake of his laws."

24 Anti'ochus felt that he was being treated with contempt, and he was suspicious of her reproachful tone. The youngest brother being still alive, Antiochus[h] not only appealed to him in words, but promised with oaths that he would make him rich and enviable if he would turn from the ways of his fathers, and that he would take him for his friend and entrust him with public affairs. [25]Since the young man would not listen to him at all, the

king called the mother to him and urged her to advise the youth to save himself. [26]After much urging on his part, she undertook to persuade her son. [27]But, leaning close to him, she spoke in their native tongue as follows, deriding the cruel tyrant: "My son, have pity on me. I carried you nine months in my womb, and nursed you for three years, and have reared you and brought you up to this point in your life, and have taken care of you.[i] [28]I beg you, my child, to look at the heaven and the earth and see everything that is in them, and recognize that God did not make them out of things that existed.[j] Thus also mankind comes into being. [29]Do not fear this butcher, but prove worthy of your brothers. Accept death, so that in God's mercy I may get you back again with your brothers."

30 While she was still speaking, the young man said, "What are you[k] waiting for? I will not obey the king's command, but I obey the command of the law that was given to our fathers through Moses. [31]But you,[l] who have contrived all sorts of evil against the Hebrews, will certainly not escape the hands of God. [32]For we are suffering because of our own sins. [33]And if our living Lord is angry for a little while, to rebuke and discipline us, he will again be reconciled with his own servants. [34]But you, unholy wretch, you most defiled of all men, do not be elated in vain and puffed up by uncertain hopes, when you raise your hand against the children of heaven. [35]You have not yet escaped the judgment of the almighty, all-seeing God. [36]For our brothers after enduring a brief suffering have drunk[m] of everflowing life under God's covenant; but you, by the judgment of God, will receive just punishment for your arrogance. [37]I, like my brothers, give up body and life for the laws of our fathers, appealing to God to show mercy soon to our nation and by afflictions and plagues to make you confess that he alone is God, [38]and through me and my brothers to

---

7:24 friend: A privileged position as part of the king's court.

7:28 not ... out of things that existed: The *Catechism of the Catholic Church* cites the mother's testimony in this passage as a witness to the doctrine of creation *ex nihilo*—that is, the idea that God created everything out of nothing rather than from preexistent material. As the *Catechism* states, it follows from this doctrine that "since God could create everything out of nothing, he can also, through the Holy Spirit, give spiritual life to sinners by creating a pure heart in them and bodily life to the dead through the Resurrection. God 'gives life to the dead and calls into existence the things that do not exist'" (Rom 4:17; CCC 297–98).

7:38 end the wrath: The martyrs' hope that their suffering will bring an end to God's wrath is fulfilled with the rise of Judas Maccabee, whose counterattack is granted success with God's wrath now being turned to mercy in 8:5. This provides the backstory to 1 Maccabees' account of Judas turning away God's wrath (1 Mac 3:8). • 2 Mac 7 offers perhaps the clearest example of substitutionary atonement before the advent of Christ. Like the Suffering Servant of Isaiah 53, the suffering of these righteous representatives of Israel serves to elicit God's mercy and provides atonement for the nation in a time when the Temple could no longer offer sacrifices to God (cf. 6:1–6). Rather than being a new Christian idea, then, the belief that the sufferings of the righteous could bring atonement for others was already made familiar in Christ's time by the Maccabean martyrs. We can then understand the sacrifices of these martyrs and Christ as similar in kind but infinitely distinct in degree; while the faithfulness of these martyrs is so great that God's wrath is turned away from an entire nation, the infinite worth of the perfect Lamb of God takes away the sin of the whole world (Jn 1:29; 1 Jn 2:2). Paul appeals to the same principle in Gal 3, where he explains how Christ

---

[f] Gk *him.*
[g] Lat: other authorities omit *Therefore.*
[h] Gk *he.*
[i] Or *have borne the burden of your education.*
[j] Or *God made them out of things that did not exist.*
[k] The Greek here for *you* is plural.
[l] The Greek here for *you* is singular.
[m] Cn: Gk *fallen.*

bring to an end the wrath of the Almighty which has justly fallen on our whole nation."

39 The king fell into a rage, and handled him worse than the others, being exasperated at his scorn. [40]So he died in his integrity, putting his whole trust in the Lord.

41 Last of all, the mother died, after her sons.

42 Let this be enough, then, about the eating of sacrifices and the extreme tortures.

The Revolt of Judas Maccabeus

8 But Judas, who was also called Mac"cabe'us, and his companions secretly entered the villages and summoned their kinsmen and enlisted those who had continued in the Jewish faith, and so they gathered about six thousand men. [2]They begged the Lord to look upon the people who were oppressed by all, and to have pity on the temple which had been profaned by ungodly men, [3]and to have mercy on the city which was being destroyed and about to be leveled to the ground, and to heed the blood that cried out to him, [4]and to remember also the lawless destruction of the innocent babies and the blasphemies committed against his name, and to show his hatred of evil.

5 As soon as Mac"cabe'us got his army organized, the Gentiles could not withstand him, for the wrath of the Lord had turned to mercy. [6]Coming without warning, he would set fire to towns and villages. He captured strategic positions and put to flight not a few of the enemy. [7]He found the nights most advantageous for such attacks. And talk of his valor spread everywhere.

8 When Philip saw that the man was gaining ground little by little, and that he was pushing ahead with more frequent successes, he wrote to Ptol'emy, the governor of Coe'lesyr'ia and Phoeni'cia, for aid to the king's government. [9]And Ptol'emy[n] promptly appointed Nica'nor the son of Patro'clus, one of the king's chief friends, and sent him, in command of no fewer than twenty thousand Gentiles of all nations, to wipe out the whole race of Judea. He associated with him Gor'gias, a general and a man of experience in military service. [10]Nica'nor determined to make up for the king the tribute due to the Romans, two thousand talents, by selling the captured Jews into slavery. [11]And he immediately sent to the cities on the seacoast, inviting them to buy Jewish slaves and promising to hand over ninety slaves for a talent, not expecting the judgment from the Almighty that was about to overtake him.

Preparation for Battle

12 Word came to Judas concerning Nica'nor's invasion; and when he told his companions of the arrival of the army, [13]those who were cowardly and distrustful of God's justice ran off and got away. [14]Others sold all their remaining property, and at the same time begged the Lord to rescue those who had been sold by the ungodly Nica'nor before he ever met them, [15]if not for their own sake, yet for the sake of the covenants made with their fathers, and because he had called them by his holy and glorious name. [16]But Mac"cabe'us gathered his men together, to the number of six thousand, and exhorted them not to be frightened by the enemy and not to fear

---

being hung on a tree as accursed, though he was sinless, means that he has taken our curses upon himself and set us free (Gal 3:13–14; cf. Deut 21:23).

7:40 died in his integrity: Why were these seven brothers and their mother martyred, while other faithful Israelites, such as Shadrach, Meshach, and Abednego, were miraculously spared in similar circumstances? According to St. Augustine, the answer is that all of them were spiritually rescued by God, although God's hidden counsel ordained for some to be delivered visibly and others invisibly. While those miraculously rescued offer a demonstration of God's power and an opportunity for their persecutors to repent (such as Nebuchadnezzar, Dan 3:28–29), the martyrs provide an example of Christlike fidelity for believers to imitate and a sign of judgment upon their persecutors, whom God judges to be unworthy to have their actions prevented by his miraculous intervention (see, e.g., *To Victorianus* 5 and *Enarrations on the Psalms* 91, 19).

7:41 Last of all, the mother died: One ancient Jewish text praises the mother with these words: "The moon in heaven, with the stars, does not stand so august as you, who, after lighting the way of your star-like seven sons to piety, stand in honor before God and are firmly set in heaven with them" (*4 Maccabees* 17, 5). • According to St. Gregory Nazianzen, this mother's sacrifice is even greater than that of Abraham, as his willingness to lose his promised son, Isaac, is

surpassed by the seven she willingly sees tortured and killed (*Oration* 15, 4).

8:3 the blood that cried out: The phrase used in Gen 4:10 to describe the innocent blood of Abel that cries out to God. See also Deut 32:43; Heb 12:24.

8:5 The wrath ... turned to mercy: The suffering of those who gave their lives for the Law in the previous chapters is shown to be effective, as Israel sees God turning their enemies' plans toward their own destruction. This is highlighted especially in the case of Nicanor in 8:34–35.

8:8 Philip: See note on 5:22. **Ptolemy:** This is likely Ptolemy son of Dorymenes, the general noted in 4:45 and 6:8 (cf. 1 Mac 3:38). **governor of Coele-syria and Phoenicia:** See note on 3:5.

8:9 Nicanor: A recurring foe in this narrative, whose significance is such that his final defeat becomes a national holiday among the Jews (cf. 1 Mac 3:38; 7:26). **Gorgias:** Judas' main opponent in this battle in the account in 1 Mac 3:38–4:25.

8:10 tribute due: The Seleucids owed massive annual tribute to the Romans in accordance with the treaty of Apamea, signed following Antiochus III's defeat in 188 B.C. They viewed the Jewish uprising as an opportunity to make up for lost finances.

8:11 ninety slaves ... a talent: A very low price for slaves—less than half the normal rate—possibly indicating Nicanor's low valuation of the Jewish people. Setting the price this low would also create a huge market for these slaves, allowing Nicanor to sell off Judea's troublesome inhabitants quickly and quell the uprising.

---

the great multitude of Gentiles who were wickedly
coming against them, but to fight nobly, [17]keeping
before their eyes the lawless outrage which the
Gentiles[o] had committed against the holy place,
and the torture of the derided city, and besides,
the overthrow of their ancestral way of life. [18]"For
they trust to arms and acts of daring," he said, "but
we trust in the Almighty God, who is able with a
single nod to strike down those who are coming
against us and even the whole world."

19 Moreover, he told them of the times when
help came to their ancestors; both the time of Sennach'erib, when one hundred and eighty-five thousand perished, [20]and the time of the battle with
the Galatians that took place in Babylonia, when
eight thousand in all went into the affair, with four
thousand Macedonians; and when the Macedonians
were hard pressed, the eight thousand, by the help
that came to them from heaven, destroyed one
hundred and twenty thousand and took much booty.

Judas Defeats Nicanor

21 With these words he filled them with good
courage and made them ready to die for their laws
and their country; then he divided his army into four
parts. [22]He appointed his brothers also, Simon and
Joseph and Jonathan, each to command a division,
putting fifteen hundred men under each. [23]Besides,
he appointed Elea'zar to read aloud[p] from the holy
book, and gave the watchword, "God's help"; then,
leading the first division himself, he joined battle
with Nica'nor.

24 With the Almighty as their ally, they slew more
than nine thousand of the enemy, and wounded and
disabled most of Nica'nor's army, and forced them all
to flee. [25]They captured the money of those who had
come to buy them as slaves. After pursuing them for
some distance, they were obliged to return because
the hour was late. [26]For it was the day before the
sabbath, and for that reason they did not continue
their pursuit. [27]And when they had collected the arms
of the enemy and stripped them of their spoils, they
kept the sabbath, giving great praise and thanks to
the Lord, who had preserved them for that day and
allotted it to them as the beginning of mercy. [28]After
the sabbath they gave some of the spoils to those who
had been tortured and to the widows and orphans,
and distributed the rest among themselves and their
children. [29]When they had done this, they made
common supplication and begged the merciful Lord
to be wholly reconciled with his servants.

30 In encounters with the forces of Timothy and
Bacchi'des they killed more than twenty thousand
of them and got possession of some exceedingly
high strongholds, and they divided very much
plunder, giving to those who had been tortured and
to the orphans and widows, and also to the aged,
shares equal to their own. [31]Collecting the arms
of the enemy,[q] they stored them all carefully in
strategic places, and carried the rest of the spoils
to Jerusalem. [32]They killed the commander of
Timothy's forces, a most unholy man, and one who
had greatly troubled the Jews. [33]While they were
celebrating the victory in the city of their fathers,

8:19 Sennacherib: Sennacherib's Assyrian empire covered a territory similar to that of the Seleucid empire in the time of the Maccabees and, thus, served as a natural analogy in the eyes of the Jewish resistance, which once again faced a much stronger foe from the north. God's defeat of Sennacherib's army against all expectations in 701 B.C. (2 Kings 18–19; Is 36–37) provides the blueprint for Jewish hopes in the Maccabean books. See also 15:22 and 1 Mac 7:41.

8:20 battle with the Galatians: While this battle was evidently well known in the time of Judas and his army, history has preserved for us no other information regarding it. The Galatians, a people from Western Europe who relocated to Asia Minor in 278 B.C., had a reputation as fierce warriors. The Jews in Babylon would presumably have been among the substantial number who remained there in the centuries following the Babylonian captivity. **Macedonians:** Likely refers to armies associated with the empire of Alexander of Macedon (= Alexander the Great).

8:21 ready to die: The same phrase used by the seven brothers in 7:2, showing the continuity between the martyrs and Judas' forces in bringing about God's deliverance.

8:22 Simon and Joseph and Jonathan: More on these brothers and their roles in the Maccabean revolt can be found in 1 Maccabees. For Simon, see 1 Mac 5:21–23 and chaps. 12–16; for Jonathan, 1 Mac 9:28—13:26. Joseph may be an alternate name for John in 1 Mac 9:35–36 or an otherwise unknown brother.

8:23 Eleazar: See 1 Mac 6:43–46. **God's help:** A watchword related to the meaning of Eleazar's name, "God has helped."

8:26 sabbath: The author highlights the victorious Maccabees' fidelity in keeping the Sabbath in accordance with the Law, in contrast with the apostates in Jerusalem, whose infidelity led to the city's downfall (4:13–17).

8:28 widows and orphans: Such provisions for the weak again illustrate the concern of Judas' army to keep the Law (e.g., Deut 14:28–29), as well as their adherence to David's example in sharing plunder with non-combatants (1 Sam 30:23–31).

8:30–33 This section summarizes material covered at greater length in 1 Mac 5, which describes Judas' campaign among the Ammonites.

8:30 Timothy: A Seleucid commander with whom the Maccabees fight on multiple occasions (see 10:24–37; 1 Mac 5). Killed at the end of chap. 10, Timothy then reappears at the beginning of chap. 12, meaning that either the compiler has arranged the events thematically rather than chronologically or that there are two Timothys. **Bacchides:** A Seleucid governor who, though only mentioned once in this narrative, is attested in 1 Maccabees to have fought many battles against the Jews. See 1 Mac 7:8–20; 9:1–72.

8:32 commander of Timothy's forces: An unknown figure, perhaps the leader of Timothy's Arab mercenaries mentioned in 1 Mac 5:37–44.

8:33 Callisthenes: Beyond that his punishment is suited to his crimes, nothing else is known of this figure.

---

[o] Gk *they*.
[p] The Greek text of this clause is uncertain.
[q] Gk *their arms*.

they burned those who had set fire to the sacred gates, Callis'thenes and some others, who had fled into one little house; so these received the proper recompense for their impiety.[r]

34 The thrice-accursed Nica'nor, who had brought the thousand merchants to buy the Jews, [35]having been humbled with the help of the Lord by opponents whom he regarded as of the least account, took off his splendid uniform and made his way alone like a runaway slave across the country till he reached Antioch, having succeeded chiefly in the destruction of his own army! [36]Thus he who had undertaken to secure tribute for the Romans by the capture of the people of Jerusalem proclaimed that the Jews had a Defender, and that therefore the Jews were invulnerable, because they followed the laws ordained by him.

The Last Campaign of Antiochus Epiphanes

9 About that time, as it happened, Anti'ochus had retreated in disorder from the region of Persia. [2]For he had entered the city called Persep'olis, and attempted to rob the temples and control the city. Therefore the people rushed to the rescue with arms, and Anti'ochus and his men were defeated,[s] with the result that Antiochus was put to flight by the inhabitants and beat a shameful retreat. [3]While he was in Ecbat'ana, news came to him of what had happened to Nica'nor and the forces of Timothy. [4]Transported with rage, he conceived the idea of turning upon the Jews the injury done by those who had put him to flight; so he ordered his charioteer to drive without stopping until he completed the journey. But the judgment of heaven rode with him! For in his arrogance he said, "When I get there I will make Jerusalem a cemetery of Jews."

5 But the all-seeing Lord, the God of Israel, struck him an incurable and unseen blow. As soon as he ceased speaking he was seized with a pain in his bowels for which there was no relief and with sharp internal tortures—[6]and that very justly, for he had tortured the bowels of others with many and strange inflictions. [7]Yet he did not in any way stop his insolence, but was even more filled with arrogance, breathing fire in his rage against the Jews, and giving orders to hasten the journey. And so it came about that he fell out of his chariot as it was rushing along, and the fall was so hard as to torture every limb of his body. [8]Thus he who had just been thinking that he could command the waves of the sea, in his superhuman arrogance, and imagining that he could weigh the high mountains in a balance, was brought down to earth and carried in a litter, making the power of God manifest to all. [9]And so the ungodly man's body swarmed with worms, and while he was still living in anguish and pain, his flesh rotted away, and because of his stench the whole army felt revulsion at his decay. [10]Because of his intolerable stench no one was able to carry the man who a little while before had thought that he could touch the stars of heaven. [11]Then it was that, broken in spirit, he began to lose much of his arrogance and to come to his senses under the scourge of God, for he was tortured with pain

---

8:34 thrice-accursed: "Thrice" is used as an intensifying prefix, as with the description of Haman in Esther 16:15.

8:35 like a runaway slave: Nicanor, who arrogantly sought to sell the Jews as slaves, is now made like a slave himself. See 8:11.

9:1–29 Antiochus' demise is also narrated in chap. 9, as well as in 1 Mac 6 and by the ancient historians Polybius, Appian, and Josephus. These accounts all report similar stories with slightly varying details, such as the timing of Antiochus' death relative to the Jerusalem Temple's purification and the site of his last Persian temple robbery. In keeping with the author's stated aim of making the material easy to memorize (2:25), these narratives may reflect a thematic organization—the judgment of Israel's oppressors after God's wrath is turned away from his chosen people—rather than a strictly chronological one.

9:1 Antiochus: See note on 1:11.

9:2 Persepolis: The capital of Persia, which had been famously ransacked by Alexander the Great's armies generations prior. The location of these events is contested: 1 Maccabees, Polybius, and Appian identify the city as Elymais; Josephus says "Elymais in Persis"; and 2 Mac 1 says simply Persia. The use of "Persepolis" here may reflect an original source that read a city (*polis*) in Persia or may be employed as the nearest Persian city to Elymais, which was well known

to the Jews, in keeping with the author's aim to present an accessible history (cf. 2:24–31). Given Polybius' testimony that Antiochus robbed most of the temples of Egypt (*Histories* 30, 26), it is also possible that the king's raids were not limited to one location.

9:3 Ecbatana: North of Elymais and Persepolis and well known as the capital of the Medes (cf. Ezra 6:2). **news came to him:** See similarly 1 Mac 6:5–7, where Lysias is the main figure whose defeats are announced.

9:4 judgment of heaven: The recompense promised by the martyred brothers now finds its fulfillment (cf. 7:17, 19, 31, 35–36). **cemetery of Jews:** A promise not only to kill the city's inhabitants, but to render the holy city ceremonially defiled.

9:7 every limb: Like the tortures in Antiochus' bowels, the injuries in every limb harken back to his threats to have the martyrs' bodies "punished limb by limb" (7:7).

9:8 command the waves: The language in this passage evokes both the pride of Xerxes (cf. 5:21) and Isaiah, as well as Ezekiel's oracles against the prideful kings of Babylon (Is 14:12–17) and Tyre (Ezek 28:2).

9:9 swarmed with worms: A common fate for rulers who make themselves God, such as Herod Agrippa in Acts 12:23 and the king of Babylon in Is 14:11. **stench:** This may be an allusion to Joel 2:20: "I will remove the northerner far from you, and drive him into a parched and desolate land ... the stench and foul smell of him will rise."

9:11 scourge of God: Like his deputy Heliodorus in 3:33–39, who was "scourged by heaven", Antiochus himself is now forced to his senses by the affliction from God.

---

[r] The Greek text of this verse is uncertain.
[s] Gk *they were defeated.*

every moment. ¹²And when he could not endure his own stench, he uttered these words: "It is right to be subject to God, and no mortal should think that he is equal to God."ᵗ

Antiochus Makes a Promise to God

13 Then the abominable fellow made a vow to the Lord, who would no longer have mercy on him, stating ¹⁴that the holy city, which he was hastening to level to the ground and to make a cemetery, he was now declaring to be free; ¹⁵and the Jews, whom he had not considered worth burying but had planned to throw out with their children to the beasts, for the birds to pick, he would make, all of them, equal to citizens of Athens; ¹⁶and the holy sanctuary, which he had formerly plundered, he would adorn with the finest offerings; and the holy vessels he would give back, all of them, many times over; and the expenses incurred for the sacrifices he would provide from his own revenues; ¹⁷and in addition to all this he also would become a Jew and would visit every inhabited place to proclaim the power of God. ¹⁸But when his sufferings did not in any way abate, for the judgment of God had justly come upon him, he gave up all hope for himself and wrote to the Jews the following letter, in the form of a supplication. This was its content:

Antiochus' Letter and Death

19 "To his worthy Jewish citizens, Anti'ochus their king and general sends hearty greetings and good wishes for their health and prosperity. ²⁰If you and your children are well and your affairs are as you wish, I am glad. As my hope is in heaven, ²¹I remember with affection your esteem and good will. On my way back from the region of Persia I suffered an annoying illness, and I have deemed it necessary to take thought for the general security of all. ²²I do not despair of my condition, for I have good hope of recovering from my illness, ²³but I observed that my father, on the occasions when he made expeditions into the upper country, appointed his successor, ²⁴so that, if anything unexpected happened or any unwelcome news came, the people throughout the realm would not be troubled, for they would know to whom the government was left. ²⁵Moreover, I understand how the princes along the borders and the neighbors to my kingdom keep watching for opportunities and waiting to see what will happen. So I have appointed my son Anti'ochus to be king, whom I have often entrusted and commended to most of you when I hastened off to the upper provinces; and I have written to him what is written here. ²⁶I therefore urge and beg you to remember the public and private services rendered to you and to maintain your present good will, each of you, toward me and my son. ²⁷For I am sure that he will follow my policy and will treat you with moderation and kindness."

28 So the murderer and blasphemer, having endured the more intense suffering, such as he had inflicted on others, came to the end of his life by a most pitiable fate, among the mountains in a strange land. ²⁹And Philip, one of his courtiers, took his body home; then, fearing the son of Anti'ochus, he betook himself to Ptol'emy Phil"ome'tor in Egypt.

The Purification of the Temple

10 Now Mac"cabe'us and his followers, the Lord leading them on, recovered the temple and the city; ²and they tore down the altars which had been built in the public square by the foreigners, and also destroyed the sacred precincts. ³They

---

9:14 declaring … free: Likely meaning a return to the policies of his father, Antiochus III, under whom the Jews enjoyed favored status and were allowed to live according to the Jewish Law.

9:15 citizens of Athens: A city with a highly favored relationship to Antiochus. Note that the last mention of Athens came with the Athenian senator in 6:1, whom Antiochus had sent to outlaw the Torah and desecrate the Jerusalem Temple!

9:16 expenses … for the sacrifices: A return to the policies of Antiochus' brother Seleucus IV Philopator (cf. 3:3).

9:17 become a Jew: After making it unlawful to confess to be a Jew in 6:6, Antiochus now vows to become one himself. The meaning of "Jew" in this context is much discussed: the term certainly signifies more than a resident of Judea and likely entails both the worship of the God of Israel and adherence to the Mosaic Law, including circumcision and Jewish food regulations. On becoming a Jew (and the fearful final step of circumcision), see Josephus on the similar case of King Izates (*Antiquities of the Jews* 20, 2).

9:18 judgment of God: If the prayer of the righteous is powerful and effective (Jas 5:16), the opposite qualities characterize the prayer of wicked Antiochus, who was obstinately unmerciful and now does not receive mercy (Jas 2:13;

cf. Mt 5:7; 6:14; 18:33-35). Antiochus' dubious sincerity is illustrated in the following epistle, where his claims regarding friendship and good hope for recovery directly contradict his statements in the prior section.

9:19-27 Antiochus' letter, written to secure loyalty to his successor, may have been sent throughout the empire with different recipients in the first line (rather than only to the Jews), as evidenced by the highly general language used throughout.

9:23 my father … upper country: Antiochus III had appointed a successor when going to war in Parthia (modern-day Iran) around 210 B.C.

9:25 my son Antiochus: Known as Antiochus V Eupator ("of a good father"), who was between nine and twelve years old when he began to reign with Lysias in control of the government as his regent (cf. 13:2).

9:28 in a strange land: The same fate as Jason in 5:9.

9:29 Philip: See note on 5:22. Antiochus making Philip regent over his son is further described in 1 Mac 6:14. **Ptolemy Philometor:** See note on 4:21.

10:1-8 For another account of the Temple's purification, see 1 Mac 4:36-59.

10:3 striking fire out of flint: The Greek literally reads "igniting stones and taking fire from them", which some translations speculate may refer to the use of flint (though flint is not actually set on fire). A more natural referent is the mysterious stones from 1:31, which last appear in the context of the

---

ᵗ Or *think thoughts proper only to God.*

purified the sanctuary, and made another altar of sacrifice; then, striking fire out of flint, they offered sacrifices, after a lapse of two years, and they burned incense and lighted lamps and set out the bread of the Presence. ⁴And when they had done this, they fell prostrate and begged the Lord that they might never again fall into such misfortunes, but that, if they should ever sin, they might be disciplined by him with forbearance and not be handed over to blasphemous and barbarous nations. ⁵It happened that on the same day on which the sanctuary had been profaned by the foreigners, the purification of the sanctuary took place, that is, on the twenty-fifth day of the same month, which was Chis'lev. ⁶And they celebrated it for eight days with rejoicing, in the manner of the feast of booths, remembering how not long before, during the feast of booths, they had been wandering in the mountains and caves like wild animals. ⁷Therefore bearing ivy-wreathed wands and beautiful branches and also fronds of palm, they offered hymns of thanksgiving to him who had given success to the purifying of his own holy place. ⁸They decreed by public ordinance and vote that the whole nation of the Jews should observe these days every year.

9 Such then was the end of Anti'ochus, who was called Epiph'anes.

10 Now we will tell what took place under Anti'ochus Eu'pator, who was the son of that ungodly man, and will give a brief summary of the principal calamities of the wars. ¹¹This man, when he succeeded to the kingdom, appointed one Lys'ias to have charge of the government and to be chief governor of Coe'le-syr'ia and Phoeni'cia. ¹²Ptol'emy, who was called Ma'cron, took the lead in showing justice to the Jews because of the wrong that had been done to them, and attempted to maintain peaceful relations with them. ¹³As a result he was accused before Eu'pator by the king's friends. He heard himself called a traitor at every turn, because he had abandoned Cyprus, which Phil"ome'tor had entrusted to him, and had gone over to Anti'ochus Epiph'anes. Unable to command the respect due his office,ᵘ he took poison and ended his life.

Campaign in Idumea

14 When Gor'gias became governor of the region, he maintained a force of mercenaries, and at every turn kept on warring against the Jews. ¹⁵Besides this, the Idume'ans, who had control of important strongholds, were harassing the Jews; they received those who were banished from Jerusalem, and endeavored to keep up the war. ¹⁶But Mac"cabe'us and his men, after making solemn supplication and begging God to fight on their side, rushed to the strongholds of the Idume'ans. ¹⁷Attacking them vigorously, they gained possession of the places, and beat off all who fought upon the wall, and slew those whom they encountered, killing no fewer than twenty thousand.

18 When no less than nine thousand took refuge in two very strong towers well equipped to withstand a siege, ¹⁹Mac"cabe'us left Simon and Joseph, and also Zacchae'us and his men, a force sufficient to besiege them; and he himself set off for places where he was more urgently needed. ²⁰But the men with Simon, who were money-hungry, were bribed by some of those who were in the towers, and on receiving seventy thousand drachmas let some of

---

Temple's rededication when Nehemiah pours out the remaining fiery naphtha liquid upon them. Now, at the Temple's second rededication, these stones become the source for the renewed fire for the Temple's sacrifices. See note on 1:31. **lapse of two years:** While both 1 and 2 Maccabees report that the Temple was profaned and rededicated on the same calendar date, the 25th of Chislev (10:5), there is a difference between this mention of "two years" and the three years attested in 1 Maccabees (see 1 Mac 1:59 and 4:52), which is surprising considering the significance of the events and the simple calculation involved. The difference is likely due to the ambiguous Greek calendar system, which usually included the present year in counting, so that translating between systems often leaves numbers varying by one (see note on 4:18).
10:5 the same day: The poetic justice here is a vindication of God's rule over the events that have taken place (cf. 1 Mac 4:54).
10:6 eight days ... feast of booths: The festival, which becomes known as Hanukkah (meaning "dedication"), is here celebrated with the same eight-day merriment as a pilgrimage feast. Just as the Feast of Booths (= Tabernacles) was meant to bring to the Israelites' remembrance of their time spent in the wilderness after their deliverance from Egypt (Lev 23:43), this

new feast uses booths to remind them of their more recent time spent in the wilderness and God's deliverance in bringing them back to his holy place. See notes on 1:9 and 2:7.
10:7 ivy-wreathed wands ... fronds of palm: Formerly forced to wear ivy in honor of Dionysus (6:7), the Jews now include it among the "boughs of leafy trees" as prescribed for the Feast of Booths/Tabernacles (Lev 23:40; cf. Jud 15:12).
10:8 decreed ... every year: Witnesses to such a decree are found at the beginning of the book (see 1:18; 2:16).
10:11 Lysias: A high-ranking Seleucid general, known from 1 Mac 3:32 to have been appointed as regent by Antiochus IV Epiphanes while he went on his campaign to the east.
10:12 Ptolemy, who was called Macron: A figure also briefly noted by the historian Polybius. This is likely a different Ptolemy from the son of Dorymenes. See note on 4:45.
10:14–23 This section likely corresponds with Judas' Idumean campaign in 1 Mac 5:1–3.
10:14 Gorgias: Introduced with Nicanor at 8:9.
10:15 Idumeans: The people of the region immediately south and southwest of Judea.
10:19 Simon and Joseph: See note on 8:22. **Zacchaeus:** Otherwise unknown.
10:20 seventy thousand drachmas: A drachma was roughly equivalent to a day's wage for a manual laborer (like a denarius in Mt 20:2), meaning that this total would represent a year's earnings for almost 200 men.

ᵘCn: The Greek text here is uncertain.

them slip away. ²¹When word of what had happened came to Mac″cabe′us, he gathered the leaders of the people, and accused these men of having sold their brethren for money by setting their enemies free to fight against them. ²²Then he slew these men who had turned traitor, and immediately captured the two towers. ²³Having success at arms in everything he undertook, he destroyed more than twenty thousand in the two strongholds.

Judas Defeats Timothy

24 Now Timothy, who had been defeated by the Jews before, gathered a tremendous force of mercenaries and collected the cavalry from Asia in no small number. He came on, intending to take Judea by storm. ²⁵As he drew near, Mac″cabe′us and his men sprinkled dust upon their heads and put on sackcloth, in supplication to God. ²⁶Falling upon the steps before the altar, they begged him to be gracious to them and to be an enemy to their enemies and an adversary to their adversaries, as the law declares. ²⁷And rising from their prayer they took up their arms and advanced a considerable distance from the city; and when they came near to the enemy they halted. ²⁸Just as dawn was breaking, the two armies joined battle, the one having as pledge of success and victory not only their valor but their reliance upon the Lord, while the other made rage their leader in the fight.

29 When the battle became fierce, there appeared to the enemy from heaven five resplendent men on horses with golden bridles, and they were leading the Jews. ³⁰Surrounding Mac″cabe′us and protecting him with their own armor and weapons, they kept him from being wounded. And they showered arrows and thunderbolts upon the enemy, so that, confused and blinded, they were thrown into disorder and cut to pieces. ³¹Twenty thousand five hundred were slaughtered, besides six hundred horsemen.

32 Timothy himself fled to a stronghold called Gaz′ra, especially well garrisoned, where Chae′reas was commander. ³³Then Mac″cabe′us and his men were glad, and they besieged the fort for four days. ³⁴The men within, relying on the strength of the place, blasphemed terribly and hurled out wicked words. ³⁵But at dawn of the fifth day, twenty young men in the army of Mac″cabe′us, fired with anger because of the blasphemies, bravely stormed the wall and with savage fury cut down every one they met. ³⁶Others who came up in the same way wheeled around against the defenders and set fire to the towers; they kindled fires and burned the blasphemers alive. Others broke open the gates and let in the rest of the force, and they occupied the city. ³⁷They killed Timothy, who was hidden in a cistern, and his brother Chae′reas, and Apolloph′anes. ³⁸When they had accomplished these things, with hymns and thanksgivings they blessed the Lord who shows great kindness to Israel and gives them the victory.

Lysias Besieges Beth-zur

11 Very soon after this, Lys′ias, the king's guardian and kinsman, who was in charge of the government, being vexed at what had happened, ²gathered about eighty thousand men and all his cavalry and came against the Jews. He intended to make the city a home for Greeks, ³and to levy tribute on the temple as he did on the sacred places of the other nations, and to put up the high priesthood for sale every year. ⁴He took no account whatever of the power of God, but was elated with his ten thousands of infantry, and his thousands of cavalry, and his eighty elephants. ⁵Invading Judea, he approached Beth-zur, which was a fortified place about five leaguesᵛ from Jerusalem, and pressed it hard.

6 When Mac″cabe′us and his men got word that Lys′iasʷ was besieging the strongholds, they and all the people, with lamentations and tears, begged the

---

10:24 Timothy: See note on 8:30. **calvary from Asia:** Famous for having the most fearsome war horses in the ancient world, further emphasizing the long odds faced by Judas' army.

10:26 as the law declares: For example, in Ex 23:22: "But if you listen attentively to his voice and do all that I say, then I will be an enemy to your enemies and an adversary to your adversaries."

10:29 five resplendent men on horses: In fulfillment of God's promise in Ex 23:22, this angelic epiphany is said to be visible to the Jews' enemies, much like the epiphany that strikes down Heliodorus in 3:25. See word study: *Appearances* at 2:21.

10:32 Gazara: Also known as Gezer (Josh 16:10; 1 Kings 9:15), a city in the foothills of the Judean mountains, on the road from Jerusalem to the coastal city of Joppa. While this reading is supported by the ancient manuscripts of the book, some suspect the original may have been "Jazer" (a city in the

Transjordan region), so that these events would correspond with those in 1 Mac 5:6–8. **Chaereas:** The brother of Timothy (see 10:37).

10:37 hidden in a cistern: God's response to the Jews' supplications in 10:25 is so great that the mighty Seleucid commander has been reduced to hiding under the earth. **Apollophanes:** Otherwise unknown.

11:1 Lysias: Lysias' self-confidence and pride in attacking Judea (11:4) set the stage for another manifestation of the power of God. The events in this section appear to correspond with the campaign described in 1 Mac 4:26–35. If so, the author would likely be organizing the series of events thematically rather than sequentially. See note on 10:11.

11:2 home for Greeks: Thus bringing the project of Hellenization described in 4:11–17 to completion.

11:3 high priesthood for sale: While the Jewish high priesthood had traditionally been hereditary and kept for the priest's lifetime, its sale would have made the high priest a vassal of the Seleucid leaders and subject to their yearly appointment.

11:5 Beth-zur: A town 20 miles southwest of Jerusalem on the border between Idumea and Judea.

ᵛ About twenty miles. The text is uncertain here.
ʷ Gk *he.*

Lord to send a good angel to save Israel. 7Mac″cabe′us himself was the first to take up arms, and he urged the others to risk their lives with him to aid their brethren. Then they eagerly rushed off together. 8And there, while they were still near Jerusalem, a horseman appeared at their head, clothed in white and brandishing weapons of gold. 9And they all together praised the merciful God, and were strengthened in heart, ready to assail not only men but the wildest beasts or walls of iron. 10They advanced in battle order, having their heavenly ally, for the Lord had mercy on them. 11They hurled themselves like lions against the enemy, and slew eleven thousand of them and sixteen hundred horsemen, and forced all the rest to flee. 12Most of them got away stripped and wounded, and Lys′ias himself escaped by disgraceful flight. 13And as he was not without intelligence, he pondered over the defeat which had befallen him, and realized that the Hebrews were invincible because the mighty God fought on their side. So he sent to them 14and persuaded them to settle everything on just terms, promising that he would persuade the king, constraining him to be their friend.ˣ 15Mac″cabe′us, having regard for the common good, agreed to all that Lys′ias urged. For the king granted every request in behalf of the Jews which Maccabeus delivered to Lysias in writing.

16 The letter written to the Jews by Lys′ias was to this effect:

"Lysias to the people of the Jews, greeting. 17John and Ab′salom, who were sent by you, have delivered your signed communication and have asked about the matters indicated therein. 18I have informed the king of everything that needed to be brought before him, and he has agreed to what was possible. 19If you will maintain your good will toward the government, I will endeavor for the future to help promote your welfare. 20And concerning these matters and their details, I have ordered these men and my representatives to confer with you. 21Farewell. The one hundred and forty-eighth year,ʸ Di″oscorin′thius twenty-fourth."

22 The king's letter ran thus:

"King Anti′ochus to his brother Lys′ias, greeting. 23Now that our father has gone on to the gods, we desire that the subjects of the kingdom be undisturbed in caring for their own affairs. 24We have heard that the Jews do not consent to our father's change to Greek customs but prefer their own way of living and ask that their own customs be allowed them. 25Accordingly, since we choose that this nation also be free from disturbance, our decision is that their temple be restored to them and that they live according to the customs of their ancestors. 26You will do well, therefore, to send word to them and give them pledges of friendship, so that they may know our policy and be of good cheer and go on happily in the conduct of their own affairs."

27 To the nation the king's letter was as follows:

"King Anti′ochus to the senate of the Jews and to the other Jews, greeting. 28If you are well, it is as we desire. We also are in good health. 29Menela′us has informed us that you wish to return home and look after your own affairs. 30Therefore those who go home by the thirtieth day of Xan′thicus will have our pledge of friendship and full permission 31for the Jews to enjoy their own food and laws, just as formerly, and none of them shall be molested in any way for what he may have done in ignorance. 32And I have also sent Menela′us to encourage you. 33Farewell. The one hundred and forty-eighth year,ᶻ Xan′thicus fifteenth."

34 The Romans also sent them a letter, which read thus:

11:8 horseman ... clothed in white: See word study: *Appearances* at 2:21.

11:13 not without intelligence: Lysias' reasoning confirms that the Jews' victory could be a result only of divine intervention, as the Seleucid armies carried the upper hand in every practical way.

11:17 John and Absalom: Not attested elsewhere. Judging by their Hebrew names, these were likely envoys from the Maccabees rather than the Hellenizing Jews.

11:21 Dioscorinthius: The name of this month is otherwise unattested, which has hindered attempts to date the letter precisely. While the original may have been another month name (such as Dios, Dystros, or Dioscouros) that was miscopied, the fact that early manuscripts do not amend it to a better-known name suggests that it was intelligible to its ancient readers.

11:22 King Antiochus: Evidently Antiochus V Eupator, judging by the reference to his father's death in the following verse. See note on 9:25.

11:27 senate of the Jews: See note on 1:10.

11:29 Menelaus: While not mentioned since 5:23, the corrupt Menelaus is presented as still the Seleucids' official representative among the Jews.

11:30 thirtieth day of Xanthicus: Xanthicus corresponds with March–April in the modern Gregorian calendar.

11:32 sent Menelaus to encourage you: The nature of this letter as genuine correspondence from the Seleucids—rather than a paraphrase or later conjecture—seems to be confirmed by the letter's positive portrayal of Menelaus, who is consistently presented elsewhere in 2 Maccabees as a source, not of encouragement, but, rather, of all the Jews' misfortunes (cf. 4:47).

11:33 Xanthicus fifteenth: This is the same date as the letter from the Romans below (11:38), and some suspect that a scribal error could have led to the date from 11:38 being used here as well. In any case, these dates may also hold theological significance: Josephus informs us that Xanthicus (Nisan, in Hebrew) was the month when Moses delivered Israel from Egypt, and the fifteenth of Xanthicus marked the very day of the Israelites' departure (*Antiquities of the Jews* 1, 81, and 2, 318).

11:34–38 These Roman envoys are unknown elsewhere, though some suspect that the second (Titus Manius) may correspond with a Roman consul (Titus Manlius Torquatus) or an ambassador to Antiochus (Manius Sergius) in this period. For

---

ˣ The Greek text here is corrupt.
ʸ 164 B.C.
ᶻ 164 B.C.

"Quint'us Mem'mius and Titus Ma'nius, envoys of the Romans, to the people of the Jews, greeting. [35]With regard to what Lys'ias the kinsman of the king has granted you, we also give consent. [36]But as to the matters which he decided are to be referred to the king, as soon as you have considered them, send some one promptly, so that we may make proposals appropriate for you. For we are on our way to Antioch. [37]Therefore make haste and send some men, so that we may have your judgment. [38]Farewell. The one hundred and forty-eighth year,[a] Xan'thicus fifteenth."

Incidents at Joppa and Jamnia

12 When this agreement had been reached, Lys'ias returned to the king, and the Jews went about their farming.

2 But some of the governors in various places, Timothy and Apollo'nius the son of Gennae'us, as well as Hi"eron'ymus and Dem'ophon, and in addition to these Nica'nor the governor of Cyprus, would not let them live quietly and in peace. [3]And some men of Joppa did so ungodly a deed as this: they invited the Jews who lived among them to embark, with their wives and children, on boats which they had provided, as though there were no ill will to the Jews;[b] [4]and this was done by public vote of the city. And when they accepted, because they wished to live peaceably and suspected nothing, the men of Joppa[c] took them out to sea and drowned them, not less than two hundred. [5]When Judas heard of the cruelty visited on his countrymen, he gave orders to his men [6]and, calling upon God the righteous Judge, attacked the murderers of his brethren. He set fire to the harbor by night, and burned the boats, and massacred those who had taken refuge there. [7]Then, because the city's gates were closed, he withdrew, intending to come again and root out the whole community of Joppa. [8]But learning that the men in Jam'nia meant in the same way to wipe out the Jews who were living among them, [9]he attacked the people of Jam'nia by night and set fire to the harbor and the fleet, so that the glow of the light was seen in Jerusalem, thirty miles[d] distant.

The Campaign in Gilead

10 When they had gone more than a mile[e] from there, on their march against Timothy, not less than five thousand Arabs with five hundred horsemen attacked them. [11]After a hard fight Judas and his men won the victory, by the help of God. The defeated nomads begged Judas to grant them pledges of friendship, promising to give him cattle and to help his people[f] in all other ways. [12]Judas, thinking that they might really be useful in many ways, agreed to make peace with them; and after receiving his pledges they departed to their tents.

13 He also attacked a certain city which was strongly fortified with earthworks[g] and walls, and inhabited by all sorts of Gentiles. Its name was Cas'pin. [14]And those who were within, relying on the strength of the walls and on their supply of provisions, behaved most insolently toward Judas and his men, railing at them and even blaspheming and saying unholy things. [15]But Judas and his men, calling upon the great Sovereign of the world, who without battering-rams or engines of war overthrew Jericho in the days of Joshua, rushed furiously upon the walls. [16]They took the city by the will of God, and slaughtered untold numbers, so that the adjoining lake, a quarter of a mile[h] wide, appeared to be running over with blood.

Judas Defeats Timothy's Army

17 When they had gone ninety-five miles[i] from there, they came to Cha'rax, to the Jews who are called Tou"bia'ni. [18]They did not find Timothy in that region, for he had by then departed from the region without accomplishing anything, though

---

more on the Romans' relationship with the Jews in this period, see 1 Mac 8, 12, 14.

11:35 Lysias ... has granted you: A reference to the matters Lysias notes in his letter at 11:18.

12:2 Timothy: Apparently a different Timothy from the previous Seleucid commander, who was introduced in 8:30 and killed in 10:37. Alternatively, if the compiler is not following strict chronological sequence, this section could be filling in details from Judas' earlier battles with Timothy. **Apollonius the son of Gennaeus:** Also distinguished from the prior Apollonius, the son of Menestheus (4:4). **Hieronymus and Demophon:** Unknown elsewhere. **Nicanor ... of Cyprus:** The text is unclear whether this figure is to be distinguished from the Nicanor who appears in chaps. 8 and 14.

12:3 Joppa: See note on 4:21.

12:8 Jamnia: A coastal town about 12 miles south of Joppa.

12:10 Arabs: Possibly a reference to one of two Arab groups in 1 Mac 5: the Nabateans in 1 Mac 5:25, who supplied Judas with information on the attacks against Jews in Gilead, or the Arabs that were part of Timothy's forces in 1 Mac 5:39.

12:13 Caspin: Perhaps the same as Chaspho in 1 Mac 5:26, a city east of the Jordan River.

12:15 engines of war: Hellenistic-era warfare included the use of a number of war machines, such as catapults, battering rams, cranes, and siege towers. **the days of Joshua:** Like the miraculous toppling of the walls of Jericho in Josh 6:1–21, here too God's aid provides the Jews with victory against a seemingly impenetrable city.

12:17 Charax: Either a place name that is unknown or a Greek word meaning "palisaded enclosure". If the latter is correct, this may correspond with the fortress of Dathema mentioned in 1 Mac 5:29. **Toubiani:** An uncertain group; it may refer to the remaining Jews in the land of Tob (cf. 1 Mac 5:13).

---

[a] 164 B.C.
[b] Gk *them.*
[c] Gk *they.*
[d] Gk *two hundred and forty stadia.*
[e] Gk *nine stadia.*
[f] Gk *them.*
[g] The Greek text here is uncertain.
[h] Gk *two stadia.*
[i] Gk *seven hundred and fifty stadia.*

in one place he had left a very strong garrison. [19]Dosith'eus and Sosip'ater, who were captains under Mac"cabe'us, marched out and destroyed those whom Timothy had left in the stronghold, more than ten thousand men. [20]But Mac"cabe'us arranged his army in divisions, set men[j] in command of the divisions, and hastened after Timothy, who had with him a hundred and twenty thousand infantry and two thousand five hundred cavalry. [21]When Timothy learned of the approach of Judas, he sent off the women and the children and also the baggage to a place called Carna'im; for that place was hard to besiege and difficult of access because of the narrowness of all the approaches. [22]But when Judas' first division appeared, terror and fear came over the enemy at the manifestation to them of him who sees all things; and they rushed off in flight and were swept on, this way and that, so that often they were injured by their own men and pierced by the points of their swords. [23]And Judas pressed the pursuit with the utmost vigor, putting the sinners to the sword, and destroyed as many as thirty thousand men.

24 Timothy himself fell into the hands of Dosith'eus and Sosip'ater and their men. With great guile he begged them to let him go in safety, because he held the parents of most of them and the brothers of some and no consideration would be shown them. [25]And when with many words he had confirmed his solemn promise to restore them unharmed, they let him go, for the sake of saving their brethren.

Judas Wins Other Victories

26 Then Judas[k] marched against Carna'im and the temple of Atar'gatis, and slaughtered twenty-five thousand people. [27]After the rout and destruction of these, he marched also against E'phron, a fortified city where Lys'ias dwelt with multitudes of people of all nationalities.[1] Stalwart young men took their stand before the walls and made a vigorous defense; and great stores of war engines and missiles were there. [28]But the Jews[m] called upon the Sovereign who with power shatters the might of his enemies, and they got the city into their hands, and killed as many as twenty-five thousand of those who were within it.

29 Setting out from there, they hastened to Scythop'olis, which is seventy-five miles[n] from Jerusalem. [30]But when the Jews who dwelt there bore witness to the good will which the people of Scythop'olis had shown them and their kind treatment of them in times of misfortune, [31]they thanked them and exhorted them to be well disposed to their race in the future also. Then they went up to Jerusalem, as the feast of weeks was close at hand.

Judas Defeats Gorgias

32 After the feast called Pentecost, they hastened against Gor'gias, the governor of Idume'a. [33]And he came out with three thousand infantry and four hundred cavalry. [34]When they joined battle, it happened that a few of the Jews fell. [35]But a certain Dosith'eus, one of Bace'nor's men, who was on horseback and was a strong man, caught hold of Gor'gias, and grasping his cloak was dragging him off by main strength, wishing to take the accursed man alive, when one of the Thracian horsemen bore down upon him and cut off his arm; so Gorgias escaped and reached Mar'isa.

36 As Es'dris and his men had been fighting for a long time and were weary, Judas called upon the Lord to show himself their ally and leader in the battle. [37]In the language of their fathers he raised the battle cry, with hymns; then he charged against Gor'gias' men when they were not expecting it, and put them to flight.

Prayers for Those Killed in Battle

38 Then Judas assembled his army and went to the city of Adul'lam. As the seventh day was coming on, they purified themselves according to the custom, and they kept the sabbath there.

12:19 Dositheus and Sosipater: Leaders of Judas' forces who appear to have been Jews native to the Toubian region, as their relatives are held hostage by Timothy (12:24).
12:21 Carnaim: A fortified city in Gilead (cf. 1 Mac 5:43–44).
12:26 Atargatis: A Syrian fish goddess (cf. 1 Mac 5:43).
12:27 Ephron: A city east of the Jordan River that appears to be a Seleucid outpost, as evidenced by Lysias' dwelling there (1 Mac 5:46–51).
12:29 Scythopolis: Also known as Beth-shan, a city south of the Sea of Galilee and 75 miles north of Jerusalem. In contrast with Joppa, Jamnia, and the succeeding towns in chap. 12, the citizens of Scythopolis have shown kindness to the Jews rather than malevolence. As a result, Judas' forces have only friendship and gratitude to offer them, showing there is no necessary enmity between Jews and Gentiles in the region.
12:31 feast of weeks: Also known as Pentecost, celebrated 50 days after Passover (Ex 34:22–24).
12:32 Gorgias: The general appointed with Nicanor to counter Judas' forces in 8:9. **Idumea:** The region south of Judea.
12:34 a few of the Jews fell: Noteworthy as the first mention of casualties among Judas' forces in the narrative.
12:35 a certain Dositheus: Likely different from the Dositheus noted in 12:19, 24. **one of Bacenor's men:** This figure is unknown, and some manuscripts read "of the Toubians" instead (= the Toubiani of 12:17). **Thracian horsemen:** Calvary units infamous for their savagery. **Marisa:** Also known as Mareshah, a Hellenized city southwest of Jerusalem along Judea's border with Idumea (1 Mac 5:66).
12:36 Esdris: Otherwise unknown. Some suspect he may be identified with the Eleazar in 8:23 and 1 Mac 6:43–46.
12:38 Adullam: A town between Marisa and Jerusalem, about 15 miles southwest of the latter.

[j] Gk *them.*
[k] Gk *he.*
[1] The Greek text of this sentence is uncertain.
[m] Gk *they.*
[n] Gk *six hundred stadia.*

39 On the next day, as by that time it had become necessary, Judas and his men went to take up the bodies of the fallen and to bring them back to lie with their kinsmen in the sepulchres of their fathers. [40]Then under the tunic of every one of the dead they found sacred tokens of the idols of Jam'nia, which the law forbids the Jews to wear. And it became clear to all that this was why these men had fallen. [41]So they all blessed the ways of the Lord, the righteous Judge, who reveals the things that are hidden; [42]and they turned to prayer, begging that the sin which had been committed might be wholly blotted out. And the noble Judas exhorted the people to keep themselves free from sin, for they had seen with their own eyes what had happened because of the sin of those who had fallen. [43]He also took up a collection, man by man, to the amount of two thousand drachmas of silver, and sent it to Jerusalem to provide for a sin offering. In doing this he acted very well and honorably, taking account

---

12:39 take up the bodies: On the importance of burying the dead in Judaism, see Tob 1:16–20.

12:40 sacred tokens: Possessing images of foreign gods was prohibited by Deut 7:25.

12:43 two thousand drachmas of silver: For context, this is considerably more than the three hundred drachmas for Jason's offering to Hercules in 4:19.

Second Maccabees and the Canon of Scripture

If one were to ask the question why Protestant Bibles are shorter than Catholic ones, a quick and easy answer would be "2 Maccabees 12". While also attested in the ancient practice of the Church, the clearest scriptural basis for praying for the dead—and hence for a doctrine of Purgatory—is found in this passage, where Judas' army takes up a collection to offer sacrifices for their fallen brethren.

If we fast-forward to 1517, we find an Augustinian monk named Martin Luther railing against the abuse of similar collections being taken on behalf of the dead, which (in his view) appears to have produced a lax Christian populace satisfied with buying their way out of Purgatory and a corrupt institutional Church only too happy to take their money. And indeed, such abuses (in the form of "indulgences" sold for profit) were recognized as problematic by nearly all sides in this period: Catholic opponents of Luther such as Cardinal Cajetan similarly condemned the sale of indulgences, and the granting of indulgences in association with any financial almsgiving was eventually banned following the Council of Trent in 1567.

For Luther, however, a more dramatic solution to the problem was found: to deny the authority of the Old Testament books not accepted in rabbinic Judaism—known today as the "deuterocanonicals"—which included 2 Maccabees. This was the tactic adopted by Luther in his famous debate with Johann Eck at Leipzig in 1519, where he cited the testimony of the Jews and St. Jerome as proof that 2 Maccabees was not inspired Scripture and, thus, that the Church's teaching on Purgatory lacked a foundation in the written word of God.

Such a move Luther deemed necessary, as he concedes in a 1519 letter to his friend Georg Spalatin that the teaching on Purgatory in 2 Mac 12 is "quite plain". Similarly, the reformer John Calvin acknowledged in his rebuttal to the Council of Trent (1547) that the Catholics could prove Purgatory's existence from 2 Maccabees. This idea of Purgatory was at the center of the conflict over the Church's authority to forgive sins, and Luther alleged that all the pope's wealth and power were built upon it, so that resistance to the Church's hierarchy necessarily meant opposition to the sources where Purgatory was attested. As a result, most Protestants followed Luther in relegating the books not accepted by rabbinic Judaism into an "apocrypha" section at the end of the Old Testament and eventually (in modern times) leaving them out altogether.

While the reformers were correct that St. Jerome and certain other Fathers, following the general practice of Jews after Christ's time, regarded books like 2 Maccabees as holding a lower status, such a view was a minority within the early Church. Instead, the broader Old Testament canon found in the Greek Septuagint—which Christians had read as Scripture since apostolic times—was more widely followed in the early Church and confirmed by the synods at Carthage and Hippo in the late fourth and early fifth centuries. Further, it represented no small irony that Luther's tactic relied on the authority of the Jews and St. Jerome, given his low opinion of them elsewhere: Luther's writings are infamous for their rhetoric against what he regarded as the deceptions of the Jews, and in *Bondage of the Will* (1521), Luther writes that Jerome's errors are so great that he has merited hell rather than heaven!

In sum, Judas' collection for his fallen soldiers in 2 Mac 12 provides the single biggest reason why Protestant Bibles are shorter than Catholic ones, as abuses in funding prayers and sacrifices for the dead led the reformers to follow the canon of rabbinic Judaism rather than the traditional Christian one. While the potential for such abuses was recognized on the Catholic side as well—as witnessed by the need to separate completely financial almsgiving from indulgences following Trent—the Church upheld both the theological validity of interceding for the dead and the canonicity of the book in which she had always found it affirmed. As Augustine wrote over a millennium earlier, to offer such care for the dead stood on the authority both of 2 Maccabees and of the universal practice of the Church, whose priests at the altar always followed Judas' lead in commending their fallen brethren to God.

of the resurrection. [44]For if he were not expecting that those who had fallen would rise again, it would have been superfluous and foolish to pray for the dead. [45]But if he was looking to the splendid reward that is laid up for those who fall asleep in godliness, it was a holy and pious thought. Therefore he made atonement for the dead, that they might be delivered from their sin.*

Menelaus Put to Death

13 In the one hundred and forty-ninth year° word came to Judas and his men that Anti'ochus Eu'pator was coming with a great army against Judea, [2]and with him Lys'ias, his guardian, who had charge of the government. Each of them had a Greek force of one hundred and ten thousand infantry, five thousand three hundred cavalry, twenty-two elephants, and three hundred chariots armed with scythes.

3 Menela'us also joined them and with utter hypocrisy urged Anti'ochus on, not for the sake of his country's welfare, but because he thought that he would be established in office. [4]But the King of kings aroused the anger of Anti'ochus against the scoundrel; and when Lys'ias informed him that this man was to blame for all the trouble, he ordered them to take him to Beroe'a and to put him to death by the method which is the custom in that place. [5]For there is a tower in that place, fifty cubits high, full of ashes, and it has a rim running around it which on all sides inclines precipitously into the ashes. [6]There they all push to destruction any man guilty of sacrilege or notorious for other crimes. [7]By such a fate it came about that Menela'us the lawbreaker died, without even burial in the earth. [8]And this was eminently just; because he had committed many sins against the altar whose fire and ashes were holy, he met his death in ashes.

A Battle Near Modein

9 The king with barbarous arrogance was coming to show the Jews things far worse than those that had been done[p] in his father's time. [10]But when Judas heard of this, he ordered the people to call upon the Lord day and night, now if ever to help those who were on the point of being deprived of the law and their country and the holy temple, [11]and not to let the people who had just begun to revive fall into the hands of the blasphemous Gentiles. [12]When they had all joined in the same petition and had begged the merciful Lord with weeping and fasting and lying prostrate for three days without ceasing, Judas exhorted them and ordered them to stand ready.

13 After consulting privately with the elders, he determined to march out and decide the matter by the help of God before the king's army could enter Judea and get possession of the city. [14]So, committing the decision to the Creator of the world and exhorting his men to fight nobly to the death for the laws, temple, city, country, and commonwealth, he pitched his camp near Mo'dein. [15]He gave his men the watchword, "God's victory," and with a picked force of the bravest young men, he attacked the king's pavilion at night and slew as many as two thousand men in the camp. He stabbed[q] the leading elephant and its rider. [16]In the end they filled the camp with terror and confusion and withdrew in

---

12:44-45 Praying for the dead, a practice here attested by Jews over a century before Christ, became common in early Christianity as well. St. Augustine's treatise *On the Care of the Dead* begins by citing the Maccabees' intercessions for the dead in this passage, which he sees as corresponding with the Church's universal practice of the priest praying for the dead at the altar. Later, in *On the Soul and Its Origin*, Augustine disputes with Vincentius Victor's claim that the sacrifice of the Eucharist can be offered for the unbaptized dead, which he had sought to establish using this passage from 2 Maccabees. Augustine counters that just as Judas made these offerings only for the circumcised (the sacrament of initiation into the Old Covenant), so too could the Church make offerings only for the baptized (the sacrament of initiation into the New). A famous story of early Christian prayers for the dead is found with the example of Perpetua, who was martyred around A.D. 202. After being inspired to pray for her brother Dinocrates, who had died of cancer when he was seven, Perpetua sees a vision of him suffering and then another where he is healed by the strength of her prayers. • "Let us help and commemorate them [the dead]. If Job's sons were purified by their father's sacrifice, why would we doubt that our offerings for the dead bring them some consolation? Let us not hesitate to help those who have died and to offer our prayers for them" (St. John Chrysostom, *Homilies on 1 Corinthians* 41, 5, cited in CCC 1032).

13:1-26 This section covers the same period described in 1 Mac 6:18-63, though the two accounts focus on different events. The figures of the Seleucid armies vary between the accounts, perhaps due to being reckoned at different points in the campaign or fluctuations in the transfer of power from Antiochus IV to Eupator.

13:1 Antiochus Eupator: See note on 9:25.

13:2 Lysias: See notes on 10:11 and 11:1.

13:3 Menelaus: See note on 4:23.

13:4 Beroea: Corresponds with modern Aleppo in Syria, about 60 miles east of Antioch.

13:5 fifty cubits: About 75 feet high. • This creates a fascinating parallel between Menelaus and wicked Haman, who is ordered by King Ahasuerus to be hung from gallows of the same height in Esther 5:14; 7:9-10.

13:8 death in ashes: Like 4:16, the death of Menelaus illustrates the Book of Wisdom's principle that "one is punished by the very things by which he sins" (Wis 11:16).

13:14 Modein: Judas' ancestral home, about 20 miles northwest of Jerusalem. See note on 1 Mac 2:1.

13:15 stabbed the leading elephant: Reminiscent of the battle of Beth-zechariah (1 Mac 6:43-47), where Judas' brother Eleazar attacks the tallest elephant and dies as a result.

---

*12:45: Vulgate has (verses 45–46): "[45]And because he considered that they who had fallen asleep with godliness had great grace laid up for them. [46]It is therefore a holy and wholesome thought to pray for the dead, that they may be loosed from sins."

° 163 B.C.

[p] Or *the worst of the things that had been done.*

[q] The Greek text here is uncertain.

triumph. [17]This happened, just as day was dawning, because the Lord's help protected him.

Antiochus Makes a Treaty with the Jews

[18] The king, having had a taste of the daring of the Jews, tried strategy in attacking their positions. [19]He advanced against Beth-zur, a strong fortress of the Jews, was turned back, attacked again,ʳ and was defeated. [20]Judas sent in to the garrison whatever was necessary. [21]But Rhod'ocus, a man from the ranks of the Jews, gave secret information to the enemy; he was sought for, caught, and put in prison. [22]The king negotiated a second time with the people in Beth-zur, gave pledges, received theirs, withdrew, attacked Judas and his men, was defeated; [23]he got word that Philip, who had been left in charge of the government, had revolted in Antioch; he was dismayed, called in the Jews, yielded and swore to observe all their rights, settled with them and offered sacrifice, honored the sanctuary and showed generosity to the holy place. [24]He received Mac"cabe'us, left Hegemon'ides as governor from Ptolema'is to Ge'rar, [25]and went to Ptolema'is. The people of Ptolemais were indignant over the treaty; in fact they were so angry that they wanted to annul its terms.ˢ [26]Lys'ias took the public platform, made the best possible defense, convinced them, appeased them, gained their good will, and set out for Antioch. This is how the king's attack and withdrawal turned out.

Alcimus Speaks against Judas

14 Three years later, word came to Judas and his men that Deme'trius, the son of Seleu'cus, had sailed into the harbor of Trip'olis with a strong army and a fleet, [2]and had taken possession of the country, having made away with Anti'ochus and his guardian Lys'ias.

[3] Now a certain Al'cimus, who had formerly been high priest but had wilfully defiled himself in the times of separation, realized that there was no way for him to be safe or to have access again to the holy altar, [4]and went to King Deme'trius in about the one hundred and fifty-first year,ᵗ presenting to him a crown of gold and a palm, and besides these some of the customary olive branches from the temple. During that day he kept quiet. [5]But he found an opportunity that furthered his mad purpose when he was invited by Deme'trius to a meeting of the council and was asked about the disposition and intentions of the Jews. He answered:

[6] "Those of the Jews who are called Hasid'eans, whose leader is Judas Mac"cabe'us, are keeping up war and stirring up sedition, and will not let the kingdom attain tranquillity. [7]Therefore I have laid aside my ancestral glory—I mean the high priesthood—and have now come here, [8]first because I am genuinely concerned for the interests of the king, and second because I have regard also for my fellow citizens. For through the folly of those whom I have mentioned our whole nation is now in no small misfortune. [9]Since you are acquainted, O king, with the details of this matter, deign to take thought for our country and our hard-pressed nation with the gracious kindness which you show to all. [10]For as long as Judas lives, it is impossible for the government to find peace."

[11] When he had said this, the rest of the king's friends, who were hostile to Judas, quickly inflamed Deme'trius still more. [12]And he immediately chose Nica'nor, who had been in command of the elephants,

---

13:19 Beth-zur: See note on 11:5.

13:21 Rhodocus: Unknown elsewhere.

13:23 Philip: See notes on 5:22 and 9:29. Another account of these events is found in 1 Mac 6:55–63.

13:24 Hegemonides: Perhaps the same as Hegemonides son of Zephyros, a figure known from epigraphic evidence to have been an ally of Eupator's father, Antiochus IV. **from Ptolemais to Gerar:** Reaching from Ptolemais (also called Acre), west of the Sea of Galilee along the Mediterranean Sea, down to the southern coast of Judea near Gaza.

13:25 people of Ptolemais: Their antipathy toward the Jews is also attested in 1 Mac 5:15.

14:1 Demetrius: Demetrius I Soter was the son of King Seleucus IV, who reigned over the empire from 187 to 175 B.C. before being deposed by his younger brother, Antiochus IV. As the son of Seleucus, Demetrius would have had a stronger claim to the throne than Antiochus V. He was a hostage in Rome from age nine (serving as a substitute for Antiochus IV) until his escape and return to Antioch at 25. **Seleucus:** Seleucus IV Philopator. See note on 3:3. **Tripolis:** A city by the sea about 150 miles south of Antioch (cf. 1 Mac 7:1).

14:3 Alcimus: A priest who was likely among the Hellenizers and not from the traditional high-priestly line of Zadok, but who had a strong enough claim of being from the "line of Aaron" to win the support of the more traditionally minded Jews (see 1 Mac 7:5, 14). **formerly been high priest:** Alcimus may have taken this role under Antiochus V following Menelaus' death, with the position needing to be confirmed under the new ruler, Demetrius.

14:4 crown of gold ... palm ... olive branches: Customary gifts for a new king.

14:6 Hasideans: Commentators disagree on who exactly the Hasideans were, and some speculate they were related to the group that was killed in the wilderness after Antiochus IV's attack on Jerusalem (1 Mac 2:29–38). Their name means "the pious" or "the devout" (from the Hebrew word ḥesed), and the Essenes and Pharisees are both usually traced back to this group. When Alcimus acquires the high priesthood at this point in the narrative in 1 Maccabees, the Hasideans give their support to Alcimus, only to be immediately betrayed by him (1 Mac 7:13–18).

14:12 Nicanor: Some commentators suggest there may be more than one Nicanor in 2 Maccabees; however, the same designation of "thrice-accursed" is used both earlier (8:34) and in this section (15:3), which implies that these refer to the same figure. See note on 8:9.

ʳ Or *faltered*.
ˢ The Greek text of this clause is uncertain.
ᵗ 161 B.C.

appointed him governor of Judea, and sent him off ¹³with orders to kill Judas and scatter his men, and to set up Al′cimus as high priest of the greatest temple. ¹⁴And the Gentiles throughout Judea, who had fled before ᵘ Judas, flocked to join Nica′nor, thinking that the misfortunes and calamities of the Jews would mean prosperity for themselves.

Nicanor Makes Friends with Judas

15 When the Jews ᵛ heard of Nica′nor's coming and the gathering of the Gentiles, they sprinkled dust upon their heads and prayed to him who established his own people for ever and always upholds his own heritage by manifesting himself. ¹⁶At the command of the leader, they ʷ set out from there immediately and engaged them in battle at a village called Des′sau. ˣ ¹⁷Simon, the brother of Judas, had encountered Nica′nor, but had been temporarily ʸ checked because of the sudden consternation created by the enemy.

18 Nevertheless Nica′nor, hearing of the valor of Judas and his men and their courage in battle for their country, shrank from deciding the issue by bloodshed. ¹⁹Therefore he sent Pos″ido′nius and Theod′otus and Mattathi′as to give and receive pledges of friendship. ²⁰When the terms had been fully considered, and the leader had informed the people, and it had appeared that they were of one mind, they agreed to the covenant. ²¹And the leaders ᶻ set a day on which to meet by themselves. A chariot came forward from each army; seats of honor were set in place; ²²Judas posted armed men in readiness at key places to prevent sudden treachery on the part of the enemy; they held the proper conference.

23 Nica′nor stayed on in Jerusalem and did nothing out of the way, but dismissed the flocks of people that had gathered. ²⁴And he kept Judas always in his presence; he was warmly attached to the man. ²⁵And he urged him to marry and have children; so he married, settled down, and shared the common life.

Nicanor Turns against Judas

26 But when Al′cimus noticed their good will for one another, he took the covenant that had been made and went to Deme′trius. He told him that

Nica′nor was disloyal to the government, for he had appointed that conspirator against the kingdom, Judas, to be his successor. ²⁷The king became excited and, provoked by the false accusations of that depraved man, wrote to Nica′nor, stating that he was displeased with the covenant and commanding him to send Mac″cabe′us to Antioch as a prisoner without delay.

28 When this message came to Nica′nor, he was troubled and grieved that he had to annul their agreement when the man had done no wrong. ²⁹Since it was not possible to oppose the king, he watched for an opportunity to accomplish this by a stratagem. ³⁰But Mac″cabe′us, noticing that Nica′nor was more austere in his dealings with him and was meeting him more rudely than had been his custom, concluded that this austerity did not spring from the best motives. So he gathered not a few of his men, and went into hiding from Nicanor.

31 When the latter became aware that he had been cleverly outwitted by the man, he went to the great ᵃ and holy temple while the priests were offering the customary sacrifices, and commanded them to hand the man over. ³²And when they declared on oath that they did not know where the man was whom he sought, ³³he stretched out his right hand toward the sanctuary, and swore this oath: "If you do not hand Judas over to me as a prisoner, I will level this precinct of God to the ground and tear down the altar, and I will build here a splendid temple to Diony′sus."

34 Having said this, he went away. Then the priests stretched forth their hands toward heaven and called upon the constant Defender of our nation, in these words: ³⁵"O Lord of all, who have need of nothing, you were pleased that there be a temple for your habitation among us; ³⁶so now, O holy One, Lord of all holiness, keep undefiled for ever this house that has been so recently purified."

Razis Dies for His Country

37 A certain Ra′zis, one of the elders of Jerusalem, was denounced to Nica′nor as a man who loved his fellow citizens and was very well thought of and for his good will was called father of the Jews. ³⁸For in former times, when there was no mingling

---

14:16 **Dessau:** Location uncertain. Suggestions include Adasa, where Nicanor's last battle is fought (1 Mac 7:40), or a village near the battle of Capharsalama (1 Mac 7:31). In either case, the village is likely north of Jerusalem.
14:17 **Simon:** See note on 8:22.

14:19 **Posidonius and Theodotus and Mattathias:** Nothing further is known of these figures.
14:24-30 The description of the goodwill between Judas and Nicanor is absent from the parallel account in 1 Mac 7. The fact that Nicanor had once been a friend of the nation may explain why, out of all the Jews' enemies in this period, only Nicanor's death is commemorated as a national holiday (15:36). To use an analogy from American history, while thousands fought on the British side of the Revolutionary War, the primary person remembered by Americans—Benedict Arnold—is the one who was once a friend.
14:33 **Dionysus:** See note on 6:7.
14:37 **Razis:** Unknown outside this section of the book (14:37-38).

ᵘ The Greek text is uncertain.
ᵛ Gk *they.*
ʷ Gk *he.*
ˣ The name is uncertain.
ʸ Other authorities read *slowly.*
ᶻ Gk *they.*
ᵃ Gk *greatest.*

with the Gentiles, he had been accused of Judaism, and for Judaism he had with all zeal risked body and life. ³⁹Nica′nor, wishing to exhibit the enmity which he had for the Jews, sent more than five hundred soldiers to arrest him; ⁴⁰for he thought that by arresting^b him he would do them an injury.

^b The Greek text here is uncertain.
^c Gk *he.*

⁴¹When the troops were about to capture the tower and were forcing the door of the courtyard, they ordered that fire be brought and the doors burned. Being surrounded, Ra′zis^c fell upon his own sword, ⁴²preferring to die nobly rather than to fall into the hands of sinners and suffer outrages unworthy of his noble birth. ⁴³But in the heat of the struggle he did not hit exactly, and the crowd was now rushing in through the doors. He bravely ran up on the wall, and manfully threw himself down into the crowd.

The Death of Razis

The death of Razis presents a number of interpretative questions: **(1)** What is the nature of Razis' death? **(2)** How does the sacred author present his death? **(3)** How should we as readers view Razis' death?

First, what is the nature of Razis' death? The issue is whether Razis' act is properly categorized as martyrdom or suicide, which is not easily answered. Razis may have been as good as dead, and commentators frequently draw parallels with other biblical figures like Samson, who forfeits his life by breaking the pillars of Dagon's temple (Judg 16:23–30). The account of the martyrdom of the mother and her sons in *4 Maccabees* may provide some analogy for Razis' actions as well, as the last son and his mother are presented as willingly jumping into the fire to embrace their fate (*4 Maccabees* 12, 19; 17, 1). The early Church also commemorated as martyrs those virgins who, in times of persecution, had thrown themselves into the river to avoid violating their consecration to God (Eusebius, *Ecclesiastical History* 8, 12, 3–4; St. Ambrose, *On Virginity* 3, 7; St. Augustine, *City of God* 1, 17). Nevertheless, while Razis dies in a context where death seems likely to have awaited him in any event, his self-inflicted wounds in this passage—which are intended to avoid his anticipated fate—are still striking and make it difficult to categorize his case as straightforward martyrdom.

Second, how does the sacred author present Razis' death? However one categorizes the demise of Razis, one must affirm both that the author regards him as a hero of the nation and that the description of his death falls far short of the praises given to the prior martyrdoms of Eleazar and the mother and seven brothers. Earlier in the narrative, the author twice explains how Eleazar sets "a noble example of how to die a good death willingly and nobly for the revered and holy laws" (6:28), and leaves "in his death an example of nobility and a memorial of courage, not only to the young but to the great body of his nation" (6:31). Eleazar's example of willing submission is then followed by the seven brothers, with the author praising the seventh brother's martyrdom by writing that "he died in his integrity, putting his whole trust in the Lord" (7:40). By contrast, while Razis is admired for his courage and hope in the resurrection, he clearly deviates from Eleazar's example by trying to die before his tormentors reach him, which does not turn out as planned (14:43). Once Razis finally does die, the author marks Razis' end with only a terse description: "This was the manner of his death" (14:46). Further, while the author conveys Razis' preference "to die nobly rather than to fall into the hands of sinners and suffer outrages unworthy of his noble birth" (14:42), it is clear that this is Razis' reasoning and not necessarily the author's. Indeed, the author's earlier repetition makes plain that it is Eleazar who sets the "example of nobility" by willingly suffering outrages at the hands of sinners, which is followed by the subsequent youths and their mother. These sufferings are presented by the author, not as ignoble, but as supremely noble and as so valuable that they turn God's wrath away from Israel (7:38).

Third, how should we view Razis' death? Whatever the precise nature of Razis' act, interpreters such as St. Augustine and St. Thomas Aquinas explain how this text cannot be used as a theological pretext for suicide. Augustine makes this point in countering the Donatists who equated suicide with martyrdom and appealed to Razis' death to validate their own practices, which included throwing themselves off cliffs and attacking passers-by to provoke violent retribution. While Razis' thoughts and actions are reported by the 2 Maccabees' author, Augustine points out that the author does not praise them, and the discerning reader will recognize that these actions violate the directives of Sirach and Exodus to suffer abuses and not take innocent life (*Letter* 204; cf. Sir 2:4; Ex 23:7). St. Thomas Aquinas likewise comments upon the Razis text that while "some, among whom was Razias, have killed themselves thinking to act from fortitude", such an act "is not true fortitude, but rather a weakness of soul unable to bear penal evils" (*Summa Theologiae* II-II, 64, 5). According to St. Thomas, the same holds true in analogous situations: while the virgins who perished in the river are commemorated by the early Church, Thomas writes that a nobler example in similar circumstances is left by the virgin martyr St. Lucy, who recognized that even if one's body suffers outrages, "without consent of the mind there is no stain on the body" (*Summa Theologiae* II-II, 64, 5).

In summary, the nature of Razis' death is ambiguous, a potential martyrdom that is interrupted by Razis' desire to preserve his nobility in death. While the sacred author praises Razis' virtuous qualities compared with the Seleucid invaders, the account of his death concludes with a terse description, which differs from the praise given to the noble examples of the earlier martyrs. As Augustine and Aquinas make clear, the Christian reader is to recognize a higher level of fortitude in those who allow themselves to suffer abuse—a fortitude indeed exemplified by none other than Christ himself.

[44]But as they quickly drew back, a space opened and he fell in the middle of the empty space. [45]Still alive and aflame with anger, he rose, and though his blood gushed forth and his wounds were severe he ran through the crowd; and standing upon a steep rock, [46]with his blood now completely drained from him, he tore out his entrails, took them with both hands and hurled them at the crowd, calling upon the Lord of life and spirit to give them back to him again. This was the manner of his death.

Nicanor's Arrogance

15 When Nica'nor heard that Judas and his men were in the region of Samar'ia, he made plans to attack them with complete safety on the day of rest. [2]And when the Jews who were compelled to follow him said, "Do not destroy so savagely and barbarously, but show respect for the day which he who sees all things has honored and hallowed above other days," [3]the thrice-accursed wretch asked if there were a sovereign in heaven who had commanded the keeping of the sabbath day. [4]And when they declared, "It is the living Lord himself, the Sovereign in heaven, who ordered us to observe the seventh day," [5]he replied, "And I am a sovereign also, on earth, and I command you to take up arms and finish the king's business." Nevertheless, he did not succeed in carrying out his abominable design.

Judas Prepares the Jews for Battle

6 This Nica'nor in his utter boastfulness and arrogance had determined to erect a public monument of victory over Judas and his men. [7]But Mac"cabe'us did not cease to trust with all confidence that he would get help from the Lord. [8]And he exhorted his men not to fear the attack of the Gentiles, but to keep in mind the former times when help had come to them from heaven, and now to look for the victory which the Almighty would give them. [9]Encouraging them from the law and the prophets, and reminding them also of the struggles they had won, he made them the more eager. [10]And when he had aroused their courage, he gave his orders, at the same time pointing out the perfidy of the Gentiles and their violation of oaths. [11]He armed each of them not so much with confidence in shields and spears as with the inspiration of brave words, and he cheered them all by relating a dream, a sort of vision,[d] which was worthy of belief.

12 What he saw was this: Oni'as, who had been high priest, a noble and good man, of modest bearing and gentle manner, one who spoke fittingly and had been trained from childhood in all that belongs to excellence, was praying with outstretched hands for the whole body of the Jews. [13]Then likewise a man appeared, distinguished by his gray hair and dignity, and of marvelous majesty and authority. [14]And Oni'as spoke, saying, "This is a man who loves the brethren and prays much for the people and the holy city, Jeremi'ah, the prophet of God." [15]Jeremi'ah stretched out his right hand and gave to Judas a golden sword, and as he gave it he addressed him thus: [16]"Take this holy sword, a gift from God, with which you will strike down your adversaries."

17 Encouraged by the words of Judas, so noble and so effective in arousing valor and awaking manliness in the souls of the young, they determined not to carry on a campaign but to attack bravely, and to decide the matter, by fighting hand to hand with all courage, because the city and the sanctuary and the temple were in danger. [18]Their concern for wives and children, and also for brethren and relatives, lay upon them less heavily; their greatest and first fear was for the consecrated sanctuary. [19]And those who had to remain in the city were in no little distress, being anxious over the encounter in the open country.

The Defeat and Death of Nicanor

20 When all were now looking forward to the coming decision, and the enemy was already close at hand with their army drawn up for battle, the elephants[e] strategically stationed and the cavalry deployed on the flanks, [21]Mac"cabe'us, perceiving the hosts that were before him and the varied supply of arms and the savagery of the elephants,[e] stretched out his hands toward heaven and called upon the Lord who works wonders; for he knew that it is not by arms, but as the Lord[f] decides, that he gains the victory for those who deserve it. [22]And he called upon him in these words: "O Lord, you

---

15:1 Samaria: The region north of Judea. **day of rest:** The Sabbath.

15:3 thrice-accursed: See note on 8:34.

15:8 help had come to them from heaven: This message ("help comes from heaven") is a constant refrain in 1 Maccabees (see 1 Mac 3:19; 12:15; 16:3).

15:12–16 Another manifestation sent by God (cf. 2:21).

15:12 Onias: The honorable Onias III, who continues interceding for his people. See note on 3:1.

15:14 loves ... prays much ... Jeremiah: The prophet Jeremiah, who is also noted in the second introductory letter (2:1–8). • Jeremiah's intercession for the nation seems to have been powerful enough that God instructs him to stop offering it when his judgment is necessary (Jer 7:16; 11:14; 14:11). • Origen of Alexandria appeals to Jeremiah in this passage as evidence that the saints who have passed from this life still love those in the world, remain concerned for our salvation, and aid us by their prayers (*Commentary on Song of Songs* 3, 7) (cf. Rev 5:8; 8:3–4; CCC 956).

15:15 a golden sword: The image of a divine weapon conquering Israel's enemies is similarly found in Is 31:8, where a sword "not of man" is promised to defeat Assyria.

15:22 Hezekiah ... camp of Sennacherib: This recollection from the history of Israel is also found in 8:19 and 1 Mac 7:41.

---

[d] The Greek text here is uncertain.

[e] Gk *beasts.*

[f] Gk *he.*

sent your angel in the time of Hezeki'ah king of Judea, and he slew fully a hundred and eighty-five thousand in the camp of Sennach'erib. ²³So now, O Sovereign of the heavens, send a good angel to carry terror and trembling before us. ²⁴By the might of your arm may these blasphemers who come against your holy people be struck down." With these words he ended his prayer.

25 Nica'nor and his men advanced with trumpets and battle songs; ²⁶and Judas and his men met the enemy in battle with invocation to God and prayers. ²⁷So, fighting with their hands and praying to God in their hearts, they laid low no less than thirty-five thousand men, and were greatly gladdened by God's manifestation.

28 When the action was over and they were returning with joy, they recognized Nica'nor, lying dead, in full armor. ²⁹Then there was shouting and tumult, and they blessed the Sovereign Lord in the language of their fathers. ³⁰And the man who was ever in body and soul the defender of his fellow citizens, the man who maintained his youthful good will toward his countrymen, ordered them to cut off Nica'nor's head and arm and carry them to Jerusalem. ³¹And when he arrived there and had called his countrymen together and stationed the priests before the altar, he sent for those who were in the citadel. ³²He showed them the vile Nica'nor's head and that profane man's arm, which

had been boastfully stretched out against the holy house of the Almighty; ³³and he cut out the tongue of the ungodly Nica'nor and said that he would give it piecemeal to the birds and hang up these rewards of his folly opposite the sanctuary. ³⁴And they all, looking to heaven, blessed the Lord who had manifested himself, saying, "Blessed is he who has kept his own place undefiled." ³⁵And he hung Nica'nor's head from the citadel, a clear and conspicuous sign to every one of the help of the Lord. ³⁶And they all decreed by public vote never to let this day go unobserved, but to celebrate the thirteenth day of the twelfth month—which is called Adar' in the Syrian language—the day before Mor'decai's day.

The Compiler's Epilogue

37 This, then, is how matters turned out with Nica'nor. And from that time the city has been in the possession of the Hebrews. So I too will here end my story. ³⁸If it is well told and to the point, that is what I myself desired; if it is poorly done and mediocre, that was the best I could do. ³⁹For just as it is harmful to drink wine alone, or, again, to drink water alone, while wine mixed with water is sweet and delicious and enhances one's enjoyment, so also the style of the story delights the ears of those who read the work. And here will be the end.

15:25–26 As St. John Chrysostom observes, the contrast between the bombast of the Seleucids and the prayers of the Maccabees demonstrates that the Jews were not fighting for their own glory, but for God's (*Treatise on Psalm 44*).

15:27 God's manifestation: This may refer either to Judas' dream or to the result of the battle that God had orchestrated.

15:30 head and arm: Having stretched out his hand toward the sanctuary with an oath to destroy it (14:33), Nicanor's arm is now returned to the place of his oath, with his severed head to go with it. • The presentation of Nicanor's head in Jerusalem by Judas evokes the similar action of David with Goliath (cf. 1 Sam 17:54).

15:31 citadel: See note on 4:12.

15:36 decreed by public vote: As with the purification of the Temple and subsequent festival in 10:8, the book similarly closes with a great victory and new festival, Nicanor's day, which rabbinic sources attest was celebrated by Jews in

the following centuries. See also 1 Mac 7:49. **Mordecai's day:** Also known as the feast of Purim (Esther 9:26).

15:37–39 Like the preface of Luke's Gospel, the author speaks of his own role in assembling the narrative of events. See note on 2:23–32.

15:38 the best I could do: The author speaks frankly about his efforts and his limitations as a storyteller. In doing so, he does not deny that his work is divinely inspired; he simply shows himself unaware of being inspired (as Paul does in 1 Cor 1:16). • The Catholic doctrine of biblical inspiration teaches that the Holy Spirit made full use of the faculties and powers of the human authors of Scripture, so that those who wrote the biblical books acted as "true authors" and were not mere stenographers taking dictation. The Spirit acted in them and through them, moving them to say everything and only those things that God wanted, and yet their humanity was not suppressed in the process (Vatican II, *Dei Verbum* 11).

STUDY QUESTIONS
2 Maccabees

Chapter 1

For understanding

1. **1:9.** In accordance with Lev 23, how and when was the Feast of Booths (or Tabernacles) celebrated? As a harvest celebration that also became a great commemoration of the Temple, when was it renewed and under whose leadership? For what feast did this celebration become the model, and how was it celebrated? Following some variant readings, what does the reference to 164 B.C. commemorate and with reference to what other date?

2. **1:18—2:15.** What does the lengthy portion of this letter recount? Why is the appeal to an array of scriptural figures—Nehemiah, Jeremiah, Solomon, Moses—essential?

3. **1:18.** How does the Greek text literally read, and to what feast does it most likely refer? To what does the fire refer? For what is this memory foundational? What prompts commentators to speculate as to why the author of 2 Maccabees credits Nehemiah with constructing the Temple and altar? Where else are similar identifications of Nehemiah as the Temple's builder found? Within the context of 2 Maccabees, why would it seem that Nehemiah's role as a builder is emphasized? To what other parallels is this added?

4. **1:31-33.** How does Christian interpretation view this mysterious fire-water? How does St. Ambrose interpret this fire-water symbol in the light of Baptism?

For application

1. **1:1-5.** If you became aware that a group of Christians in Iraq were in a precarious situation such as imminent persecution, what would you say to encourage them in their faith? How might this introduction serve as a model?

2. **1:18—2:15.** The note for these verses states that they provide the rationale for establishing a new feast not prescribed in the Torah. Aside from Christmas and Easter, what are some important feasts that the Church has established? What do they commemorate? Why devote several feasts to various aspects of the lives of Jesus and Mary or of John the Baptist and St. Paul?

3. **1:22.** What fire does the Feast of Pentecost celebrate? What does the association of fire with the Holy Spirit mean? How does one obtain that fire?

Chapter 2

For understanding

1. **2:1.** Though this narrative is not present in the canonical book of Jeremiah, what action of Jeremiah/Baruch do several early Jewish sources discuss? On what does Eupolemus, a Jewish historian contemporary with the Maccabees, also comment? Why did Jeremiah hold a distinct significance for Jews in Egypt?

2. **2:7.** What hope is the focal point of this second letter, and with what is it linked? For what does the inclusion of Jeremiah's testimony about the future reappearance of the ark and God's glory serve as an encouragement? What desire may these "gathering" references indicate? While little testimony survives from this period, what feast do we know that Jesus observed?

3. **Word Study: Appearances (2:21).** What does the Greek word *epiphaneia* mean, and for what English word is it the source? What can this word be used to describe? How is the second sense of *epiphaneia*, common in 2 Maccabees, employed? Why did Antiochus give himself the nickname Epiphanes? Throughout 2 Maccabees, how are the wicked plans of this "God Manifest" countered? How is this theme in 2 Maccabees further developed in the Gospel of John?

4. **2:23-32.** Where do we find the closest scriptural parallel to the author's account of his own writing? What was the effect of God's inspiration? What Church teaching about the authors of Scripture did Vatican II reaffirm?

For application

1. **2:2-3.** Immigrants from other countries are usually expected to assimilate to the prevailing culture, as were European immigrants to United States in the last century. What are the advantages of assimilation for them? From a religious perspective, what are the disadvantages of assimilation? How can immigrants adapt to the new culture and still retain their religious beliefs?

2. **2:7-8.** What do you expect will happen at the Last Judgment, when God gathers his people together for the revelation of his sons? What will it reveal that now remains hidden (CCC 1038-41)?

3. **2:19-22.** The story of the Maccabees against the Seleucids is presented as a war between two personal antagonists. In reality, what might be said of most people, those in the middle who joined neither side? Whom might they have favored? How might they have tried to avoid committing themselves to either side? In today's secular culture, who are the antagonists? What does Jesus say about the effort to avoid taking sides (cf. Mk 8:34-38)?

4. **2:24-32.** Have you ever had to present information to an audience? What was your purpose? What background research did you have to do? With what intent or according to what schema did you organize your material? How successful was your presentation?

Chapter 3

For understanding

1. **3:5.** Who is Apollonius of Tarsus? As what province are Coele-syria and Phoenecia also known, and what area did it include? What is the term Coele-syria also used more narrowly to describe?

2. **3:7.** Who is Heliodorus, and how is he identified by the Greek historian Appian? What did archaeologists at Tell Maresha in Judea discover about him? Bearing the date of 178 B.C., what did the stele detail?

3. **3:11.** What is known from the Jewish historian Josephus about Hyrcanus, son of Tobias? What context can help readers understand the value of four hundred talents of silver and two hundred of gold?
4. **3:39.** What is the significance of the statement in this verse? What principle does Heliodorus' unsuccessful invasion establish, and what does it have to do with the Temple's later desecration under Antiochus?

For application
1. **3:4–6.** When you have a disagreement with a religious or spiritual authority, how do you resolve it? What do you do if there is no one higher in authority to whom to appeal? How appropriate is it to appeal to an outside source?
2. **3:25.** How does this figure resemble St. Michael the Archangel? What is the usual role of this archangel? Do you ever recite the prayer to St. Michael? If so, when?
3. **3:26.** In the New Testament, when do two strong young men make their appearance (cf. Lk 24:4)? To whom do they appear, and what do they do? According to the *Catechism*, what is the role of angels in the life of the Church (CCC 334–36)?
4. **3:38.** Where are some locations where one might experience the power of God's presence? Have you ever experienced such an encounter? If so, what did it teach you about God's love and mercy toward you?

Chapter 4

For understanding
1. **4:9.** Rather than enrolling the men of Jerusalem as citizens in the far-off Seleucid capital of Antioch, what would this proposal have meant? Into what would Jerusalem have been made?
2. **4:12.** What kind of institution was a Greek gymnasium? What was the citadel? What was a Greek hat?
3. **4:18.** Though called the quadrennial games, what were they literally? How did the Greek system of counting years make the games equivalent to quadrennial? By whom were the games inaugurated?
4. **4:23–25.** As whom is Menelaus here presented, and why would he be unqualified for the high priesthood? However, what ancestry do some manuscripts of 3:4 offer in place of Benjamin? How does Josephus' later testimony complicate the issue even more? While a conclusive solution is not possible at present, how is the Septuagint's reading of "Benjamin" here taken?

For application
1. **4:1.** Against which commandment is the sin of slander or calumny an offense? What virtues does this offense oppose? What does slander do to one against whom it is directed (CCC 2477, 2479)? How can social media contribute to the spread of slander?
2. **4:4–6.** According to Mt 18:15–17, what procedure should one follow to resolve a dispute with a fellow Christian? Why not have recourse to the highest authority as the first step rather than the last?
3. **4:7–9.** What is simony, and why is it a sin? According to the *Catechism*, why is it "impossible to appropriate to oneself spiritual goods and behave toward them as their owner or master" (CCC 2118, 2121)?
4. **4:13–14.** What is the likely influence on subordinates when their leader either neglects his duties or positively disregards them? For example, if a religious leader such as a bishop were to become secularized and use Church goods for his own benefit, how intent on the performance of their ministries are his priests likely to be? Considering his influence on the priesthood, what sin might the bishop be committing?

Chapter 5
For understanding

1. **5:19.** Similarly to this maxim, what does Christ teach regarding why the Lord gives institutions? Just as the Sabbath is created for man, rather than man for the Sabbath, for whose sake is the Temple made?
2. **5:21.** How was the tremendous sum of eighteen hundred talents likely generated? To whom is the allusion of sailing on land and walking on the sea made? In a famous passage, of what does Xerxes' uncle warn him, and to whom else does this warning apply?
3. **5:22.** In what way are Antiochus' actions described in the same terms as Pharaoh's? Who is Philip, the Phrygian?
4. **5:27.** By taking refuge in the wilderness, whose pattern are Judas and his companions following? Rather than eat unclean food, how do Judas and his friends sustain themselves?

For application
1. **5:2–3.** When confronted with a heavenly apparition or a private revelation, what principles should one use to determine whether it is true or false? To what sources might one go to locate or clarify these principles?
2. **5:12–14.** What are some of the names we give to the wanton killing of large numbers of people? Why are we appalled at the murder of even one innocent human being? If that is so, how are we to respond to wholesale slaughters of entire communities?
3. **5:19.** Read the note for this verse. Applying the same teaching, why are attendance at Mass on Sundays and holy days as well as certain penitential seasons mandated?
4. **5:21.** Is it always the case that pride goes before a fall (cf. Prov 16:18)? What does Paul mean when he warns Christians who think they are standing to beware of falling (1 Cor 10:12)?

Chapter 6

For understanding
1. **6:1.** Who is the Athenian senator referred to here? Why was Antiochus' compulsion to suppress the Jewish way of life unusual? How did Antiochus likely see Torah observance?

2.   **6:12–17.** Which one of the book's central themes does the author make explicit? Where else in Scripture does this biblical principle appear?
3.   **6:19.** What is the rack? How does Heb 11:35 allude to this event?
4.   **6:24.** For whom did Eleazar's testimony become an example? With what strikingly similar language does the martyr Polycarp reply to the Roman proconsul?

For application
1.   **6:6.** In our society, how dangerous is it for one to profess himself a Christian? If it is not currently dangerous, why do some Christians hide not only the profession but the practice of their faith? What does Scripture say about the consequences of being ashamed of the faith (cf. Mt 5:13; 10:32)?
2.   **6:12–17.** According to the text of these verses, what is the Lord's motive for disciplining his people? According to the Book of Hebrews, why does he administer discipline (Heb 12:4–10)? How do you respond to setbacks, hardships, desolations, or other forms of divine discipline?
3.   **6:24–25.** Why does Eleazar refuse to pretend to cooperate with his tormentors? What sin is he trying to avoid? To what lengths are you prepared to go to avoid committing this same sin?
4.   **6:31.** What kind of example does the martyrdom of Christians give to the Church? What thought have you given to the possibility of your own martyrdom? How is living an exemplary Christian life in ordinary circumstances a kind of martyrdom?

Chapter 7

For understanding
1.   **7:1.** Of whom is no mention made in this account? How does St. Cyprian explain this omission? Although the text does not identify the location of these events, where does evidence from early reception suggest they took place? As what kind of food does the Torah list pigs? While *4 Maccabees* 8, 25, testifies that the Law of Moses would not have condemned the brothers to death for this violation, why did they choose to lose their lives?
2.   **Topical Essay: Resurrection in the Old Testament.** What evidence is there to support the claim that the Old Testament presents no clear vision of life after death? What are some definite exceptions to this rule, however? While commentators rightly point out that some resurrection passages, particularly those in Ezekiel and Isaiah, serve as analogies for what will happen when the nation of Israel is restored from exile, how does this very point serve to demonstrate the existence of some notion of physical resurrection in these contexts? Why can we regard the Old Testament's testimony on the resurrection as well represented by the conflict between the Sadducees and Pharisees in Acts 23:6–8?
3.   **7:28.** To which doctrine does the *Catechism of the Catholic Church* cite the mother's testimony in this passage as a witness? As the *Catechism* states, what follows from this doctrine?
4.   **7:38.** How is the martyrs' hope that their suffering will bring an end to God's wrath fulfilled? Of what does 2 Mac 7 offer perhaps the clearest example before the advent of Christ? Like the Suffering Servant of Isaiah 53, what does the suffering of these righteous representatives of Israel serve to elicit, and for what does it provide atonement? When was the belief that the sufferings of the righteous could bring atonement for others made familiar? While the sacrifices of these martyrs and Christ are similar in kind but infinitely distinct in degree, what did the faithfulness of these martyrs accomplish? What appeal to the same principle does Paul make in Gal 3?

For application
1.   **7:1–2.** Do you have any religious emblems (crucifixes, bibles, icons, etc.) around your home? If these were outlawed under severe penalties for their possession, what would you do with them? To what lengths would you go to protect them and continue their use?
2.   **7:7–8.** St. Dominic Savio had as his personal motto, "Death rather than sin". To what lengths are you willing to go to maintain moral purity in your life? Or what compromises are you willing to make to preserve your life?
3.   **7:28–29.** What impresses you about the creative power of God? What moves him to create? Of all the persons he could have created, why did he create you?
4.   **7:36.** Read Jn 3:13–16, 36. What is your understanding of the eternal life that Jesus promises? When does it begin? How is it completed?

Chapter 8

For understanding
1.   **8:11.** What did the very low price for slaves possibly indicate about Nicanor? What would setting the price this low do to the slave market?
2.   **8:19.** Because Sennacherib's Assyrian empire covered a territory similar to that of the Seleucid empire in the time of the Maccabees, how did it serve as a natural analogy in the eyes of the Jewish resistance? What blueprint does God's defeat of Sennacherib's army against all expectations in 701 B.C. provide for them?
3.   **8:26.** What does the author highlight in this verse, and in contrast to what?
4.   **8:30.** Who is Timothy? Killed at the end of chap. 10, how can Timothy then reappear at the beginning of chap. 12? Who is Bacchides, and what is he attested to have done in 1 Maccabees?

For application
1.   **8:2–4.** This prayer lists seven evils from which the faithful Jews need deliverance. When praying for help, why list the troubles you face? According to Jesus, what seems to motivate the Lord to act (cf. Mt 9:22; Mk 10:52; Lk 8:50)?
2.   **8:10.** Although selling human beings into slavery has been outlawed in this country, it is still practiced here. What forms does it take? What makes enslaving other people such an abominable crime?
3.   **8:18.** According to Ps 20:7–8, ancient armies trusted in horses and chariots for military strength. What are the modern equivalents of such equipment? The psalm praises those of faith who place their trust in the Lord. Why is it still necessary for people of faith to trust in him rather than in armies?

Study Questions

Chapter 9

For understanding
1. **9:1-29.** Where else is Antiochus' demise narrated? With what slightly varying details do these accounts report similar stories? In keeping with the author's stated aim of making the material easy to memorize (2:25), what kind of organization may these narratives reflect?
2. **9:4.** What judgment of heaven finds its fulfillment here? What does Antiochus' promise include?
3. **9:17.** After making it unlawful to confess to be a Jew in 6:6, what does Antiochus now vow? What is the meaning of "Jew" in this context?
4. **9:18.** If the prayer of the righteous is powerful and effective (Jas 5:16), what qualities characterize the prayer of wicked Antiochus? How is Antiochus' dubious sincerity illustrated?

For application
1. **9:8.** While this verse drips with sarcasm regarding Antiochus, what person is actually able to command the waves of the sea and weigh the mountains in a balance? When Jesus commanded the waves and the sea, what was the disciples' reaction (cf. Mt 8:27; Mk 4:41)?
2. **9:11.** Although broken in spirit, how much of his arrogance did Antiochus actually relinquish? When the Lord allows a person's spirit to be broken, what is his purpose? According to Ps 51:17, upon what kind of spirit does the Lord look favorably?
3. **9:13-17.** What is Antiochus attempting to do with his vow? Have you ever tried to bargain with God to give you some benefit or relieve you of some problem? What does God look for in those who pray to him?
4. **9:27.** What is the irony in this verse? What ironies often lie hidden in the promises of politicians, whether intentionally or not?

Chapter 10

For understanding
1. **10:3.** How does the Greek read literally, and to what do some translations speculate these words may refer? What is a more natural referent? Now, at the Temple's second rededication, for what do these stones become the source? While both 1 and 2 Maccabees report that the Temple was profaned and rededicated on the same date, the 25th of Chislev, what is the difference in years between these two books, and why is this surprising? To what is the difference likely due?
2. **10:6.** How is this festival, which becomes known as Hanukkah (meaning "dedication"), here celebrated? Just as the Feast of Booths (= Tabernacles) was meant to bring to the Israelites' remembrance of their time spent in the wilderness after their deliverance from Egypt, how does this new feast use booths?
3. **10:7.** Formerly forced to wear ivy in honor of Dionysus, how do Jews now use it?
4. **10:20.** To what was a drachma roughly equivalent, and to what would the total of seventy thousand drachmas amount?

For application
1. **10:1-4.** In the dedication or rededication of a church, the building and its altar are sprinkled with holy water, anointed with chrism, and incensed. What is the significance of using sacred chrism, especially on the altar? The incensing of the altar signifies the pleasing nature of Christ's sacrifice; what does the incensing of the nave of the church signify?
2. **10:6.** How long does the celebration of Christmas last? For how many days do Christians celebrate Easter? What feast concludes the Easter celebration? How similar are these feasts to the Jewish feasts of Hanukkah, Passover, and Pentecost (Shavuot)?
3. **10:13.** Against what commandment is suicide an offense? How does it offend love of neighbor? What factors can diminish the responsibility for one who commits suicide (CCC 2281-82)?
4. **10:20-23.** Under the rules of most armies, commanders may execute those under their command for a variety of serious reasons. What are some of them? Since these executions are usually public, what is their purpose? How do they accord with the fifth commandment?

Chapter 11

For understanding
1. **11:1.** For what manifestation does Lysias' self-confidence and pride in attacking Judea set the stage? With what do the events in this section appear to correspond? If so, how would the author likely be organizing the series of events?
2. **11:3.** While the Jewish high priesthood was traditionally hereditary and kept for the priest's lifetime, what would its sale have made the high priest?
3. **11:32.** How does the nature of this letter as genuine correspondence from the Seleucids seem to be confirmed?
4. **11:33.** Of what significance is the date of Xanthicus the fifteenth? In any case, what theological significance may these dates hold?

For application
1. **11:3.** What would happen to the Church if the papacy were for sale to the highest bidder or if a political power were to impose a candidate? What protections have recent popes placed on the conclave to prevent such abuses from happening? Why do conclaves begin with the invocation to the Holy Spirit?
2. **11:6-8.** What is the Catholic doctrine concerning guardian angels? How have angels intervened in human history (cf. CCC 331-36)? What is the role of the Archangel Michael (cf. Dan 10:13; 12:1)?
3. **11:15.** How does the *Catechism*, quoting *Gaudium et Spes*, define what the common good is? What are its essential elements, and what are the responsibilities of authorities with respect to them (CCC 1906-9)? To what is the common good always ordered, and on what is it founded (CCC 1912)?

Chapter 12

For understanding
1. **12:15.** What war machines did Hellenistic-era warfare include? Like the miraculous toppling of the walls of Jericho in Josh 6:1–21, with what does God's aid provide the Jews?
2. **12:29.** Where is Scythopolis, also known as Beth-shan? In contrast with Joppa, Jamnia, and the succeeding towns in chap. 12, how do the citizens of Scythopolis regard the Jews? As a result, what do Judas' forces have to offer them, and what does that show?
3. **Topical Essay: Second Maccabees and the Canon of Scripture.** Why would "2 Maccabees 12" provide a quick and easy answer to why Protestant Bibles are shorter than Catholic ones? What in Martin Luther's opinion did the abuse of collections being taken on behalf of the dead appear to have produced? For Luther, what more dramatic solution to the problem was found? Why did such a move seem necessary to Luther and, similarly, to Calvin? While the reformers were correct that St. Jerome and certain other Fathers, following the general practice of Jews after Christ's time, regarded books like 2 Maccabees as holding a lower status, how was the broader Old Testament canon found in the Greek Septuagint followed in the early Church? While the potential for abuses was recognized on the Catholic side as well as the Protestant side, what doctrine did the Church uphold, and how did she regard the canonicity of Scripture?
4. **12:44–45.** For whom did the practice of praying for the dead, here attested by Jews over a century before Christ, become common as well? How does St. Augustine's treatise *On the Care of the Dead* begin? In his dispute with Vincentius Victor's claim that the sacrifice of the Eucharist can be offered for the unbaptized dead, how does Augustine counter? What famous story of early Christian prayers for the dead is found with the example of Perpetua, who was martyred around A.D. 202? According to St. John Chrysostom, why should Christians pray for the dead?

For application
1. **12:3–6.** What Old Testament principle does Judas follow in taking revenge on Joppa for the murder of two hundred Jews (cf. Ex 21:23; Lev 24:19–20)? How do you think modern Christians would respond to such an incident?
2. **12:8–9.** Would you consider Judas' nighttime attack on Jamnia an offensive or a defensive operation? Granted that nations have a right to legitimate defense, according to the "just war" doctrine, what is the moral legitimacy of a preemptive strike?
3. **12:40.** What is the morality of carrying with you some good luck charm such as a rabbit's foot? How do you interpret the *Catechism*'s definition of superstition, particularly the last sentence (CCC 2111)? What might be some examples of using sacramentals in a superstitious manner?
4. **12:43–45.** Why does the Church refer to those in Purgatory as *holy souls*? Do you ever pray for them?

Chapter 13

For understanding
1. **13:1–26.** What period does this section cover? Why do the figures of the Seleucid armies vary between the accounts?
2. **13:5.** How high are fifty cubits? What fascinating parallel between Menelaus and wicked Haman does this create?
3. **13:8.** What principle in the Book of Wisdom does the death of Menelaus illustrate?

For application
1. **13:8.** Look up Wis 11:16. What examples can you think of to illustrate this principle (hint: how overindulgence in food negatively affects one's health)? How has this principle shown itself in your own experience?
2. **13:10–12.** What kind of preparation does Judas make in these verses as he and all Judea face this military threat? For the devout Christian facing a difficult situation, why should prayer be the first step taken? What danger might be inherent in deciding to skip prayer and act first?
3. **13:21.** What crime against the Jews did Rhodocus commit? In the military, what would be the normal punishment for such a crime?

Chapter 14

For understanding
1. **14:3.** Who was Alcimus, and what claim did he have to win the support of the more traditionally minded Jews? When might Alcimus have taken this role, and with whose confirmation being required?
2. **14:6.** Who do commentators say the Hasideans were? What does their name mean, and how are they related to the Essenes and Pharisees? When Alcimus acquires the high priesthood at this point in the narrative in 1 Maccabees, what happens to the Hasideans?
3. **14:24–30.** What description is absent from the parallel account in 1 Mac 7? What may explain why, out of all the Jews' enemies in this period, only Nicanor's death is commemorated as a national holiday? What analogy from American history illustrates this?
4. **Topical Essay: The Death of Razis.** What interpretative questions does the death of Razis present? First, what is the answer regarding the question of whether Razis' death was martyrdom or suicide? Second, although the author regards him as a hero of the nation, how does the description of his death fall far short of the praises given to the prior martyrdoms of Eleazar and the mother and seven brothers? Third, how do interpreters such as St. Augustine and St. Thomas Aquinas explain how this text cannot be used as a theological pretext for presenting suicide as martyrdom? In summary, how is the Christian reader to understand the ambiguous nature of Razis' death?

For application
1. **14:3–4.** Statesmen frequently offer gifts to one another upon their first meeting. If you wished to make a presentation to a new superior but were uncertain of your reception, how might you obtain a favorable hearing? For example, what would you try to learn about the superior before your meeting?

2. **14:6-10.** Note how Alcimus replies to the king's request for information. What misinformation does he provide regarding Judas and even about himself? When you encounter misinformation calculated to undermine the faith, how can you counter it?
3. **14:28.** Have you ever been ordered by a higher authority to renege on an agreement you have just made and to do the opposite? If so, what moral or ethical problems did the order raise for you? What did you do in response? Afterward, what second thoughts did you have about your response?
4. **14:37-46.** Read the essay *The Death of Razis*, especially the next-to-last paragraph. Using these criteria, how would you evaluate the death of King Saul (1 Sam 31:4)? How would St. Thomas' dictum ("without consent of the mind, there is no stain on the body") apply to victims of abuse such as rape?

Chapter 15

For understanding
1. **15:14.** How powerful does Jeremiah's intercession seem to have been for the nation? Why does Origen of Alexandria appeal to Jeremiah in this passage as evidence of saints' prayers after their death?
2. **15:25-26.** As St. John Chrysostom observes, what does the contrast between the bombast of the Seleucids and the prayers of the Maccabees demonstrate?
3. **15:36.** As with the purification of the Temple and subsequent festival in 10:8, how does the book close? How is Mordecai's day also known?
4. **15:38.** Although the author speaks frankly about his efforts and his limitations as a storyteller, how aware is he of being divinely inspired? What does the Catholic doctrine of biblical inspiration teach?

For application
1. **15:7.** When have you most needed help from the Lord? How hard was it for you to maintain your trust in such a difficult situation? How did you stir up confidence in him?
2. **15:14.** If Jesus is the one Mediator between God and man, why do Catholics pray to saints? To which saint do you most frequently pray? What attracts you to him or her?
3. **15:17.** Whom do you know who is the most effective in encouraging others to persevere in confidence or effort? How does this person do it? What encouragement have you drawn from this person? How have you worked to encourage others when their confidence flags?
4. **15:38.** What is your understanding of the historical reliability of the Gospels? How important is it for the doctrine of biblical inspiration that the Gospels be historically reliable? Have you devoted any time to studying the subject? How does their reliability influence your faith?

BOOKS OF THE BIBLE

THE OLD TESTAMENT (OT)

Gen	Genesis
Ex	Exodus
Lev	Leviticus
Num	Numbers
Deut	Deuteronomy
Josh	Joshua
Judg	Judges
Ruth	Ruth
1 Sam	1 Samuel
2 Sam	2 Samuel
1 Kings	1 Kings
2 Kings	2 Kings
1 Chron	1 Chronicles
2 Chron	2 Chronicles
Ezra	Ezra
Neh	Nehemiah
Tob	Tobit
Jud	Judith
Esther	Esther
Job	Job
Ps	Psalms
Prov	Proverbs
Eccles	Ecclesiastes
Song	Song of Solomon
Wis	Wisdom
Sir	Sirach (Ecclesiasticus)
Is	Isaiah
Jer	Jeremiah
Lam	Lamentations
Bar	Baruch
Ezek	Ezekiel
Dan	Daniel
Hos	Hosea
Joel	Joel
Amos	Amos
Obad	Obadiah
Jon	Jonah
Mic	Micah
Nahum	Nahum
Hab	Habakkuk
Zeph	Zephaniah
Hag	Haggai
Zech	Zechariah
Mal	Malachi
1 Mac	1 Maccabees
2 Mac	2 Maccabees

THE NEW TESTAMENT (NT)

Mt	Matthew
Mk	Mark
Lk	Luke
Jn	John
Acts	Acts of the Apostles
Rom	Romans
1 Cor	1 Corinthians
2 Cor	2 Corinthians
Gal	Galatians
Eph	Ephesians
Phil	Philippians
Col	Colossians
1 Thess	1 Thessalonians
2 Thess	2 Thessalonians
1 Tim	1 Timothy
2 Tim	2 Timothy
Tit	Titus
Philem	Philemon
Heb	Hebrews
Jas	James
1 Pet	1 Peter
2 Pet	2 Peter
1 Jn	1 John
2 Jn	2 John
3 Jn	3 John
Jude	Jude
Rev	Revelation (Apocalypse)